The Arts and Crafts Movement in the Cotswolds

Contributors

Maureen Batkin is a lecturer and ceramics historian, and the author of numerous books, including *Wedgwood Ceramics 1846–1959* (Richard Dennis, 1982).

Annette Carruthers is a museum curator, formerly at Cheltenham Art Gallery and Museums, now doing research for St Andrew's University, Scotland.

Catherine Gordon has just completed her PhD on Arts and Crafts architecture.

Barley Roscoe is curator of the Holburne Museum, Bath. She has a deep interest in twentieth-century crafts and writes and lectures on the subject.

The Arts and Crafts Movement in the Cotswolds

MARY GREENSTED

ALAN SUTTON

First published in the United Kingdom in 1993
Alan Sutton Publishing Ltd · Phoenix Mill · Far Thrupp
Stroud · Gloucestershire

First published in the United States of America in 1993
Alan Sutton Publishing Inc · 83 Washington Street · Dover NH 03820

British Library Cataloguing in Publication Data

Greensted, Mary
The Arts and Crafts
Movement in the Cotswolds
I. Title
745.09424

ISBN 0-86299-942-1

Library of Congress Cataloguing in Publication Data applied for

Typeset in Perpetua 11/13.
Typesetting and origination by
Alan Sutton Publishing Limited,
Colour separation by Yeo Graphics Reproductions Ltd.
Printed and bound in Great Britain by
Biddles Ltd, Guildford and King's Lynn

Contents

List of Illustrations   vii

Acknowledgements   xi

Map of Gloucestershire and its surrounds   xii

1. The Arts and Crafts Movement and the Cotswolds   1

2. London Days   12

3. Gimson and the Barnsleys   22

4. The Guild of Handicraft at Chipping Campden   44
   ANNETTE CARRUTHERS

5. The Arts and Crafts Architecture of the Cotswold Region   59
   CATHERINE GORDON

6. The Simple Life in the Cotswolds   78

7. Alfred and Louise Powell   92
   MAUREEN BATKIN

8. William and Eve Simmonds   110

9. Phyllis Barron and Dorothy Larcher   122
   BARLEY ROSCOE

10. The Craft Workshops between the Wars   140

11. Gordon Russell   154

12. A Living Tradition   167

Notes   179

Select Bibliography   186

Index   189

Illustrations

	Map of Gloucestershire and its surrounds	xii
1.1	Pine table, probably designed by William Morris	4
1.2	Broadway Tower, Worcestershire	5
1.3	Wedgwood bowl, painted by Alfred Powell	6
1.4	Daneway House near Sapperton, at one time Ernest Gimson's showrooms	7
1.5	*Gloucestershire Waggon and Team*, carved chestnut panel by William Simmonds	8
1.6	*The Chair-maker*, line engraving by Stanley Anderson	10
2.1	A pencil drawing of C.R. Ashbee, by William Strang	14
2.2	Buckle in silver, designed and possibly made by C.R. Ashbee	16
2.3	Sporting cup, designed by C.R. Ashbee	17
2.4	Green glass decanter mounted in silver, by the Guild of Handicraft	18
2.5	A view of the 1891 Kenton and Co. exhibition, including an oak table and mahogany chair designed by Ernest Gimson	19
2.6	The hall in Ernest Barnsley's house at Sapperton showing a Kenton and Co. dresser and decorative plasterwork, both by Ernest Gimson	20
2.7	Chest in oak, designed by William Lethaby	21
3.1	Group photograph at Pinbury	23
3.2	Joint workshop at Pinbury	25
3.3	Ladderback chair, by Ernest Gimson	26
3.4	Sidney Barnsley's living room at Pinbury	28
3.5	One of the showrooms at Daneway House	30
3.6	Four toasting forks, designed by Ernest Gimson and made by Alfred Bucknell	34
3.7	Design for a candlesconce, by Ernest Gimson	35
3.8	Settee or daybed in English oak, designed and made by Sidney Barnsley	37
3.9	Segmental sideboard in oak, designed by Ernest Gimson	38
3.10	Memorial cross, designed by Ernest Gimson	39
3.11	Design by Ernest Gimson for a china cabinet in mahogany	42
4.1	William Grevel's house in Chipping Campden, by E.H. New	45

4.2	The Guild Workshops at Chipping Campden, by E.H. New	47
4.3	Jim Pyment in the Guild of Handicraft machine shop	48
4.4	Cabinet, designed by C.R. Ashbee and made by the Guild of Handicraft	49
4.5	A simple oak chest of drawers, from a catalogue of the Guild of Handicraft Limited	50
4.6	Silver macehead set with green pearl blisters, designed by C.R. Ashbee	51
4.7	Silver brooch, designed by C.R. Ashbee	52
4.8	Silver buttons, designed by Ashbee and made by the Guild of Handicraft	53
4.9	Alec Miller in his workshop	57
5.1	Well's Folly, Evenlode, by Guy Dawber	62
5.2	The building of Rodmarton Manor	64
5.3	Izod's House, Chipping Campden, designed by C.R. Ashbee	66
5.4	Design by Sidney Barnsley for a pair of cottages, Painswick	67
5.5	Thimble Cottage, Prescott, architect unknown	69
5.6	War memorial, Minchinhampton, designed by Sidney Barnsley	70
5.7	Seynckley House, Amberley, altered by Sidney Barnsley	73
5.8	Norman Jewson, photographed by his father-in-law, Ernest Barnsley	74
5.9	Leadwork for Cotswold Farm, designed by Norman Jewson	75
5.10	Iles Farm, Far Oakridge, altered and enlarged by Norman Jewson	76
6.1	The yard outside Sidney Barnsley's cottage, Pinbury	79
6.2	Drawing of a shepherd wearing a smock, by Freda Derrick	80
6.3	Group photograph at Pinbury	81
6.4	Janet Ashbee, painted by William Strang	83
6.5	The cast of *As You Like It*, performed by the Guild of Handicraft and Friends	85
6.6	A page from *The Essex House Song-book*, by C.R. and Janet Ashbee	86
6.7	Ernest Gimson's living room at Pinbury, drawn by Alfred Powell	88
6.8	A class in the Chipping Campden Summer School	90
7.1	Interior of the Powells' studio cottage at Tarlton	94
7.2	Lessore family photograph	95
7.3	Dante's *Divine Comedy,* written out and decorated by Louise Powell	96
7.4	Altar frontal for St Andrew's church, Roker, by Louise Powell	98
7.5	Exhibition of Wedgwood pottery, decorated by Alfred Powell and assistants	101

7.6	Gimson dresser with Wedgwood pottery, decorated by Alfred Powell	103
7.7	Detail of 'Woodpecker' cabinet, made by Peter Waals and painted by Louise Powell	104
7.8	Wedgwood earthenware, decorated by Grace Barnsley	105
7.9	The Handcraft Studio at Barlaston	107
8.1	Small ivory carvings, by William Simmonds	112
8.2	'Flora', an embroidered panel in coloured worsteds, by Eve Simmonds	114
8.3	*Three Leverets*, an oak carving, by William Simmonds	115
8.4	*Calf*, a marble carving, by William Simmonds	116
8.5	William Simmonds with two hand puppets	117
8.6	*Mouse* and *Wren on a Beech Leaf*, carved by William Simmonds	119
8.7	Drawing of Norman Jewson and his daughter, Mary, by William Simmonds	120
9.1	Hambutts House, Painswick	122
9.2	Dorothy Larcher and Eve Simmonds at Hambutts House, drawn by William Simmonds	124
9.3	Phyllis Barron and Dorothy Larcher at Hambutts House	125
9.4	'Large Feather', indigo resist on organdie	127
9.5	'Elizabethan', designed by Phyllis Barron	130
9.6	'Basket', the third block Dorothy Larcher designed	131
9.7	Dorothy Larcher and Phyllis Barron on holiday in France	132
9.8	The workshop at Hambutts House	133
9.9	A sofa upholstered in 'Diagonal' and a cushion printed with 'Chanel'	134
10.1	Silver cup and cover, by George Hart	141
10.2	Bill Thornton in his smithy	143
10.3	Chestnut roaster, by Charlie Downer	144
10.4	*Dick*, a relief portrait, by Alec Miller	145
10.5	Peter Waals	146
10.6	The workshop at Chalford	147
10.7	Drop-front writing cabinet, designed by Peter Waals	149
10.8	Design by Peter Waals for a cabinet	151
10.9	Box in walnut, designed by George Trevelyan and made by Ernest Smith	152
11.1	'The Rubaiyat of Omar Khayyam', calligraphy by Gordon Russell	157
11.2	'A Model Cafe', designed by Gordon Russell and made by Russell and Sons	159
11.3	Cabinet in English walnut, designed by Gordon Russell	160

11.4   Glassware, designed by Gordon Russell   161
11.5   Advertisement, designed by Gordon Russell   162
11.6   The cabinet-making workshop at Broadway   163
11.7   Polished steel fender, designed by Gordon Russell   164
11.8   Garden seat, designed by Gordon Russell   165
12.1   Jug in slip-decorated earthenware, made by Michael Cardew   170
12.2   The Winchcombe Pottery   171
12.3   Folding table in English walnut, made by Fred Foster   173
12.4   'The Cotswold Tradition' exhibition at Cirencester   174
12.5   Sideboard in English walnut, designed and made by Harry Davoll   175
12.6   Christchurch, Chalford   176
12.7   Metal screen, designed by Alan Evans   178

Colour Plates

I   Marquetry cabinet, designed by Ernest Gimson
II   Detail of the ceiling of the church of the Wisdom of God, Lower
            Kingswood, designed and painted by Sidney Barnsley
III   Oak coffer, designed and made by Sidney Barnsley, painted by
            Alfred Powell
IV   Ewer, Wedgwood earthenware, painted by Louise Powell
V   Cupboard, designed by Ernest Gimson and painted by Alfred
            Powell
VI   Guild of Handicraft silverwork, with enamelled decoration by
            Fleetwood Varley and William Mark
VII   'The Whitebeam Tree', hanging designed by Louise Powell and
            embroidered by Eve Simmonds
VIII   *Autumn Calf*, carved and painted by William Simmonds
IX   *A Christmas party*, a watercolour, by Edward Payne
X   Block and sample print of 'Lizard' in indigo discharge on cotton
XI   Detail of a firedog, designed by Ernest Gimson
XII   Jacket and skirt made up from 'Peach' and printed in black on velvet

Acknowledgements

One of my pleasures in writing this book has been in working closely with the contributors, Maureen Batkin, Annette Carruthers, Catherine Gordon and Barley Roscoe – they have each added a unique element to the overall picture. Over the years I have been fortunate enough to get to know a number of individuals connected with the Arts and Crafts Movement in the Cotswolds, including the late Edward Barnsley, the late Mrs Mary Biddulph, Norman Bucknell, Donald Gimson, Ray Finch, the late Nancy Jewson, Oliver Morel, the late Edward Payne, Alan Peters, the late Sir Gordon Russell, Sir George Trevelyan, who have provided me with a great deal of information and inspiration. I would also like to thank Karin Antonini and the Edward Barnsley Educational Trust, Mr and Mrs Simon Biddulph, George Breeze, Alan Crawford, Anthony Davies, Alan Evans, Charles, Oscar and John Greensted, Frank Johnson and the Guild of Handicraft Trust, Allan Lupton, Helen and Stephen McDonnell, Mike McGrath, Jan Marsh, Jane May (Leicestershire Arts, Museums and Records Service), the families of Oliver and Roger Powell, the families of Oliver and Roger Powell, Alan Powers, Lady Elizabeth and the late Sir John Rothenstein, Amanda Silk, Jennifer Harris and Ann Tullo of the Whitworth Art Gallery (University of Manchester). I am particularly grateful to George Breeze, Chief Art Gallery and Museums Officer at Cheltenham, for permission to use the rich archive of photographs, and to my colleagues at that institution, especially Jonathan Benington, Helen Brown, Alan Morrall and Sophia Wilson. Above all, I must thank Annette Carruthers – her organizational talents have created a valuable archive at Cheltenham which has made my work much easier, and her support and advice throughout have been invaluable.

Mary Greensted
Cheltenham, 1992

Gloucestershire and its surrounds, showing many of the places connected with the Arts and Crafts Movement in the Cotswolds

Chapter One

The Arts and Crafts Movement and the Cotswolds

For twenty years or so after the turn of the century, the Cotswolds were synonymous with craftsmanship. Even as late as 1939 the link was such as to generate some gentle abuse from the pen of Osbert Lancaster:

> . . . ever since the 'eighties in the byways of Chelsea and the lost valleys of the Cotswolds a handful of devoted Artists and Craftsmen had been living the simple life according to the doctrines of William Morris, surrounded by hand-woven linens, vegetable dyed, and plain unstained oak furniture by 'goode workmen wel ywrought'.[1]

Craft activity was divided into two loose groups: one focusing on the Guild of Handicraft in Chipping Campden and the other centred on Sapperton and adjacent villages south-west of Cirencester. After the upheaval of the First World War, new areas of craft activity emerged based at Ditchling in Sussex and St Ives in Cornwall, but the Arts and Crafts tradition continued to play an important role in the Cotswolds. The variety and quality of the work carried out in the area between 1890 and 1940 was quite unique. Some of the designers, craftsmen and women involved are national, even international figures, others are hardly known outside a small circle of enthusiasts. Yet all contributed to the richness and variety of the twentieth-century craft tradition in the Cotswolds.

Between 1890 and 1920, British design achieved prominence in Europe and the United States of America. It received many accolades, including, in 1898, one from Samuel Bing, the Parisian art dealer and popularizer of art nouveau. He wrote: 'When English creations began to appear, a cry of delight sounded throughout Europe. Its echo can still be heard in every country.'[2]

The reason for this success, after many years of dogged endeavour and pedantic design reform, was the emergence, like a breath of fresh air, of the Arts and Crafts Movement. Its products can be seen as individual designs, stylish and novel, having links with the contemporary Aesthetic Movement and continental art nouveau. But, unlike these other styles, the Arts and Crafts Movement had a fundamental moral and social purpose: its concern was not solely for the end products but also for the society that shaped them, for the men and women who designed and made them and for the people who bought them. According to Charles Robert Ashbee, 'The Arts and Crafts movement . . . means Standard, whether of work or of life, the protection of standard, whether in the product or the producer, and it means that these things must be taken together.'[3]

The basic characteristics of the Movement are threefold. A strong reaction against the superficial inventiveness of High Victorian design and the proliferation of cheap ornamentation inspired the idea of 'honesty'. In practice this involved a concentration on simple lines, surface textures and the extension of constructional details to decoration. There was also a strong element of national pride running through the Movement which found its expression in a love of nature and English traditions. Finally, and possibly most crucial of all to the Arts and Crafts Movement, was the idea that creative manual work could provide personal fulfilment.

The roots of the Arts and Craft Movement lie as far back as the eighteenth century. As one of the first countries to undergo the process of industrialization, Britain had developed a version of the neoclassical style that combined refinement with fitness for purpose and sophistication with purity of form. In an atmosphere of optimism and confidence, British design and British products dominated Europe. The work of Robert Adam, Thomas Sheraton, Josiah Wedgwood and others became known and imitated throughout the western world. Yet by the 1830s, many commentators, politicians and even manufacturers felt that the Industrial Revolution had not fulfilled its original promise and saw it as a negative force. New industrial centres developed throughout the country changing its face for ever, and Britain was left holding the two-faced bad penny of rural depopulation and urban slums. Communities were broken up and traditional ways of working were no longer possible. Above all, the idea that goods could be made and decorated cheaply using mechanical means led to a growing contempt for craftsmanship. As early as 1829, Thomas Carlyle railed against the effects of industrialization, writing that: 'Men are grown mechanical in head and heart, as well as in hand. They have lost faith in individual endeavour and in natural force of any kind.'[4]

Looking back at this period at a later date, G.K. Chesterton summed it up in the idea that, 'the word "master" ceased to mean a man who was master of his craft and came to mean a man who was master of others.'[5]

Design standards fared no better, for the Victorians used industrialization to apply more decoration to an increasing number of products: they equated design with ornament. By the mid-nineteenth century, French design was pre-eminent. There was official concern about the competitiveness (or lack of it) of British manufactured goods at an international level. The civil servant, Henry Cole, and Prince Albert were driving forces behind the Great Exhibition of 1851 which, despite its financial success, served only to bring home to organizers and critics alike the sorry state of British design.

Many of the critics were architects who, as a profession, had maintained a privileged status in society while pursuing their traditional concern for interior decoration and the building arts. Most vociferous among them was A.W.N. Pugin, a Catholic convert who had espoused the Gothic style with an equally religious zeal. As well as writing and practising as an architect, Pugin also designed furniture and fittings for his buildings which were made by commercial firms. He employed assistants to produce stained glass, metalwork, textiles and jewellery to his own design.

The Gothic Revival style pioneered by Pugin was seized upon by the newly prosperous middle classes because of its supposedly 'English' characteristics (Gothic and Elizabethan were interchangeable terms at this time), and because it was seen as breaking away from the Classical style espoused by the aristocratic establishment. This coincided with a revival of interest in pre-Renaissance art and a romanticized view of medieval England. This idealization of the Middle Ages is seen in the work of the two most important theorists of the Arts and Crafts Movement, John Ruskin and William Morris. Ruskin was a writer and art critic who saw the medieval craftsman as expressing 'man's delight in God's work'. His writings remained pertinent and influential for succeeding generations. In the second volume of *The Stones of Venice* he wrote:

> It would be well if all of us were good handicraftsmen in some kind, and the dishonour of manual labour done away with altogether . . . It is not that men are ill-fed, but that they have no pleasure in the work by which they make their bread, and therefore look to wealth as their only pleasure.[6]

In 1853, the year that this volume of *The Stones of Venice* was published, William Morris arrived in Oxford as a young undergraduate and quickly absorbed Ruskin's teachings. Through his friend, Edward Burne Jones, he also became drawn into the circle of the Pre-Raphaelite Brotherhood. After leaving university, Morris trained briefly with the Gothic Revival architect, G.E. Street, together with Philip Webb, who was to remain his lifelong friend. He abandoned architecture for painting, set up a studio in Red Lion Square, London and also designed, for his own use, what was described as 'intensely medieval furniture' made for him in deal by a local carpenter (Fig. 1.1).[7]

In 1860 the newly married William Morris and Jane Burden, together with many friends, were deeply absorbed in the decoration and furnishing of their new home, known as Red House, built for them by Philip Webb. From this stage it was a smooth transition to the founding of the firm of Morris, Marshall, Faulkner and Company in 1861. It was this project that for the first time gave Morris a real sense of purpose. He wanted to use the firm to break down barriers between artists and craftsmen, and to bring a new awareness of their surroundings to peoples' lives. His dictum was:

1.1   Pine table, probably designed by William Morris, c. 1856. Scrubbed top, the underframing was painted green at a later date (Woodley and Quick for CAGM)

'Have nothing in your houses that you do not know to be useful or believe to be beautiful.'[8] His writings, lectures and practical example through the next twenty years inspired the younger generation of architects and designers.

William Morris was also at the forefront of a stream of middle-class individuals responding to the lure of the countryside. Early in 1871 he had seen an advertisement in a house agent's catalogue for Kelmscott Manor near Lechlade, not far from the source of the Thames in the Cotswold hills. On an exploratory visit he found a typical Cotswold stone house with a gabled front and tall chimneys, built in the seventeenth century in a conservative vernacular style. He was entranced by the house and its rural setting amidst fields and water. That summer he and the Pre-Raphaelite painter and poet, Dante Gabriel Rossetti, jointly acquired the lease to the manor house.

Kelmscott Manor was intended to serve as a summer house – a refuge where Rossetti and Janey Morris could indulge their emotional, romantic attachment without the constraints of society, and where the Morris girls and friends of the family could enjoy an uncluttered existence. Rossetti commented that, at Kelmscott, Morris's two daughters, Jenny and May, were 'able to amuse themselves all day long without needing to be thought about by their elders'.[9] Among the novel outings during summers at Kelmscott were visits to Broadway Tower (Fig. 1.2), the tall turretted folly rented by Cormell Price, an old friend from Morris's university days. Jane and May Morris in particular threw themselves into these escapades with childlike enthusiasm. May described the setting as:

> . . . the most inconvenient and the most delightful place ever seen – to simple folks like ourselves, who could do without almost everything with great cheerfulness: . . . The Tower was certainly absurd – the men had to bathe on the roof, when the wind didn't blow the soap away and there was water enough . . . but how the clean aromatic wind blew the aches out of our tired bodies and how good it all was.[10]

Kelmscott Manor itself provided the minimum of domestic conveniences and was sparsely furnished. The only improvement made by the new tenants was to lay down plain flagstone floors. The house and its interior are described in *News from Nowhere*, Morris's utopian romance published in 1890:

1.2 Broadway Tower, Worcestershire (Broadway Tower Country Park)

Everywhere there was but little furniture and that only the most necessary, and of the simplest form. The extravagant love of ornament which I had noted in this people elsewhere seemed here to have given place to the feeling that the house itself and its associations was the ornament of the country life amidst which it had been left stranded from old times, and that to re-ornament it would but take away its use as a piece of natural beauty.[11]

Although Morris himself never spent that much time there, the house remained important to him and an influence on his work. While at Kelmscott he would try out old vegetable recipes for textile dyes, choosing leaves, twigs and other raw materials while fishing. For Morris and for the Arts and Crafts Movement, nature was the vital source of inspiration for pattern. He wrote: 'I, as a Western man and a picture-lover, must still insist on plenty of meaning in your patterns; I must have unmistakeable [*sic*] suggestions of gardens and fields, and strange trees, boughs and tendrils.'[12]

As an outsider, Morris was quick to appreciate the natural beauty of the Cotswolds, although 'at that time they were a mystery land of difficult hills and deeply wooded valleys'.[13] The countryside, its surface scarred by the limestone outcrops,

1.3 Wedgwood bowl, painted by Alfred Powell with a growing tree, a recurrent source of inspiration for the Arts and Crafts Movement (F.C. Scorey for CAGM)

was too austere for earlier tastes. William Cobbett's *Rural Rides*, written in 1821, described it as 'cheerless', reflecting the prejudices of his age and the current economic conditions. The Cotswold hills provided ideal pasture for sheep farming. In the Middle Ages the wool trade had been a source of great wealth and trading links. As the local wool trade declined in the eighteenth century with the emergence of new industrial centres in the north, so the area's reliance on farming as a source of wealth increased. The collapse of agriculture in the 1870s as prices were undercut by cheaper imported food also had severe repercussions on local communities. As a result the rural population declined drastically at a time when the overall population was rising.

Apart from the major ecclesiastical monuments – Gloucester Cathedral, Tewkesbury and Evesham Abbeys – the Cotswolds were unknown territory for architects and artists. Until the mid-nineteenth century there was very little new building in the area. Then a spate of country houses and churches were commissioned by the newly wealthy middle classes from Birmingham and its surrounds. In 1862, Morris and Co. were commissioned to produce stained glass for one such building, Selsley Church, designed by G.F. Bodley for Sir Samuel Stephens Marling. The following year, work began on

1.4   Daneway House near Sapperton. A typical fourteenth-century Cotswold manor house with seventeenth-century additions including magnificent plasterwork ceilings. During the twentieth century it served as Ernest Gimson's showrooms for about eighteen years, and subsequent tenants included Emery Walker, co-founder of the Doves Press, and the designer Oliver Hill (CAGM)

1.5   Gloucestershire Waggon and Team, *carved chestnut panel by William Simmonds, c. 1937 (F.C. Scorey for CAGM)*

Rendcomb Manor designed by P.C. Hardwick for Sir F.H. Goldsmid. Like most of the Cotswold architecture of the period, these two buildings relied on French and Italian Gothic models rather than the local architectural traditions.

The vernacular traditions of Cotswold building came to be recognized only in the late nineteenth century. The main building material in the area is the limestone, which is so much part of the landscape that each hillside 'looks as if it has been the quarry out of which has come at least the stone for fencing walls, if not for the houses'.[14] The Cotswold vernacular style has its roots in the architecture of the Elizabethan period. The skills of the mastermason, in the choice and shaping of the stone and in the mixture and application of the mortar, reigned supreme, not only in the churches and manor houses but in the cottages, farmhouses and farmbuildings.

Morris was one of the first to appreciate the restrained and orderly qualities of Cotswold building. His own Cotswold manor house at Kelmscott he lovingly described as being built:

   . . . of well-laid rubble stone of the district, the wall of the latter part being buttered over, so as to say, with thin plaster which has now weathered to the same colour as the stone of the walls; the roofs are covered with the beautiful

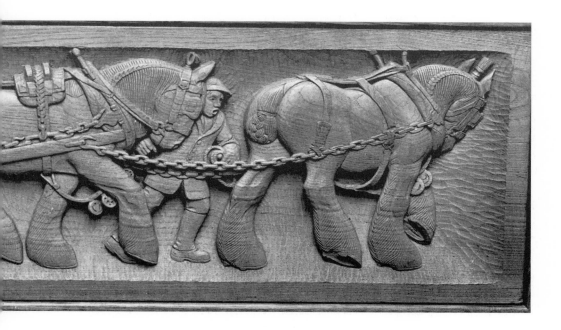

stone slates of the district, the most lovely covering which a roof can have, especially when, as here, and in all the traditional old houses of the countryside, they are sized down, the smaller ones at the top and bigger towards the eaves, which gives one the same sort of pleasure in their orderly beauty as a fish's scales or a bird's feather.[15]

His admiration for smaller-scale traditional buildings – tithe barns, village churches and the like – was such that it led him to make a lasting contribution to their conservation. In September 1876, on a journey that took him through Burford, the sight of over-zealous restorers scraping away at the village church gave him the initial impetus to found the Society for the Protection of Ancient Buildings which is still active today.

The Cotswolds held a particular appeal for the Arts and Crafts Movement, partly because the years of decline and neglect had left them relatively untouched by the changes that were going on elsewhere in the country. The area was dominated by wealthy landowners who were traditionally conservative in their approach to architectural styles. Craft traditions, too, had survived more or less intact. There was still a respect for workmanship which had all but disappeared elsewhere. Philip Webb

1.6   The Chair-maker, *line engraving by Stanley Anderson (CAGM)*

described his experiences with local workmen in Sussex in a letter to Alfred Powell: 'Most of the Estate workmen are decent fellows but rough in their work; and inclined to say "O, that will do" – when it should not . . . . When they look at the work as finished, they say, "that will stand for years" as if endurance was a kind of vice.'[16]

A different work ethic could still be found in the Cotswolds. According to Edward Barnsley, writing about the early years of the twentieth century:

> It was in those days, in the rural areas like Sapperton, IMPOSSIBLE for an artisan to produce less than his best. Everybody in the village knew the maker had done it, and if it was judged less than his best work, if the wheel axle pin squeaked, if the beam had sapwood in it, if the haystack leaned, if the layered hedge didn't face towards London and was patchy, then my word didn't the culprit hear about it . . . he just didn't dare show his face in the local . . .

Traditionally craftsmen had taken personal pride in their work. In the Cotswold villages everyone still knew who was responsible for each job and, in theory at least, no one could get away with 'that's good enough'.

Chapter Two

London Days

Ernest Gimson, born in 1864, was one of the younger generation of architects and designers who came under Morris's influence at an early age. The Gimson family, who ran a heavy engineering company in Leicester, were also interested in the arts and good handiwork. They were leading members of the Leicester Secular Society and entertained Morris in their home when he talked to the Society in 1884 on one of his many lecture tours. Gimson fell under his spell and followed his advice to complete his architectural training in London. With letters of recommendation from Morris, he joined the office of the ecclesiastical architect, John Sedding. Among his fellow students was Ernest Barnsley. The latter's brother, Sidney Barnsley, entered the office of Norman Shaw. Sedding's and Shaw's offices were probably the best training ground that any young architect could have desired. They provided inspiration as well as a theoretical and practical grounding. The list of their students reads like a roll call of the Arts and Crafts Movement: William Lethaby, Henry Wilson, Alfred Powell and Robert Weir Schultz, as well as Gimson and the Barnsleys.

Ernest Gimson and the Barnsley brothers were typical of the young men involved in the Arts and Crafts Movement. All three were from well-off middle-class families. The family business of John Barnsley and Sons was one of the major firms of builders in Victorian Birmingham. Like the Gimsons, the Barnsleys had prospered on the crest of the wave of industrialization but had maintained a strong social conscience that often accompanies non-conformity in religion. Above all, the three men were all younger sons. Their elder brothers carried on in business while they were free, and had the financial independence, to make their own choice of career.

Having decided to pursue their architectural training in London in the 1880s, they were very quickly caught up into the new groupings that were emerging. Architects were at the forefront of efforts to make artistic endeavour more relevant to everyday life, to improve the design of household goods and even to improve the quality of peoples' lives. Many diaries and autobiographies of this period write of the feeling of excitement among the younger generation of architects and designers in London, and of meetings of the Society for the Protection of Ancient Buildings, founded and patronized by Morris, where discussions were more often about the future of architecture and the arts than the day-to-day problems of Britain's threatened architectural heritage. These meetings were almost inevitably continued over the road at Gatti's, an eating house in the Strand, with Morris and Philip Webb inspiring the younger generation with their dreams of a new society. In 1884, some of that generation including William Lethaby founded the Art Workers' Guild to break down barriers between artists, architects, designers and craftsmen. Lectures and demonstrations were held regularly and the Art Workers' Guild also provided a forum for lively discussions. Gimson described some of the meetings he attended in letters he wrote to Ernest Barnsley, who completed his training in 1887 and returned to Birmingham to set up his own architectural practice: 'On Friday we had the delight of listening to Morris on art at the Art Workers' Guild. Lethaby, Schultz and Butler were in their element applauding his socialism to the echo. It's a d——d wicked world.'[18]

William Morris encouraged all his acquaintances to take up a manual skill. In 1890, Ernest Gimson learned the basic techniques of two crafts. From a London firm of plasterers, Messrs Whitcombe and Priestley, he learned how to make the decorative plaster panels that other architects, such as John Sedding and Philip Webb, were designing. Mr Whitcombe couldn't understand a gentleman like Gimson 'messing about with plaster, dirty stuff', but finally explained it as 'just his hobby'.[19] At the meetings of the Art Workers' Guild in Queen Square, Bloomsbury, Gimson was entranced by the simple rush-seated ladderback chairs which had been acquired from Philip Clissett, a traditional chair bodger from the village of Bosbury, Herefordshire. In 1890, Gimson spent a few weeks with Clissett learning how to use a simple pole lathe. From his subsequent recollections as related by a colleague, one can visualize Clissett as William Morris's ideal craftsman. Gimson told Edward Gardiner '. . . how quickly Clissett could turn out his work from cleft ash poles on his pole lathe, steam, bend and all the rest. He seems to have made a chair a day for 6/6d and rushed it in his cottage kitchen singing as he worked. According to old Philip Clissett if you were not singing you were not happy.'[20]

As well as acquiring manual skills, the younger generation of architects and designers also followed William Morris's example by becoming involved in the decorative arts. One of the first to follow in the footsteps of Morris and Co. was A.H. Mackmurdo, who set up the Century Guild in 1882 after becoming disillusioned with his architectural training. He and other like-minded young men designed furniture, metalwork and textiles and produced an influential journal, *The Hobby Horse*. In 1888, another young architect, Charles Robert Ashbee, first developed his own version of the Guild ideal.

Ashbee typified the romantic phase of socialism, described as 'essentially a response to class divisions . . . a mixture of angry youthful idealism and of upper class notions of duty tinged with panic: the important thing was to get in touch with the working class, and to get at the common humanity below the differences of class.'[21]

He had developed his ideas about the influence of society on the nature of its artistic production at university in Cambridge, under the influence of Walt Whitman and

2.1   *Charles Robert Ashbee, a pencil drawing by William Strang, 1903 (Art Workers' Guild)*

Edward Carpenter, as well as Ruskin and Morris. He also came to terms with his own sexuality. For him and others of his circle, homosexuality introduced notions of male comradeship and was seen as a force to break down barriers in society. One of his closest friends at Cambridge, Goldsworthy Lowes Dickinson, 'admired Ashbee's capacity for practical philanthropic work, his "saner, more concrete views"'.[22] Ashbee put these views into practice while training as an architect with G.F. Bodley in London. Instead of returning to his family home in Bloomsbury he moved into Toynbee Hall, a university settlement in the East End of London, where graduates devoted their free time to social and educational work with the local population.

Despite setting up a successful reading class to study the works of John Ruskin, Toynbee Hall was a disappointment to Ashbee. His impressions written on an initial visit proved to be correct:

> I arrived here last night, my object to explore. I hope perhaps to live here later for a while, but rather as a sop to my own conscience, having now for three years talked philanthropy I'm desirous of doing something. Yet I mistrust myself and this place also; myself for insincerity, Toynbee Hall for what seems at first sight a top hatty philosophy.[23]

However, the Ruskin reading class became involved in some practical work and this formed the basis of Ashbee's major venture, the Guild and School of Handicraft, formally opened in 1888.

Despite his flair for self-publicity, demonstrated in a circular sent to all the leading figures in the art world advertising his plans and inviting comments, the Guild and School began on a small scale, with three members and a working capital of £50. Its aim was to attract young journeymen and train them in design for their specific craft. At the same time workshops run by the Guildsmen would produce and sell professional handicrafts to help support the School. Ashbee himself ran a class in design until 1895: pupils were taught to work out a design and then, with the help of the Guildsmen, to apply it in a range of different media. The Guildsmen were often people whom Ashbee found 'interesting'; he was antagonistic towards anyone with an art or trade school background. In a comradely atmosphere his mixed bunch of craftsmen, including a cat's meat barrow boy, a clerk in the City and an assistant in a bookshop, acquired new skills by a process of trial and error. The main areas of activity were cabinet-making, metalwork and decoration. The Guild was run democratically on a co-operative basis and took over the lives of those involved. Ashbee put as much effort into organizing after-hours activities, with evening classes, lectures, plays and holiday weekends playing an important part in Guild life.

The Guild quickly flourished and expanded and, in 1890, the enterprise was moved to Essex House, a somewhat dilapidated Georgian house in the Mile End

*2.2   Buckle in silver, 1890. The left-hand portion consisits of a cast and chiselled profile of Mrs Ashbee, C.R.
Ashbee's mother. Designed and possibly made by C.R. Ashbee (F.C. Scorey for CAGM)*

Road. Essex House was in the heart of the East End, an area of even greater urban
deprivation and decay. The first spring, however, saw the appearance of masses of
white pinks in the garden and this flower became closely connected with the Guild, a
symbol of hope and renewal. With one of those uneasy contrasts that plague the Arts
and Crafts Movement, Ashbee leased retail premises for the Guild at 16a Brook
Street in the West End of London. Silver, metalwork and jewellery, in particular,
gradually established the Guild's reputation for innovative design and became its staple products. Ashbee designed most of the pieces but his drawings were often modified at a later stage in discussion with the craftsmen. After the first days of experiment were over he rarely made anything himself. His designs were influenced by the
robust shapes of medieval silver, the work of Renaissance designers (particularly
Benvenuto Cellini) and the use of naturalistic motifs, often stylized in a way that
makes them precursors of art nouveau.

By 1900 The Magpie and Stump, the house in Cheyne Walk, Chelsea that Ashbee
had built for his mother, had been decorated and furnished by the Guild to great critical acclaim. The Guild's work had received international recognition with the commission from the Grand Duke of Hesse to carry out designs by Baillie Scott, another
Arts and Crafts architect/designer, for the ducal palace at Darmstadt in Germany.
Ashbee and the Guild of Handicraft were at the height of their success. Spurred on by
the expiry of the lease to Essex House, Ashbee decided that the future development
of the Guild lay outside London in a very different setting.

Ernest Gimson and William Lethaby were the leading spirits behind a third venture: a 'furniture shop scheme' to produce well-designed and well-made furniture.

2.3 Sporting cup of hammered and cast gilt copper, designed by C.R. Ashbee, c. 1895 (CAGM)

In 1890, Gimson persuaded Sidney Barnsley to return from his scholarship study of Byzantine architecture in Greece and join them. Two slightly older architects, Reginald Blomfield and Mervyn Macartney, made up the working partners with a sixth business partner, Colonel Mallet. The company was prosaically named Kenton and Co. after Kenton Street, just round the corner from their premises in Bloomsbury.

The furniture designed by the five architects was made by a team of professional cabinet-makers. In keeping with the ideals of the Arts and Crafts Movement, the contributions of both designer and maker were acknowledged by stamped initials on each piece.

There was no house style at Kenton and Co.; each of the architects produced individual designs reflecting his own interests and experience. Blomfield commented: 'we made no attempt to interfere with each other's idiosyncracies'.[24] Both he and Mervyn Macartney looked to English furniture of the eighteenth and early nineteenth centuries for their inspiration. Sidney Barnsley's designs, only a few of which are documented, show the influence of his Byzantine studies in their use of inlays and veneers to achieve bold geometric patterns of shape, colour and texture. Among Grimson's contributions were three striking cabinets on stands which illustrate both his interest in seventeenth-and early eighteenth-century furniture, and his fresh and decorative approach to design.

2.4   Green glass decanter mounted in silver by the Guild of Handicraft, 1901. These popular items were made from 1897 onwards with variations in design (CAGM)

2.5   A view of the 1891 Kenton and Co. exhibition, including an oak table and mahogany chair designed by Ernest Gimson (CAGM)

Reginald Blomfield described Lethaby's and Gimson's inventions as 'simple designs of admirable form in oak'.[25] Gimson designed a simple unpolished oak dresser in which the sole decoration was provided by a precise and somewhat self-conscious use of chamfering on the plate rack (Fig. 2.6). The same, rather laboured attempt to produce 'country' furniture can be seen in the series of pieces designed by Lethaby with subject inlays including sheep (Fig. 2.7) and ships. It was Lethaby who also developed the open construction work on the furniture of this period which was to be so important in the future.

The climax of Kenton and Co.'s short existence was an exhibition held at Barnards Inn in the Inns of Court in December 1891. This was both a financial and a critical success, with sales totalling £700. It made a strong impression on a number of visitors, including C.R. Ashbee who, some 15 years later in his polemic work, *Craftsmanship in Competitive Industry*, described the event 'One of the most beautiful of modern exhibitions of furniture . . . where the pieces shown, many of them simple, straightforward & useful pieces, bore the names of Lethaby, . . . Barnsley, Gimson, and others with whom the Arts and Crafts movement is identified.'[26]

2.6   *The hall in Ernest Barnsley's house at Sapperton showing a Kenton and Co. dresser and decorative plasterwork, both by Ernest Gimson (CAGM)*

However, by the following year the enthusiasm for the 'furniture shop scheme' was on the wane. Col Mallet was unwilling to provide further financial backing, but more significant was the lack of commitment among the five active participants. According to Reginald Blomfield, they saw that the time had come to 'make a definite choice between the practice of architecture and the practice of designing and making furniture'.[27] Both he and Mervyn Macartney went on to become respected figures in the architectural profession. Lethaby continued in the Arts and Crafts mainstream as an architect, designer, writer and educationalist. In 1896 he became co-director and principal of the Central School of Arts and Crafts. For these men, Kenton and Co. had been a youthful venture set up in the flush of their rebellion against the establishment and their enthusiasm for the new ideas about unity in the arts. By the end of 1892 the company was wound up, stocks of materials were disposed of and any unsold furniture was shared out between the partners. Lethaby saw it as a rather jolly experiment:

To my share fell what we still call 'the Gimson Cabinet' of walnut 'left clean' and unpolished but now mellow and glossy from use; another cabinet which

2.7   Chest in oak inlaid with ebony and walnut, designed by William Lethaby for Kenton and Co., 1890 (F.C. Scorey for CAGM)

we call 'Blomfield', 'Barnsley's table', 'my Oak Chair' and a little revolving bookcase designed by Macartney. After all, these five pieces were not a bad return for £100 down.[28]

Chapter Three

Gimson and the Barnsleys

The intellectual excitement of London was not enough for Ernest Gimson and Sidney Barnsley. The yearning for a different way of life, for something more spiritual and natural, was very much part of the Arts and Crafts Movement. Alfred Powell expressed the longing for notional country traditions in this description of the rooms that Gimson and Sidney Barnsley shared as students:

> . . . it was wonderful in old smoky London to find yourself in those fresh clean rooms, furnished with good oak furniture and a trestle table that at seasonable hours surrendered its drawing-boards to a good English meal, in which figured, if I remember right, at least on guest nights, a great stone jar of the best ale.[29]

In the late 1880s, Ernest Gimson began to conceive of a romantic vision that was to colour the rest of his life. At first he planned simply to rent a country cottage where he and his friends could gather to cleanse their minds and bodies of their urban existence, draw from nature at first hand and find fresh inspiration from vernacular architecture and traditional crafts. In June 1890, Gimson wrote to Ernest Barnsley saying, 'I have been spending my spare time in hunts after country cottages'. Later that year, in October, he seemed to be on the verge of success, enthusiastically describing a cottage in Kent that he and Lethaby were thinking of taking as 'a charming place that might be as far from London as the Yorkshire Hills'. The discussions on these trips, according to Lethaby, were 'of the necessity of keeping near to nature'.

While for the older members of the group Kenton and Co. had been something of an aberration from their chosen path, for Ernest Gimson and Sidney Barnsley it was the first step towards a new way of life. Despite their involvement with architectural projects, they wanted to take the experiment a stage further. They felt '. . . a desire to make closer contact with Nature than they felt was possible over the drawing board in a City office, and they held the belief that the revival of architecture lay in the revival of the crafts'.[30]

They saw themselves as establishing an ideal country-based community where they would 'get hold of a few capable and trustworthy craftsmen and . . . all join together and form a nucleus around which in time others would attach themselves'.[31]

According to Alfred Powell, 'they scoured the countryside from Yorkshire to the South Downs', before moving, in 1893, to Ewen, a small hamlet south-west of

Cirencester, which they used as a temporary base while seeking a permanent home in the south Cotswolds. It is likely that they would have sought advice and guidance from those they most respected before embarking on this new venture: their families, and friends such as Philip Webb and even William Morris himself. The two young men were fortunate in managing to persuade Ernest Barnsley to give up his architectural practice in Birmingham and uproot his somewhat reluctant wife and two young daughters from their newly built home in Barnt Green, Worcestershire. He exchanged a comfortable professional life for the uncertain prospect of practising the arts of building and handcrafts in an isolated rural setting.

Initially Ernest Barnsley took over as the leader and senior figure in the group. He shared none of the diffidence of Gimson and his younger brother. Their shyness and awkwardness with strangers could easily have been a serious disability had they set up a City practice as architects. In contrast, Ernest Barnsley loved company and was at ease in almost any social situation. He was outgoing, full of fun and a connoisseur of good food, drink, and antiques. Norman Jewson, who subsequently married his eldest daughter, Mary, saw him as a 'real *bon viveur*'. From his family background, Ernest Barnsley had also inherited a sound business sense and an ability to handle

3.1   Group photograph at Pinbury, c. 1896. From left to right: Sidney Barnsley, Lucy Morley, Ernest Gimson (seated and looking uncharacteristically morose), Ernest Barnsley with his wife, Alice, and two daughters, Mary and Ethel (CAGM)

23

money matters with tact and authority. However he preferred to work at his own pace and somehow lacked the fierce sense of purpose and dedication of his younger brother and friend.

Ernest Barnsley was thus the ideal person to take on the role of spokesman and negotiator for the three men. His first major task came when his younger brother came upon Pinbury Park during a walk and decided that it would be ideal for their purposes. Pinbury Park was an Elizabethan house on the estate of Lord Bathurst in a beautiful setting near the village of Sapperton. Subsequently it also captivated Freda Derrick who wrote:

> I went to Pinbury first in 1951 . . . Through the wood beyond [Sapperton], along the cart track that emerges on the green valley; and I knew why Sidney Barnsley said 'We must have this!' when he found Pinbury. It was like the unspoiled landscape in a romance by William Morris, in which each common plant and tree had the rare beauty of such things in tapestry . . .[32]

Over the years, the house had been converted into a farm and allowed to fall into disrepair. Ernest Barnsley arranged a repairing lease of £75 per annum with the estate which allowed him and his family to occupy the main house while carrying out agreed work to the fabric of the building. Gimson and Sidney Barnsley moved into adjacent cottages converted from former farm buildings. Another outbuilding was to be used as a joint workshop.

From the first there was a strong romantic element in the move to the Cotswolds, echoing the utopian dreams of William Morris. Gimson and the Barnsleys were all city-born and bred and had never had to deal with the day-to-day practicalities of rural life. Yet they were determined to live like country folk, albeit country folk of independent means: baking their own bread, brewing cider and sloe gin, and keeping hens and goats. Alice Barnsley was no country housekeeper and her lack of enthusiasm for her husband's change of course seems to have coloured her life. So they invited one of Gimson's cousins, Lucy Morley, to join them. She had grown up on a farm in Lincolnshire where Gimson had been sent to recuperate from frequent childhood illnesses. Despite having gone deaf at the age of nineteen through a congenital problem that also affected five of her six sisters, she was a strong, supportive and amazingly capable woman. She appreciated the work that Gimson and the Barnsleys were trying to do and set about organizing the practicalities of daily life with great efficiency and good sense. In 1895, Lucy Morley and Sidney Barnsley were married. Subsequently, Sidney Barnsley was able to pass on practical advice to Philip Webb who, in 1901, had rented his own country cottage near Crawley in Sussex: 'The enclosed instructions of heating a brick oven I trust you will find useful, our experiences when we first tried were anything but successful.'[33]

3.2   Joint workshop at Pinbury, c. 1896 (CAGM)

The three men shared a single workshop at Pinbury and the photograph of the interior (Fig. 3.2) taken by Herbert Barnsley, elder brother of Ernest and Sidney and a keen amateur photographer, shows the close proximity in which they worked at this stage in their careers. As well as working on two architectural commissions – summer cottages in the Charnwood Forest near Leicester – Gimson was designing and making decorative plaster panels. He continued his close working relationship with Lethaby and produced plasterwork for a number of houses designed by his friend during this period. He also found a ready market for his turned ladderback chairs.

Ernest Barnsley, too, was primarily concerned with architectural projects during the early days at Pinbury. He was responsible for carrying out the work on Pinbury Park required by their lease and was also commissioned by the estate to undertake restoration work on the nearby Daneway House. In addition, he began designing and making furniture, the latter apparently for the first time. The workshop photograph shows part of an oak music-chest and workbox which Ernest Barnsley exhibited at the 1896 Arts and Crafts Exhibition. This piece of furniture, which is only known from photographs, was made in two parts. The solid carcase upper part had a half-hexagonal top which lifted to reveal 'the usual holes and corners, lined with pencil cedar, for the materials of the needlewoman'. The basic frame construction of the lower part had doors with fielded panels enclosing shelves for music. Decoration was

3.3   Ladderback chair in ash with an unusual basket-woven rush seat, by Ernest Gimson, c. 1895 (CAGM)

provided by well-cut dovetails and bold chevron stringing. All in all, the relatively sophisticated construction of this piece at this stage in the men's careers remains something of a puzzle. More typical of the period is the 'chick' chest in which Ernest Barnsley echoed the inlaid pieces designed by William Lethaby for Kenton and Co.

Of the three men it was Sidney Barnsley who at this stage concentrated all his efforts on mastering the techniques of cabinet-making by a process of trial and error. His son, Edward, recalled the scene in the Pinbury workshops as related to him by his mother: 'She would make the cakes for the mid-morning break, and the drinks, and taking them in find SHB hard at work at the bench, the other two standing by, often hands in pockets, whistling Gilbert and Sullivan tunes.'[34]

Sidney Barnsley's contribution in the last decade of the nineteenth century was vital in laying the foundations, both technically and stylistically, for all their later work.

His was a solitary character which has sometimes been described as austere, mainly because he shared the enthusiasm of many of his contemporaries for such rugged physical disciplines as cold baths. Above all he enjoyed the simple pleasures of long walks in the surrounding countryside with his dog and the more sociable sport of tennis on summer evenings. He avoided unnecessary or unwelcome social contact, but also tried hard to overcome his awkwardness with strangers with an open and smiling manner. He derived great satisfaction from all physical and manual tasks and believed it was wrong to delegate any of the processes of woodworking, however laborious or mundane. His personality shines through in this comment written to Philip Webb:

> Talking of using the axe and saw, don't you find the wood vanishes quickly. My winter store is just being hauled and when it is all piled up it looks sufficient for a lifetime. 16 tons a year I find I burn – and that means a good deal of sawing and carrying – still, as Thoreau says, it is economical in that one gets warmed twice – once in sawing it and then in burning it, and the pleasure of splitting a big log and thinking of the future pleasure of watching it burn is worth a good deal.[35]

Sidney Barnsley's enjoyment of woodworking was such that he was the only furniture designer in the Arts and Crafts Movement who took its ideology to its logical conclusion and made up almost all his own designs.

As an architectural student, Sidney Barnsley had built up a basic understanding of the principles of cabinet-making from his detailed observations of old furniture in museums, churches and country houses. In the Cotswolds he also acquired a great many of the standard techniques of carpentry from Richard Harrison, the local wheelwright in the village of Sapperton. As well as providing much of the timber for the needs of the three men at Pinbury, he was also the source of a great deal of practical advice. Norman Jewson vividly described him as:

> . . . a short little man with his face reddened by exposure, small, humorous blue eyes and a tight mouth holding entirely toothless jaws . . . If ever a man loved his work, old Richard did. He seemed to live for nothing else, starting work at 6 in the morning and often working as long as it was light in the evening.[36]

It is interesting, bearing in mind this close relationship between wheelwright and furniture maker, that one of Sidney Barnsley's first pieces made at Pinbury was described in *The Cabinet Maker and Art Furnisher* as having 'the lines of the coachbuilder'. This was a reference to the oak chest, the two ends of which can be seen in the workshop photograph. Its open construction work also gave rise to comment, in particular 'his excellent dovetails' which stand proud from the curve of the coffered top so 'that if you happen to sit on them you feel them'. In his design, Sidney Barnsley combined three elements: the traditional techniques of country carpentry such as chamfering, the open construction work pioneered by William Lethaby, and a sense of mass and proportion derived from early English and continental furniture. Over the years these elements were crystallized in the work of Gimson and the Barnsleys into a style that was quite fresh and unique.

Sidney Barnsley subsequently told his son, Edward, that the inspiration for one of the most influential pieces of furniture made at Pinbury came directly from William Morris. The oak bow-fronted dresser which dominated Sidney Barnsley's living room (Fig. 3.4) was designed and made to Morris's dictum that furniture 'should be made of timber rather than walking sticks'. The initial impact of this massive piece of furniture is an awareness of the sheer physical and mental stamina that it must have required of its maker. Particularly impressive is the unadorned beauty of the figure on the planks of quartered oak and the subtle planing to form the facets of the bow front. It was in the construction of this piece that he first developed the double-dovetail or butterfly joint to join two pieces of wood in the same plane: a piece of wood was dovetailed horizontally and vertically, thus forming a key joint reinforced by thin wedges. The wedges were inserted end-grain up, adding to the decorative effect of this constructional technique. It became a distinctive feature of Arts and Crafts furniture, even to the extent of being used by others as a purely decorative device.

3.4   Sidney Barnsley's living room at Pinbury, showing his bow-fronted oak dresser, c. 1897 (the Barnsley family and Edward Barnsley Educational Trust Archive)

Ernest Barnsley's furniture designs tended to follow on from those of his brother. In 1899, for example, he designed and made a cupboard closely related to the oak bow-fronted dresser. Sidney Barnsley also played a part in some of the earliest furniture designed by Ernest Gimson. At the sixth Arts and Crafts Exhibition in 1899, Gimson exhibited an oak box inlaid with pearl that had been made by Sidney Barnsley to Gimson's design. The turn of the century, however, brought changes to the craft community at Pinbury. In 1900, spurred to action by some sharp comments on his lack of commitment from his close friend, Alfred Powell, Gimson decided to concentrate his energies on furniture design. Together with Ernest Barnsley he rented a second workshop in the yard of the Fleece Hotel in Cirencester. The two men decided to embark on a formal partnership and to employ trained cabinet-makers to carry out their designs.

For Ernest Barnsley and Ernest Gimson, having workshops at Cirencester and living about five miles away at Pinbury Park was not an ideal arrangement. It was also obvious that their living accommodation was no longer very suitable. The converted farmbuildings had been perfectly adequate for the needs of two bachelors, but Sidney and Lucy Barnsley now had a young family (Grace born in 1896 and Edward in 1900) while, also in 1900, Gimson married Emily Tompson, daughter of the vicar of Skipsea in Yorkshire, whom he had met on one of his sketching tours.

They were fortunate that their requirements coincided with those of their landlord. In 1901, Lord Bathurst was due to return from an army posting overseas. He was newly married and he and his wife wanted their young family to spend part of each year in the Cotswolds. They considered commissioning Ernest Barnsley to build them a new house, but were persuaded to make their home at Pinbury Park. The Bathursts, who were keen supporters of the new craft community in their midst, were eager to make adequate provisions to ensure its continuation. In return for giving up their lease to Pinbury, Gimson and the Barnsleys were to be given the use of Daneway House in the village of Sapperton which, together with its outbuildings, would provide showrooms and workshops. They were also given a strip of land below Sapperton church on which they could build, for the estate, three houses to be occupied at the same rent as they were already paying.

The three men were thus able to design and supervise the building of their own homes at Sapperton. Upper Dorvel House, the largest of the three, was built by Ernest Barnsley on sloping ground just below the church. He seems to have relished the opportunity to put his ideas about architecture and building into practice, incorporating an existing stone cottage, using local materials, methods and craftsmen, and supervising the work down to the smallest detail. Sidney Barnsley's house was the next down the lane, with Gimson's originally thatched cottage lying furthest from the village.

Although Sidney Barnsley, tongue-in-cheek, described his brother's house as a

3.5   *One of the showrooms at Daneway House, c. 1903. This view shows two cabinets on stands designed by Gimson, and a chamfered oak chest of drawers designed by Ernest Barnsley. The small inlaid box is probably Indian in origin, illustrating an important influence on their work (CAGM)*

'mansion', all three were relatively modest and even spartan homes, simply decorated with oak floors, whitewashed walls and a mixture of old furniture and examples of their own work. Writing to Philip Webb, Sidney Barnsley gave a glimpse of their day-to-day lives: 'We still live the same life you knew at Pinbury, cooking and eating in the kitchen with the added luxury of a retiring room now, where we sit in the evenings and the children have their lessons, and in this way we have a sunny room all the day.'[37]

In July 1902, Sidney Barnsley was able to give a buoyant account of these new developments in his correspondence with Philip Webb:

> My brother and Gimson have already started workshops at Daneway having 4 or 5 cabinet makers or boys so far, with the hopes of chairmakers and modellers in the near future. I am remaining an outsider from this movement — still going on making furniture by myself and handing over to them any orders I cannot undertake, and orders seem to come in too quickly now as we are getting known.[38]

Sidney Barnsley made it clear that he was wary of family and friends going into business together. He had no real interest in running a workshop and having authority and responsibility over other men. One incident from the past remained firmly in his memory, shaping the way he was to work for the rest of his life:

> I remember when Kenton's closed down, how Hall our famous foreman rejoiced to make some furniture for himself in the shop we lent him until our lease was up — overmantels of bevelled plate glass & turned balusters glued on — Oh! such things as you've never seen and it was that made me decide never to employ men — a stupid selfish decision I know — but that was how I was made![39]

Sidney Barnsley's strong objections to designing for others were not shared by his brother or Gimson, neither did they have the same physical stamina. Instead, having made a commitment to furniture design, Gimson in particular wanted trained cabinet-makers to enable him to bring his many ideas to fruition. Between 1901 and 1904 the nucleus of craftsmen was employed. Harry Davoll, who had been working as a cabinet-maker in Liverpool for nearly ten years, heard of the Gloucestershire vacancy through his Trade Union secretary. He came down to start work at Cirencester in November 1901. He started work at 8d. (4p) an hour, working from 7.00 a.m. to 5.30 p.m. on weekdays and until 1 p.m. on Saturdays. He was soon joined by Percy Burchett and Ernest Smith, both of whom had completed cabinet-making apprenticeships in London. The indifferent approach to workmanship characterized by the expression, 'that will do', was an anathema to Gimson and the Barnsleys, and their attitude came as quite a shock to men who had worked in the trade. Once they got used to it, however, they appreciated the emphasis on quality. The most significant appointment was that of a Dutchman, Peter van der Waals, as foreman. He had worked extensively as a cabinet-maker on the continent before coming to England in about 1900, and his meticulous approach and high standards of craftsmanship were a constant source of inspiration.

By March 1902, the workshops in the outbuildings at Daneway were in use and work was progressing on the house itself. The main rooms of Daneway House, with plasterwork friezes and ceiling decorations dating from the sixteenth century, were a constant source of inspiration for Ernest Gimson. The estate stipulated that access to these rooms should be available to interested visitors. They were thus ideally suited to act as showrooms for the furniture made there. The presence of trained cabinet-makers obviously extended the range of furniture that could be produced. Gimson's design for a cabinet on a stand, dated 1902, harks back to some of his cabinets for Kenton and Co., in particular its bold shaped ebony base and the use of decorative veneered panels. However, despite producing a greater proportion of decorative pieces, Ernest Gimson and Ernest Barnsley never lost sight of the basic framework of design and construction established by Sidney Barnsley at Pinbury.

Sidney Barnsley continued to work on his own, having built himself a workshop in the garden of his new house at Sapperton. In May 1904 he wrote contentedly to Philip Webb:

> My workshop which I have to my lone self is a great improvement upon the Pinbury one, much better lighted and being thatched is warmer and drier, and from the end window I have a most wonderful view across the valley to the hanging wood you would remember. I am still occupied in making good solid oak furniture with occasional pieces of a more delicate kind as a rest and a change. I have just finished two tables out of English oak, 12'0" × 3'6" each, the tops out of 3 inch with only one joint in the width and they have given me a fair dressing down and by night time I have felt fair tired out.[40]

Inevitably, there were times when, despite his ingenuity, Sidney Barnsley needed an extra pair of hands. According to his son, he made a point of going to Gimson's gardener rather than any of the craftsmen for assistance. However, the proximity of trained cabinet-makers had an impact on his work and more sophisticated techniques, including fielded panels, quickly appeared in his own pieces.

Sadly, and all too soon, Sidney Barnsley was proved right in his distrust of mixing business with friendship. By about 1905 the partnership between Gimson and Ernest Barnsley had broken up amid a pervasive bitterness, aggravated by tensions between their wives, which was never resolved. Such was the rancour aroused that Sidney Barnsley and Gimson were only able to continue their friendship of longstanding outside their homes. Because of the lack of written material and the reluctance of subsequent generations to talk about what was still a very painful subject, it is only possible to hazard a guess at the root cause and at the difficulties that the split created in the day-to-day life of such a small community. After 1905, Ernest Barnsley gave up any serious idea of furniture-making and concentrated on his architectural work. His main achievement was the building of Rodmarton Manor, begun in 1909 and completed, three years after his death, in 1929. This large country house was commissioned by Claud Biddulph and built, more or less by hand, using local materials and traditional craft techniques. Both the client and the architect saw the commission partly as a means of reviving local traditions of craftsmanship.

It was Ernest Gimson who carried on and expanded the Daneway workshops. Although just in his forties, it was only at this point that he found a real sense of purpose. On their first meeting in the summer of 1907, Norman Jewson described him:

A tall, well-built man with a slight stoop, a large rather heavy face, except when he smiled, a brown moustache and wide-open contemplative eyes. His expression was that of a man entirely at peace with himself and all the world. His tweed suit hung loosely on him over a soft shirt and collar, with a silk tie threaded through a ring. Being summer he wore a panama hat instead of his usual cloth cap, but in all seasons he wore heavy hobnailed boots, made for him by a cobbler at Chalford.[41]

Gimson was a good judge of character and built up a strong, trusting relationship with Peter Waals which was mutually beneficial. Sir George Trevelyan, who subsequently worked as a cabinet-maker with Waals, described Gimson as 'the inspiration and genius' who 'used Waals from the outset in close co-operation'. One important aspect of Gimson's 'genius' was that, despite never practising any craft other than plasterwork and chair-making '. . . he could put himself completely into the understanding and experience of a craft, so that as far as makes no matter, he WAS the craftsman in that skill. He thought as a craftsman, knowing exactly what he could ask of the men and he had their complete confidence through the inevitable 'rightness' of each design.'[42]

Because he held their confidence and respect, his craftsmen accepted his authority over them. In many cases he was able to extend their skill far beyond their own conception of their capabilities. This is well-illustrated by the way the chair-making workshop was set up. Gimson soon found that he had more orders for the turned ladderback chairs than he could complete himself, so he sent designs to workshops in what was then the centre for chair-making, High Wycombe. He was disappointed by the finished products: the quality of the wood was inferior and the workmanship poor. He therefore looked into the possibility of setting up a chair-making workshop, using the waterwheel at the Daneway sawmill to drive the lathe. He taught Edward Gardiner, the young son of the sawmill owner, the basics of the craft and then:

> After making a few chairs in plain turning, Mr Gimson brought down his first design in bead turning for chairs, soon followed by a design for a beaded settee. I was much disquieted by this, being only a beginner, as Mr Gimson was treating me like an experienced craftsman and I was not at all sure I could rise to it.
>
> I had by this time got to know the men at Daneway House, and appreciate the quality of the work they were doing and I did not intend that my work should be in any way inferior to theirs in quality and accuracy, therefore I took great pains to make a perfect job of each chair.[43]

The demand for light, movable chairs, first catered for by Morris and Co. with the 'Sussex' chair in the 1860s, was such that the chair-making workshop flourished under Gimson's and Edward Gardiner's joint partnership. Several assistants and apprentices were taken on between 1904 and 1913, when Edward Gardiner left Daneway intending to establish a workshop in Warwickshire.

Another development was the setting up of a smithy. Once again, Gimson could not get suitable metal fittings elsewhere for his architectural work and furniture. His friend, Alfred Powell, had asked the village blacksmith at Tunley to make him some hinges for his own house. The blacksmith, Billy Bucknell, passed on the work to his son, Alfred. When he saw the finished pieces, Gimson was very impressed. He gave Alfred Bucknell some work and set him up with his own smithy in the wheelwright's yard at Sapperton in about 1903. As well as making the basic architectural fittings to Gimson's design, the two men worked closely together to devise techniques to carry out intricate and fine designs in brass, iron, polished steel and silver. Heavy firedogs, polished steel fire irons, often with spiral twist decoration, pierced and chased candlesticks and sconces were produced, as well as the distinctive handles for the furniture made in the Daneway workshops. There were usually about four men working in the smithy. As well as Alfred Bucknell, Steve Mustoe who worked at Daneway for

3.6   Four toasting forks, designed by Ernest Gimson and made by Alfred Bucknell, c. 1910–1925 (F.C. Scorey for CAGM)

3.7   *Design for a candlesconce by Ernest Gimson, June 1910 (CAGM)*

many years had had some training as a blacksmith. A number of local boys were taken on over the years as apprentices, including Fritz Whiting and Harry Gardiner.

By 1914 the workshops had expanded considerably. About nine woodworkers were employed, ranging from skilled cabinet-makers to apprentices under the daily supervision of the foreman, Peter Waals. The smithy employed between four and five men and apprentices, two or three of whom were involved in chair-making. The Daneway workshops were run on the principle that one man should have responsibility for each job, although this was not always the case. Craftsmen were paid an hourly rate according to their experience and the particular job they were doing. Before the 1914–18 War, the average weekly wage at Daneway was between 20 and 30s. (£1 and £1.50), about 5 to 10s. (25 to 50p) a week more than the average weekly earnings of an agricultural labourer. Peter Waals's wages as a cabinet-maker were supplemented by a weekly sum of £2 10 s. (£2.50) due to him as foreman. Gimson and his wife took a keen interest in the craftsmen's general welfare. Hill House Farm, the other side of Daneway from Gimson's house, was leased to provide a home for the unmarried craftsmen.

Gimson's daily life was described by Norman Jewson, who joined him as an architectural assistant in 1907:

> Gimson generally started the morning in his drawing office. Then he dropped in for a short chat with Sidney at his workshop, after which he went on to the blacksmiths' shops. Most afternoons were spent in his drawing office, but he walked across to Daneway two or three times a week. Work in the drawing office was varied by afternoons in the open shed below when there was modelled plasterwork to be done.[44]

Both Jewson and Emily Gimson acted on occasion as assistants in the execution of decorative plasterwork. Jewson described it as 'inevitably a messy job, and I remember a chimney sweep remarking with a grin, "Well, Sir, we're both of us dirty, only mine's black dirt and yours is white".'[45]

After the move to the Cotswolds, Gimson and the Barnsleys had abandoned the practice adopted by Kenton and Co. of stamping pieces with the initials of designer and maker. Items of their furniture therefore normally bear no mark. None of Ernest Barnsley's working drawings have survived. Neither Ernest Gimson nor Sidney Barnsley found it necessary to use full-size drawings; they usually worked to 1:8 or 1:12 scale. Edward Barnsley recollected Gimson working with a pencil in his right hand and a ruler in his left, thus allowing himself to draw quickly to scale. Without the evidence of drawings or provenance, it is very difficult to tell apart the work of Gimson and Sidney Barnsley. Both men designed very similar domestic furniture in oak and other locally obtainable woods, including elm, ash and various fruitwoods.

3.8   Settee or daybed in English oak, designed and made by Sidney Barnsley, c. 1912 (F.C. Scorey for CAGM)

They were also responsible for inspiring a revival of interest in the use of English walnut, a timber that had fallen out of favour in the early eighteenth century because of the savage winter of 1709, its susceptibility to woodworm and the growing popularity of imported mahogany. Continuing to build on Sidney Barnsley's experimental work at Pinbury, both men's concept of design was one of reducing a piece of furniture to its essentials while still bearing in mind its functional needs and proportion.

Sidney Barnsley's early enthusiasm for vernacular woodworking traditions survived in both men's work, with hayrake and wishbone stretchers often used for underframing and the curves on the rail backs. The wheelwright's technique of through-jointing was also regularly employed in the design of such pieces. The techniques of the wheelwright and country carpenter can also be seen in the decorative features of the two men's furniture. Chamfering continued to be used, both to lighten furniture and to add visual interest. The wood was shaped using a draw knife and spokeshave, and was left showing the marks of the tools. They liked an oak table top, for example, left with the very slight marks of the plane rather than finished with a scraper or sandpaper. With a very sharp plane, a craftsman could achieve an almost faultless surface which still had an almost imperceptible sparkle left from the tool marks.

They also employed the methods traditionally used by craftsmen to express their natural enjoyment of woodworking. Gouging was one such technique. Sidney Barnsley used to call the relatively quick process of making lines of gouged decoration on a piece of furniture, 'tickling' the wood. Another method used to emphasize the lines of a piece of furniture and to add visual interest was chip-carving. Shallow

3.9   Segmental sideboard in oak with chip-carved decoration, designed by Ernst Gimson, c. 1910 (F.C. Scorey for CAGM)

chisel cuts were made to create a repeating pattern of squares or diamonds. One writer on cabinet-making describes it as 'a pleasant way to whittle away idle hours and have something to show for it'.[46]

A greater emphasis on decoration is found on pieces by Gimson and Sidney Barnsley which can be classified as what Morris described as 'state furniture intended quite as much for Beauty's sake as for use'. Some cabinets, sideboards, dressers, small boxes and church furniture were among the types that fall into this category. They were still functional, but the materials used, their decorative nature and the hours expended serve to classify them as luxury items. In their designs, Gimson and Sidney Barnsley made use of their close observation of historical pieces. Particularly popular with both men was the cabinet, often with numerous drawers and cupboards, on a stand that originated with the varguenos made in six-teenth- and seventeenth-century Spain and Portugal. Both men often used a dark and light inlay, usually in holly and ebony. In such cabinets the inlay would be used to emphasize the structure and the pattern of drawers. This distinctive feature of their work was derived from the bold inlay found on English and Dutch chests of the sixteenth-century.

The inspiration for some of the decorative inlaid work, often in mother of pearl or ivory, came from further afield: from Byzantine and Islamic sources. Other striking

3.10   Memorial cross in ebony, inlaid with silver and mother of pearl, designed by Ernest Gimson, 1912. (CAGM)

pieces made at Sapperton were painted in oils by Alfred and Louise Powell. Although there was a tradition of painted furniture in the nineteenth century from the Victorian Gothic architects through to William Morris, the inspiration came directly from Sidney Barnsley's Byzantine studies. In 1890 he had received his first architectural commission, for a church at Lower Kingswood, Surrey, to be built on a Byzantine plan, and he had painted the wooden ceiling with a simple flowing pattern of flowers and leaves. The same effect was achieved by Alfred Powell in his first attempt at painting furniture in 1908. He decorated an oak coffer by Sidney Barnsley with an all-over design of little white flowers (Plate 3).

These pieces were sometimes made in English wood using particularly beautiful pieces of walnut or oak. The timber, which they seasoned themselves, was air rather than kiln-dried and the oak was quartered to show off the grain to best advantage. They exploited unusual grain formations, such as burrs, to obtain a decorative effect. Exotic foreign woods, including macassar ebony, Cuban and Honduras mahogany, satinwood and zebrawood, were also used, sometimes in unusual combinations or for striking inlays. Such wood was bought from London by Peter Waals who prided himself on his ability to select the right piece of timber for each job. Waals was also particularly keen on panelled work and helped to develop the octagonal fielded panels with half-ovolo mouldings which became a distinctive feature of the work of Gimson and Sidney Barnsley.

In the elaborate inlaid pieces designed by Ernest Gimson, one can appreciate his natural ability as a pattern designer, a quality he shared with William Morris. Like Morris he looked to nature for his inspiration and he used his close observation to produce masterfully restrained and flowing designs for embroideries, bookplates, plasterwork and metalwork as well as furniture. The nature of plasterwork, for example, demanded a soft approach which Gimson characterized as 'dulness', while much sharper lines were suitable for metalwork using chased decoration to provide an element of texture. Alfred Powell recalled a friend saying that Gimson 'came out wonderfully to children', and there is something childlike in his fanciful delight in birds, animals and flowers. Alfred Powell was one of those who shared some of the qualities he saw in Gimson:

> Much insight into his inner life was to be had at Daneway House among all his furniture. At the first glance all was of an extraordinary interest. Then one saw the beauty of the work, the substance, the development of the various woods, of the ivory, the silver, the brass, of inlays of coloured woods & shell. It was inevitable that you should find in the work now and then a humorous use of peculiar materials, an enjoyment of surprise; and for the work itself I have seen educated men & women, who might have been expected to behave differently, unable, short of actual laughter, to satisfy their delight in such perfect union of good workmanship with happy thought.[47]

The work of Gimson and the Barnsleys is often, and quite rightly, associated with the use of oak in its natural state. Although this timber had been traditionally used in the manufacture of cottage furniture by wheelwrights and village carpenters, by the mid-nineteenth century it had become too expensive and most villagers had to make do with cheaper wood, such as deal or pine. Just as William Morris had realized in the 1880s that he could not reach the masses with the products of Morris and Co., so did Gimson and the Barnsleys by the early years of the twentieth century. Gimson had talked of making a chest of drawers for £5, but never quite achieved this.

As well as the quality of the materials used, the cost of their furniture was determined by the hours expended in its construction. They were not prepared to compromise the quality of the finished article by either employing more machinery or having lower standards. Gimson, having more manpower at his command, had the minimum of machinery in the Daneway workshops. He had a small circular saw, suitable only for such delicate work as cutting out lines for inlay, etc. He considered it important that the craftsmen themselves should carry out the heavier work, so as to be closely in touch with their materials at every stage. It has to be remembered that the machinery available was noisy, dangerous and cumbersome, and not really suitable for small workshops. It was also closely connected with the factory sweatshops of the nineteenth century and a far cry from the power tools available today. Because he worked entirely on his own, Sidney Barnsley had a much larger circular saw, 'a magnificent saw for its time, hand and foot powered, made by the Britannia Co.'. Coming under strong pressure from William Lethaby to join the Design and Industries Association in 1916 and to design for machine production, Gimson responded to his friend's arguments, emphasizing the needs of his craftsmen. Edward Barnsley put the case in a somewhat stronger fashion when he wrote that 'Gimson etc. were against the horrible sacrificing of the lives of men, to the greed of commercialism'.[48]

It is typical of the art world that it is Ernest Gimson's and Sidney Barnsley's 'state' furniture that is best known today. Much of this fine work was seen in exhibitions and periodicals in London and on the continent. One of Gimson's important clients, Sir Ernest Debenham, also provided him with a major showcase for his work when, in 1907, he offered him an exhibition in his London department store, Debenham and Freebody. It is impressive that Gimson was able to produce eighty items for sale at this exhibition. As well as turned chairs and metalwork, the exhibition included forty-five items of furniture and represented a tremendous input, both of materials and hours, for the Daneway workshops. It is unlikely that any contemporary furniture-maker could make the same commitment to an exhibition today. Gimson and the Barnsleys were, of course, in a privileged position in that they had modest private incomes and did not need to make much of a profit from their work. They also received constant support and encouragement from their families and friends, and fellow architects such as William Lethaby, Francis Troup and Robert Weir Schultz. Most of their clients were from the socially aware and artistically inclined middle classes. They included C.H. St John Hornby (co-founder of the Ashendene Press and owner of W.H. Smith & Sons), the Cadbury family, Ambrose Heal of Heal & Sons and Harry Peach (founder of the Dryad Workshops in Leicester). A surprising number and range of visitors, from Britain and overseas, found their way to the Daneway workshops despite their relatively isolated location.

Although Gimson and the Barnsleys used traditional or vernacular elements in their work, there was rarely any self-conscious element of quaintness or historicism. Sources were absorbed and then incorporated into their designs because they answered some need in a straightforward and honest manner. Gimson's own words on the subject were quoted by Fred Griggs in writing his obituary: 'I never felt myself apart from my own times by harking back to the past – to be complete we must live in all the tenses – past, future as well as present.'[49]

By combining these various elements with their own emphasis on proportion, restraint and solid craftsmanship, they created something that was quite new, yet

3.11   *Design by Ernest Gimson for a china cabinet in mahogany, 1901. Note the early use of flush surfaces*
(CAGM)

with its roots in English traditions and with a timeless quality that evokes a response from each new generation. For Norman Jewson 'It was a completely new style, but one that had nothing tentative about it. Indeed it had the assured mastery which only genius could have achieved.'[50]

Gimson died relatively young on 12 August 1919 at the age of fifty-five. Neither he nor the Daneway workshops ever really recovered after the First World War. However, while fighting the cancer that eventually killed him, he was also planning for future developments, working on a scheme for setting up a second workshop to provide rural employment and training for apprentices. Although he was conscious of a certain disappointment at his lack of architectural commissions, Gimson was never downhearted; he had 'a vision unshaken by the world'. Alfred Powell also commented on this aspect of his character: 'His outlook was always hopeful; he saw continually vistas that led to an ampler life, to a life of more real association for work and under better conditions. His enthusiasm seemed to increase with the years, surviving all rebuffs and difficulties, and led him towards wider and firmer ideals.'[51]

After Gimson's death, Sidney Barnsley took over the management of the Daneway workshops until its affairs could be wound up. By 1924, he himself was finding physical work at the bench too taxing. He began passing work over to his son, Edward, who had taken over a workshop at Froxfield, near Petersfield, Hampshire. The two brothers died in the same year: Ernest Barnsley on 6 January 1926, leaving his son-in-law, Norman Jewson, to complete the work at Rodmarton Manor, and Sidney on 25 September. The three designer/craftsmen are buried side by side at Sapperton, their graves marked with plain granite slabs.

Chapter Four

The Guild of Handicraft at Chipping Campden

A N N E T T E   C A R R U T H E R S

While Gimson and the Barnsleys worked quietly to the end of their lives in Gloucestershire, C.R. Ashbee's stay in the county was rather more dramatic in nature but of shorter duration.[52] It was inspired by many of the same aims. Like the Sapperton group, Ashbee wanted to provide an alternative to the factory-based industrial work which seemed increasingly inevitable in British manufacturing. Like them too, he wished to provide opportunities for interesting work in beautiful sur-roundings, to get back to an idea of the simple life in the country, and to revive dis-appearing craft skills. The similarities of the achievements of the two groups derive from the common influence on them of William Morris and from their shared ambi-tions. The disparities lie not only in the very different personalities of the individuals involved, but also in the places they chose for their work.

Pinbury is an isolated house, Sapperton was, and is, a small village, and Daneway lies just off a country lane so narrow that it is surprising how many visitors found their way to Gimson's showrooms. Chipping Campden, by contrast, was a small country market town, the focus of villages and hamlets for miles around, and the site of a monthly sheepmarket which attracted farmers and tradespeople to the shops and inns. When it was discovered by Ashbee in 1901 it had certainly seen better days; wealthy wool merchants had built its fine church in the Middle Ages and another period of prosperity and architectural achievement had accompanied the growth of silk-weaving in the area in the eighteenth century. The long main street consisted of a string of solid yeomen's houses built in the honey-coloured local stone with, here and there, a stylish reminder that some Campden people knew what the fashion was. William Grevel's house of the late fourteenth century, with its Perpendicular trac-eried bay window, and the richly classical Bedfont House of the 1740s are among the finest examples.

The silk trade virtually died out in Gloucestershire in the mid-nineteenth century and Campden became simply a market centre. Long years of a depressing slump in farming from the 1870s meant that many buildings were left uninhabited and became

4.1   *William Grevel's house, High Street, Chipping Campden, drawn by E.H. New. From* A Description of the Work of the Guild of Handicraft *by C.R. Ashbee, 1902*

increasingly delapidated, and the architecture of previous centuries remained untouched, whereas in more wealthy areas buildings were torn down and redeveloped.

This combination of archaic beauty and empty cottages had an obvious appeal for Ashbee, who was not the first of the artistic middle classes to be attracted to the town. Its location made it a convenient travelling distance from Birmingham. Its proximity to Broadway, which already attracted tourists in the 1880s, had led to its discovery by artist such as John Singer Sargent and Edwin Abbey, though its position away from the major routes has ensured that it has never attracted the vast number of visitors that throng the streets of Broadway in the summer.

When the lease of Essex House was near its end and he was actively looking for somewhere else to continue the business, Ashbee was introduced to Chipping Campden by Rob Martin Holland, a supporter of the Guild whose family house was nearby at Overbury. He saw the empty silk mill which seemed ideal for the workshops, and the many neglected cottages which he was told were available for rent from the Earl of Gainsborough's estate. More importantly, he saw an opportunity to get back to roots and to enjoy permanently the fresh air and sunshine that were so invigorating on Guild expeditions to the countryside. The contrast between city and country air in the late nineteenth century is less easy to imagine now that smokeless zones ensure a cleaner atmosphere in built-up areas, but this was a period of legendary 'pea-soupers' in London and the quality of the air was a very real consideration.

Ashbee saw Campden poetically as his 'City of the Sun'.[53] He had romantic visions of a sleeping beauty ready to be reawakened by himself and the Guild and stirred into life for its own good. After visiting the town with the foremen of the different workshops in November 1901, Ashbee put the case for the move to the Guildsmen in London and succeeded in persuading them of his dream. Not all were convinced and some had strong family ties that kept them in London, but the decision was made in favour, and those ready to take the chance began to prepare for the exodus to the rural Utopia.

The people of Campden saw the situation rather differently. It is hardly surprising that there was some resistance when in 1902 their town, then with a population of about 1500, was invaded by about 150 Londoners, comprising about 70 Guildsmen and their families. Ashbee was not told until later, but some of the cottages taken over by the Guild had not originally been empty and tenants had been turned out so that the houses could be made available at a higher rent, causing understandable resentment. Then, some of the Londoners made it plain that they found the condition of the cottages shockingly primitive in comparison with their East End flats, and among the children insults flew from both sides about matters of speech, dialect and comprehension. Many Campdonians refused to talk to Londoners and for a while some charged the newcomers higher prices in the shops.

Soon, however, the Guild had settled in to the town and the workshops were established in the silk mill, which was renamed Essex House. Offices and showrooms were on the ground floor, silversmithing and jewellery workshops on the first floor, with cabinet-making and woodcarving above. The smithy was in an outhouse because of the fire risk and noise associated with the forge. Power for the mill was provided by an oil engine in a shed in the garden and woodworking machinery, comprising a circular saw, bandsaw and planer, was also installed there.

Cottages nearby were rented for the married Guildsmen and Braithwaite House in the High Street was taken as lodgings for the younger men and as a guesthouse for visitors. Ashbee saw this as a kind of university hall of residence on the American college model, designed to offer easy-going hospitality and camaraderie. Ashbee and his wife, Janet, moved in to another house further down the High Street, the partly fourteenth-century Woolstaplers' Hall, which Ashbee stripped of later additions and turned into an attractive, somewhat spartan but fitting home.

Janet Forbes and Ashbee were married in 1898 after an unconventional courtship. By now they were established in an unusual marriage in which Janet accepted the proffered role of 'comerade wife'.[54] She had eagerly embraced the freedom from convention offered by the life of the Guild, took an active part in Guild outings,

4.2 The Guild Workshops at Chipping Campden, drawn by E.H. New. From A Description of the Work of the Guild of Handicraft *by C.R. Ashbee, 1902*

bathing expeditions and sing-songs, and was able to express her own creativity in song-books and other literary works. Much loved and admired by the Guildsmen, she was like a big sister to them, as indeed she was to Ashbee himself. She was able to point out to him when he was being impossibly romantic about the Guild, but most importantly, through her enthusiasm, cheerfulness and her personal concern for the Guildsmen, she leavened the atmosphere, which Ashbee himself could make too intense. In Campden she not only charmed the Guildsmen, but soon had a following of local children who would trail after her to the fields around the town, singing and playing games or recounting ghost stories.

As soon as the Guild was established in the silk mill, it was joined by a number of young men who had already trained in the crafts and had heard of Ashbee's work. Fred Partridge, a rather bohemian jeweller, had attended a metalworking class in his native Barnstaple run by Jack Baily, one of the Guild's silversmiths. Partridge arrived in Campden in June 1902, as did Sidney Reeve who came to the metal shop after working as a school teacher in Worcestershire. Alec Miller had been in touch with Ashbee before the move and journeyed to Campden as soon as the workshop was ready to receive him. He left a vivid record of his impressions of the town: 'as foreign as Cathay and as romantic as the architecture of fairy-tale illustrations'.[55] The contrast with inner-city Glasgow where he was born and brought up must have been

4.3   Jim Pyment (foreground) in the Guild of Handicraft machine shop, c. 1905

especially intense. Miller's interest in the Guild idea derived from his knowledge of Ashbee's *A Few Chapters in Workshop Re-Construction and Citizenship*.[56] As a highly skilled craftsman who had taught himself by wide reading about philosophy, literature and art, Miller gained Ashbee's considerable respect and friendship.

Very quickly the workshops were in operation, producing the range of work the Guild had developed in its years in London. About a dozen cabinet-makers made panelling and architectural fittings, as well as individual items of furniture. Pieces were executed for designers like M.H. Baillie Scott and F.C. Eden, as well as to Ashbee's designs. They varied considerably from highly elaborate exhibition pieces, such as desks with inlay, carving and decorative metal fittings, made to show off the full range of the Guild's craft skills, to bedsteads and washstands so plain that few have been identified as survivors in recent years. The woodworkers' major achievement of the Campden years was the decoration of the library at Madresfield Court, Worcestershire, the home of the seventh Earl of Beauchamp. This house was enlivened by quirky symbolic figures and flowing images of the roots and branches of the Tree of Life and the Tree of Knowledge. Ashbee's designs were translated into delicately carved low relief by Will Hart and Alec Miller, while the doors were also embellished with pewter fittings covered in repoussé decoration.

4.4   Cabinet designed by C.R. Ashbee and made by the Guild of Handicraft, c. 1902. Veneered in holly and ebony, with fittings of wrought iron and silver plate, and carved and painted feet, it is typical of the eclectic style of Ashbee's 'state' furniture (CAGM)

As well as such important commissions as Madresfield Court, the carvers in the woodwork shop made the originals for castings for the metalworkers and jewellers, of whom there were about twenty to twenty-five altogether. The Guild's metalworking activities started in London with the production of large dishes and vases in brass and copper, with bold embossed patterns of scrolling plants and fish. These were made at first by John Pearson and John Williams. Pearson is said to have worked at William De Morgan's pottery, where many of the motifs of the lush decoration must have come from. Both men left the Guild in 1892 and from then on such pieces were made in smaller numbers, though the skills involved were still used on light fittings, etc.

Soon after the Guild started, Ashbee also wanted to produce work in precious metals. He experimented with lost-wax casting to make distinctive feet and handles for cups and table silver, often based on sixteenth- and seventeenth-century Dutch and German examples seen in the South Kensington Museum (from 1899 the Victoria and Albert Museum). Low-relief flower and leaf motifs for jewellery were made by casting. Experiments were also carried out with the techniques of painting with enamels, following the example of Alexander Fisher, whose enthusiasm for the brilliant colour effects of enamel had a widespread influence at this time.

4.5   *Simple oak chest of drawers with hammered steel handles, from a catalogue of the Guild of Handicraft Limited, c. 1905–6*

4.6 Silver macehead set with green pearl blisters, designed by C.R. Ashbee, c. 1903, to serve as a trophy for the Chipping Campden Sports Club, 'to be competed for by the girls who race at the Annual Swimming Sports for a silken smock'. (Brian Donnan for CAGM)

Enamelled copper plaques were fitted like tiles to the hall fireplace made for Ashbee's mother's house, the Magpie and Stump in Cheyne Walk, Chelsea. Also, a plain enamel plate would occasionally provide an attractive expanse of colour on a piece of silverware.

This experimental phase lasted until 1896 when the Guild showed a large number of items of metalwork and jewellery at the Arts and Crafts Exhibition. Between then and the move to Campden, the simple flowing shapes and decoration with twisted wires or stylized plant designs reached an assurance that found a ready market in the Guild's London shop in Brook Street. Most of the designs were by Ashbee, but the Guildsmen were encouraged to make variations on the shapes and to exercise their own discrimination in choosing suitable stones for setting. The attraction of the work lies in the subtlety of the forms, the sweeping curves of handles and feet with an art nouveau flavour, the small touches of brilliant colour from stones or enamels, and the gently shimmering surface on which the marks of the silversmith's hammer gave evidence of the human maker, in contrast with the perfectly smooth finish of contemporary trade silver. Further experiments with enamels produced plaques glowing in vivid colours with flowers, landscapes and figurative subjects. The arrival of Fleetwood Varley and William Mark to join the Guild in about 1900 brought further

4.7   Silver brooch set with pearls and moonstones, designed by C.R. Ashbee, c. 1905 (F.C. Scorey for CAGM)

new skills and imagination to the enamelling. When the Guild moved to Campden it was known as one of the leaders in 'art metalwork' and Ashbee was lauded in a *Studio* book of 1902 by Aymer Vallance as a pioneer of the artistic jewellery movement.[57]

Ashbee's jewellery was as innovative as his silverwork, using many of the same simple techniques involving twisted wires, cast flower designs, and plain collar-settings for semi-precious stones and pieces of mother-of-pearl. Ashbee disliked the display of wealth implied by gold and diamonds, and most of the Guild pieces were made of silver, with cheap stones that were not faceted and twinkling but smoothly rounded into cabochons to show off their rich colours. Reflecting the wide range of skills of the Guildsmen, the production varied considerably from very simple pieces to rich and ornate jewels, of which several peacock brooches are among the finest examples. The peacock provided inspiration for innumerable

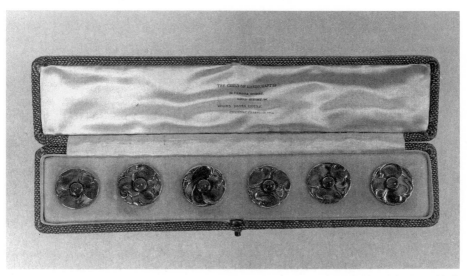

4.8   *Silver buttons set with chrysoprases in their original case, designed by C.R. Ashbee and made by the Guild of Handicraft, c. 1903 (Brian Donnan for CAGM)*

Arts and Crafts embroideries, enamels, mosaics, metalwork and jewellery, and was a favourite motif for Ashbee.

As well as small-scale silversmithing and jewellery, the Guild also undertook more substantial metalwork in wrought iron. Three blacksmiths made firescreens, gates, well-heads and other architectural fittings, and they also worked on handles and strap hinges for the furniture made by their colleagues in the woodwork shop.

When the workshops were settled, Ashbee, who was always a good publicist, produced a pamphlet about the move to Campden. It was illustrated with views of the silk mill and High Street by E.H. New, a Birmingham artist, who provided the plates for several Essex House books (Figs 4.1 & 4.2). The Essex House Press itself transferred from London to Campden in August 1902, the last of the Guild enterprises to arrive, and was set up on the ground floor next to the showroom and offices. Its presses and other equipment had come to the Guild only four years before from William Morris's Kelmscott Press, accompanied by three skilled printers. Ashbee attempted to maintain the quality of Morris's work and to follow his example in creating new typefaces. His own Endeavour and Prayer Book types were designed in 1900 and used in his massive *The Prayer Book of King Edward VII*, published in 1903.

Like the Kelmscott Press books, publications from the Essex House Press were usually printed in rich, dark type on handmade paper or on vellum, with decorated initials and bold wood-engraved illustrations by Ashbee or by a number of other artists, including William Strang, Reginald Savage, Laurence Housman, and Paul Woodroffe. Most were bound in plain cream-coloured vellum or in dull matt-textured paper, but some were in leather with gold tooling, in solid oak boards, or occasionally had decoration of enamelled plaques. The bindery was under the supervision of Annie Power, who had studied in London with Douglas Cockerell and was one of the few women involved in the work of the Guild.

From its new base the Essex House Press gave forth a stream of uplifting literary works and a number of Ashbee's polemical essays explaining the work of the Guild and the ideas behind it in an attempt to enlighten and inspire.

The educational role of the Guild was fundamental to Ashbee's aims, and in Chipping Campden he was at last able to revive the School of Handicraft. The School had been forced to close in 1895 when financial assistance from the London County Council was not forthcoming. Gloucestershire County Council agreed to provide a grant for technical education in 1904 and the Campden School of Arts and Crafts opened at Elm Tree House, where Ashbee also had an architectural office. Among those invited to the grand opening by Lord Redesdale was Ernest Barnsley,[58] whose signature also appears in the visitor's book of the Guild of Handicraft. Classes at the School of Handicraft were aimed not just at the Guildsmen and their families, but at all the people of Campden and the surrounding area. They included practical lessons in cookery, laundry work and gardening, as well as crafts, literature, history and music. Among the lecturers invited from all over Britain were John Masefield, Walter Crane, Patrick Geddes and Edward Carpenter.

As well as these temporary visitors, others were attracted to settle in Campden by the artistic activity of the area, including Paul Woodroffe, the illustrator and stained glass artist. Woodroffe had been a frequent visitor in the 1890s to friends in Westington on the edge of Campden, where he established a workshop employing about nine assistants in 1904. In the same year, Fred Griggs arrived to draw illustrations for *Highways and Byways in Oxford and the Cotswolds*[59] and, entranced by Campden, arranged to stay, lodging at first in Braithwaite House where he found congenial company among the Guildsmen.

Thus the Guild of Handicraft made its impact on Chipping Campden, though the town had never been quite as moribund as it suited Ashbee to believe. Campden had its own reforming politicians, had provided itself with gas lighting and proper pavements before the Guild arrived, and had made its own arrangements for technical education for agricultural labourers.[60] Nevertheless, it was in many ways revitalized by the presence of so many outsiders. Local traditions of popular entertainment and sport were given a new impetus by the enthusiasm of the Guild for outdoor activities, such as boating and swimming, and the bathing pool already planned by the Parish Council was at last achieved with a loan from Ashbee and Rob Martin Holland. Indoor activities like plays, masques and musical evenings proved attractive to all, and distinctions between the Guild and Campden began to blur, helped by the work of the School of Handicraft and the summer schools. The latter began in 1906 and were taught by Guildsmen and associated artists like Woodroffe. Local people attended as well as students from, for example, Leicester College of Art, where the principal, Benjamin Fletcher, was himself involved in Arts and Crafts activities and where Sidney Reeve, one of the Guild metalworkers, taught after leaving Campden in 1906.

Unfortunately, the business that provided the base for all this educational and cultural activity was showing signs of trouble. As early as 1904 the works were put on short time and the number of men had to be reduced. A financial loss was made in 1905 and 1906, and by the following year it was clear that, in spite of attempts to improve efficiency by the appointment of a manager, the Guild of Handicraft could not last much longer. The Essex House Press was forced to close in 1906. Efforts to find customers by reducing prices had failed, and from its hey-day of supplying furniture to the Grand Duke of Hesse, the Guild had sunk to catering for a cheaper market, resulting in the production of some very pedestrian silverwares and what Janet Ashbee referred to as 'vile brooches'.[61] Ashbee was still able to create fresh new designs, and his *Modern English Silverwork*, published in 1909,[62] demonstrates his capabilities with more ornately worked decoration than hitherto. However, his patient financial backers were unable to support the failing business any longer, and the large staff proved too heavy a burden for the firm to carry. In London when times were hard, the Guildsmen could find temporary jobs with other employers and return to the Guild when there was more work, but in Campden this was not an option and expensive stock accumulated unsold in the storerooms. The distance from London also affected the Guild's ability to attract publicity and customers. Ashbee believed that the healthy market that had existed for his innovative silverwork and jewellery in the 1890s had been taken away by the commercial production of Liberty's and other imitators. Clearly there was an element of truth in this, but the collapse of the company was largely brought about by the move to the country.

Ironically, Edward Barnsley remembered his father expressing something close to envy of Ashbee's success in setting up the community in Chipping Campden,[63] though the Sapperton group survived long after the Guild's dispersal. Ostensibly the two groups were trying to do the same kind of work, but while Gimson and the Barnsleys had a real love of the country and of the quiet country ways of life and work, Ashbee was in love with an idea: it was typical of his sense of drama and romance to express the idea of the move as 'better to leave Babylon and go home to the land'.[64] They wanted to fit in, to contribute to a gradual process of change, while Ashbee was impatient to change the place to suit his vision of how it should be. Gimson was rather pleased to be taken for a farmer on one of his occasional visits to London, while Ashbee was a cosmopolitan who travelled frequently to the USA, Europe and later, the Middle East. He was not a countryman but a dedicated

Londoner, and for most of the time the Guild was based in Campden he commuted regularly to his office in Chelsea on the excellent train service. When he enthused to his wife about the interesting country people he had met in Essex and elsewhere, she bluntly pointed out that there were many such characters in the Campden area but that he was always too busy to take any notice of them. This is not to diminish his achievement in creating the Guild, which was an ambitious enterprise and proved to be a formative and immensely valuable experience for many of those involved, but it does partly explain why the experiment could not be sustained.

The Guild of Handicraft Limited was formally wound up in 1908. Many of the Guildsmen had already dispersed, returning to London and elsewhere, but some felt so comfortable with the local community that they decided to stay in Campden and carried on working in the silk mill. Ananda Coomaraswamy, the Anglo-Sinhalese scholar for whom Ashbee had converted the Norman Chapel at Broad Campden into a house, took over responsibility for the Essex House Press and ran it until 1910, publishing several of his own works and a few of Ashbee's. Soon after the liquidation of the company, Ashbee also enlisted the help of a wealthy American, Joseph Fels, who bought the workshops and some agricultural land at Broad Campden and leased them to the remnants of the Guild, now formed into a Trust. This arrangement lasted until Fels died in 1914, when his heirs agreed to renew the lease.

Thus the work of the Guild carried on, considerably reduced in scale and absorbed into the normal activities of a small country town. This was, perhaps, the only possible way for it to survive in the long term. The members that remained at the silk mill continued to hold meetings with Ashbee, like the earlier Guild meetings, but essentially they now began separate businesses, each specializing in his own craft.

Jim Pyment's firm of builders and joiners, which included Charlie Plunkett and William Wall, became well known for its good standard of work and reliability. By 1917, Pyment was well enough established to buy the silk mill and surrounding property, which he continued to lease to the other craftsmen.

William Mark worked on for some years at his enamelling and Ted Horwood at his jewellery, while George Hart and Jack Baily kept on the silversmithing workshop. They received many commissions from local people and from churches all round the country, often through Ashbee, who continued to design metalwork. Baily left in 1912 to work for himself in Stratford-on-Avon. Hart worked with others, including Reynell Huyshe, his stepbrother, and Harry Warmington, a local boy who had became interested through the School of Handicraft classes. The Hart family were more interested in farming than many of the other Guildsmen, so when the Guild property was split in 1917 they bought the farm at Broad Campden.

The Guild blacksmiths, Bill Thornton and Charlie Downer, also decided to stay on in Campden and found a ready local market for their work, making architectural screens and fittings and smaller domestic items such as fire irons.

4.9   Alec Miller in his workshop, c. 1909 (Mrs A.H. Bishop)

Of the carvers, Alec Miller, his brother Fred and Will Hart remained in the work-shop. Miller was confident of his ability to make a living because he had a large order in hand. Although it was not always easy, he succeeded in finding further commissions, sometimes with the help of Ashbee who, in 1910, recommended him for work at Bryn Mawr College in Pennsylvania. Much of his work was for churches, including a massive carved and painted figure of St Michael for the Cathedral at Coventry, which along with screens, an altar cross and a Bishop's throne, all carved by him, was destroyed in the bombing of 1940. He also worked on many memorials of the First World War for the towns and villages of the area, and in 1921/2 gave to Campden his work on the war memorial designed for the town by Fred Griggs.

As well as architectural carving, Miller also began to make small portrait studies, initially of family and friends, then commissioned works, and later, small classical figures. In these he was able to apply a more personal vision and they opened up new possibilities for him.

The summer schools of the Guild of Handicraft continued with the assistance of all those craftsman who stayed on, along with others from the area such as Woodroffe, Philippe Mairet and Griggs. Ashbee, too, was involved in this, and was dismayed and disappointed when the County Council withdrew its grant in 1916 because of the war. In spite of the lack of a formal School of Handicraft, the Guild continued to have an influence on the training and encouragement of others. Hart's workshop remained an open house where keen metalworkers could come to learn, and Harry Warmington is remembered with affection for his teaching abilities at classes in the town. Alec Miller, too, took on trainees, including Jack Brookes, who began his training at Leicester College of Art and later went on to a distinguished career in education.

Ashbee continued to live in the area with his now rapidly increasing family, moving to the coveted Norman Chapel at Broad Campden when Ananda Coomaraswamy decided to stay in India in 1910. He still concerned himself with Guild affairs, attended meetings of the Guild of Handicraft Trust and devised schemes for houses and allotments in Campden, which came to nothing. He was constantly busy, writing books about the Guild experience, lecturing frequently in the USA, designing buildings and working on town-planning schemes. But he had no real focus for his work until 1919, when he, Janet and their four daughters left Campden for Jerusalem. Here he was employed to revive the crafts and advise on the reconstruction of the city.

In January 1919, Ashbee and the remaining Guild members in Campden gathered together and dissolved the Guild of Handicraft, purely a formality since all had been working independently for some time. The business, the school, the trust – all were over. And so the quiet town of Chipping Campden survived, still a little sleepy, but with its beauty enhanced by Ashbee's subtle and sympathetic renovations and additions, and its architecture now to an extent protected by a local awareness of Arts and Crafts attitudes to conservation.

Chapter Five

The Arts and Crafts Architecture of the Cotswold Region

CATHERINE GORDON

Towards the end of the nineteenth century, many prominent architects began to regard traditional buildings as a valuable reference source that could free their work from the restrictions of historical style. They admired their integrity, propriety, diversity and craftsmanship, qualities that were becoming increasingly undermined as mechanization, rural decline and the introduction of cheap new materials took their toll on regional building traditions.

Cotswold architecture attracted particular attention, partly due to the growing popularity of the region as a rural retreat and its associations with William Morris and his circle and, more specifically, to the detailed and enthusiastic articles by Guy Dawber that appeared in the architectural press. Dawber extolled the quality and quantity of traditional buildings that had survived in the Cotswolds. They seemed to exemplify the fundamental design principles that he and many architects associated with the Arts and Crafts Movement sought to express in their work. The abundance of readily obtainable and easily worked limestone had enabled the Cotswold masons to evolve a pattern of building of admirable character and variety. It gave form and feature to the broad, sweeping uplands and had a remarkable homogeneity with the natural features of the landscape. Sustained by the wealth of the medieval wool trade, the Cotswold style reached its peak between the late sixteenth and mid-seventeenth centuries. Various features, such as the tall gables, mullioned windows and Tudor arches, were adapted from the Gothic Perpendicular to form an important element of the style. Yet it was not dependent on these specific features for its effect but rather the colour and texture of the limestone, the simple logic of plan and elevation, and the lack of pretension throughout. It is to the credit of the local masons that they were not tempted to mould the accommodating freestone into vulgar and ostentatious demonstrations of their talents. As Dawber so rightly observed: 'carving is almost entirely absent, but when it is used in the building, it tells its purpose and has point and meaning and justifies its own presence'.[65] By the end of the seventeenth century the local style was gradually replaced by the elegant, symmetrical elevations, wooden window sashes and central doorcases of the Georgian period. During the following two hundred years of decline and hardship, the Cotswold buildings were little altered and many fell into disrepair. Even the new surge of building activity during the mid-nineteenth century made little impression, as there was no attempt to relate the new estate work to the local traditions and landowners generally preferred to build anew rather than convert existing structures. By the turn of the century, dereliction was rife. In 1904, Ashbee recorded that 'the population of Campden alone has dropped 25 per cent in 30 years . . . Other Cotswold villages would tell the same story and the little roofless houses and empty cottages to be seen . . . are the practical illustration of the economic fact.'[66]

This vast resource was ripe for reappraisal by the young and talented architects associated with the Arts and Crafts Movement. Their interest in vernacular architecture had its origins in Ruskin's ideas about the important relationship between landscape and building and, more directly, in the work of A.W.N. Pugin, who had praised the integrity of the ancient builders and their ability 'to adapt their edifices to localities'.[67] It was left to Morris and Webb to develop Pugin's ideas and provide them with a social and moral purpose. They believed the architectural profession could learn much from what Webb described as 'the common tradition of honest building', and that the emphasis on academic training and office discipline had resulted in superficial design and an obsession with historical style.[68] They argued that only by designing buildings in the traditional way according to their functional requirements, site and locality, and in close collaboration with the local craftsmen, would a truly creative architecture emerge. These ideas had particular appeal to men such as Ernest Gimson, W.R. Lethaby, C.R. Ashbee, Detmar Blow, Alfred Powell, and Ernest and Sidney Barnsley. They were all enthusiastic members of the Society for the Protection of Ancient Buildings (SPAB) which became a valuable platform for the dissemination of Morris's and Webb's ideas, and which helped to form and nurture the architectural ideology of the Movement. The commitment to creativity, craftsmanship and individuality led to a great diversity of architectural expression. Arts and Crafts buildings might incorporate complex symbolism, various stylistic references or even reduce detail to the bare minimum. The rigid disciplines of architectural drawing became less important than the creative talents of the craftsman and the selection and handling of materials such as handmade brick, rubble walling, weatherboarding and thatch. The buildings were generally planned with regard to practicality and convenience rather than effect, and always related to their site and locality – a house with its garden, interior with exterior – taking the principles of Morris and Webb to their physical and logical conclusion. The love of England and English traditions is also evident in the innate conservatism of many Arts and Crafts buildings, in their combination of whim and practicality, reserve and individualism, and in their reverence for nature.

It was Morris who first drew the attention of the Arts and Crafts architects to the Cotswolds. It is clear from his essays, such as *The Prospects of Architecture in Civilisation* of 1880 and *The Influence of Building materials upon Architecture* of 1892, and from his glowing descriptions of Kelmscott Manor that he deeply admired the work of the Cotswold craftsmen. His views were shared by Dawber, but the undoubted depth of feeling with which Dawber described Broadway in the *The Builder*, in 1888, gave way to a more prosaic and analytical style in his later articles as he grew more familiar with the region. For a brief period from 1900 to 1901, Dawber ran a practice at Bourton-on-the-Hill, renting a room at the Village Institute for 9d. a week. His research was eventually published by Batsford in 1905 as *Old Cottages, Farmhouses and Other Stone Buildings of the Cotswold Region*. His enthusiasm was shared by many architects and students who followed him to the Cotswolds during the 1890s, and whose sketches and detailed drawings were regularly published in the architectural journals. Most of them came from London or Birmingham but Edgar Wood, the Manchester Arts and Crafts architect, made several sketching trips to the region during the 1890s, and C.R. Mackintosh also visited the North Cotswolds in 1894 as his very first sketching trip outside Scotland.

Many leading architects associated with the Movement worked in the Cotswolds between 1890 and 1920. They undertook an impressive range of commissions from major country houses to small cottage alterations. Much of the work was concentrated in the north of the region. In Broadway the wealthy middle-class newcomers ensured that the talents of architects such as C.E. Bateman and Andrew Prentice were in continual demand; in and around Chipping Campden, Ashbee carried out a substantial amount of new and repair work; and in Overbury, Ernest Newton transformed the small village on the south side of Bredon Hill into one of the most attractive in the region. Further south, architectural activity was mainly confined to an area bounded by Painswick, Cirencester and Minchinhampton, and focused on the relatively few buildings executed by Gimson and the Barnsleys, Alfred Powell and Detmar Blow. In spite of their common admiration for the local traditions, the work was surprisingly varied in interpretation. For example, Ashbee would exercise the utmost respect and restraint but occasionally chose to defy tradition altogether. Dawber and C.E. Bateman were very professional in their outlook and less constrained by tradition, whereas purists, such as Gimson, Blow and Powell, could take their theoretical beliefs to uncompromising extremes.

The small country house was much in demand as either a weekend retreat or a manageable permanent home. Dawber was the popular choice for many of these commissions owing to his knowledge of the area, the quiet dignity of his designs and his experience of country house building in the office of Ernest George & Peto. One of his earliest houses of this type in the Cotswolds was Nether Swell Manor, near Stow-on-the-Wold. This was built between 1903 and 1909 for Walter Montagu

Scott. It is constructed of local coursed rubble, with ashlar dressings in a lighter stone from the Farmington quarries and a stone slate roof. It was designed in a simple Cotswold Jacobean style, the only ornate flourishes confined to the pierced and scrolled parapets above the bay windows and the detailing of the two-storey porch. The house was extended as work progressed and appears as an informal group of steep roofs, gabled wings and projecting bays, clustered around the squat central tower. It nestles into the side of the hill, accommodating the changes in level, and the composition is united by its simple detailing, and the texture and colour of the materials. Practical considerations were of paramount importance for, as Lawrence Weaver noted in *Country Life* in 1910, even the kitchen wing was ingeniously planned 'to the defeating of the flies'.[69] However only the French statuary and vases in the formal garden prepare one for the interior decoration. Dawber's client was the brother of John Murray Scott who helped transfer the treasures of the Wallace Collection to Britain. Some of these found their way to Nether Swell Manor. A suitable setting was provided for them by M. Marcel Boulanger, who decorated the study with intricate French panelling and plasterwork, and the billiard room with fittings inspired by Versailles. Such a compromise of taste is indicative of Dawber's business sense, and consequently Nether Swell Manor became an unsatisfactory combination of formal and informal elements. A more interesting result was achieved at Wells

5.1   Well's Folly, Evenlode, by Guy Dawber, 1910 (Catherine Gordon)

Folly (formerly Coldicote), Evenlode, which was built in 1910 (Fig. 5.1). Here Dawber's handling of mass and material is shown to good advantage. The house is partly constructed of coursed local rubble. Any shaping of the stone and dressings is reduced to the bare minimum and the joints are raked out to heighten the surface texture. The building stands on an open upland site, sheltered on the entrance side by a belt of trees. Dawber made the most of this situation by giving the building a striking profile. The entrance elevation is dominated by the long line of the roof ridge broken only by one large cross-wing to the right of centre. Detailing is restrained and possibly dictated by cost. Windows are plain wooden casements, the chimneys are built in brick, and ashlar mouldings are confined to the two-storey porch. The rear elevation presents a complete contrast. It is rough-cast and intimate in scale, surmounted by a row of three gables, and encloses a small courtyard on three sides. This U-shaped plan is extended by a large brick stable courtyard which continues the line of the front elevation, drawing the eye towards its wide archways, corner turret and bell-cote. Internally the house is compact and, apart from the painted ceiling in the large billiard room, continues to rely on good materials and strong lines for its impact. The staircase leading from the hallway is flanked by a pair of doors and echoes the design of Lutyens's Tigbourne Court, Surrey, of 1899. The contrasting elevations, the bold use of different materials and the exaggerated voussoirs of the garden archway also tempt comparison with the contemporary work of Lutyens. He also worked briefly in Ernest George's office between 1887 and 1888. There is little doubt that he provided the inspiration for the mannerist detailing at Bibsworth, a house Dawber built in Broadway in 1903 for Henry Gordon Clegg. This has a similar staircase plan to Wells Folly and was probably the house that caused Lutyens to remark in 1906: 'oh how naughty . . . a fearless copy of some of my work, yet dreadful and oh so foreign to the county and its materials'.[70]

Materials were used to even greater effect at Hilles, Harescombe, the house Detmar Blow built for himself in 1914 but never finished due to a lack of funds. Hilles is a throwback to the pure craftsmanship of Blow's early career when he worked as an apprentice stonemason in Newcastle-upon-Tyne from 1894 to 1895. Here he collaborated with Gimson, Powell and E.S. Prior on a number of projects. The house stands on the steep western escarpment of the Cotswold hills overlooking the Severn valley. It is built of local coursed rubble and was originally thatched. This is a surprising choice considering its size and the widespread use of stone slates in the region, but an economical and also a practical one in view of its multi-gabled roofline. Thatch was popular with many Arts and Crafts architects because of its organic and textural qualities and Blow had used it before in Happisburgh House, Norfolk, a similar-sized house of about 1900. The massive walls of Hilles and its high terraced retaining wall appear to merge with the steep hillside to heighten this organic effect. The entrance front has two, two-storey bay windows oddly situated at the junction of three prominent gables. Despite the stunning views, the windows are all modestly sized with small, round-headed lights which further emphasize the impression of solidity and mass. The choice and use of materials dominate the interior too. All the internal partitions are of timber, with plain boarded or flagstone floors and boarded ceilings. These provided a simple background for Morris tapestries, needlework rugs, paintings, and block-printed linen curtains by Phyllis Barron and Dorothy Larcher. As work progressed, Blow is said to have arranged for the stonemasons to eat at the same table as the family, but the scheme had to be dropped owing to the embarrassment of both parties. Hilles achieved much as an architectural if not a social experiment, for it redefined the conventional elements of a Cotswold country house in a very personal and uncompromising way.

Rodmarton Manor may lack the more interesting idiosyncracies of Hilles, but it exemplified not merely the architectural ideals of the Movement but also its social and moral principles. Rodmarton was Ernest Barnsley's major architectural work and was built between 1906 and 1929 for the Hon. Claud Biddulph (Fig. 5.2). Sidney Barnsley supervised operations after his brother's death in January 1926 and Norman Jewson finally completed the chapel in 1929. Claud Biddulph originally intended to

5.2   The building of Rodmarton Manor, c. 1912 (Mr and Mrs Simon Biddulph)

spend £5000 a year to build a modest house on his Rodmarton estate. He was the ideal client – very sympathetic and supportive – and Ernest Barnsley's affable and enthusiastic nature persuaded him to finance a much larger project that would provide a focal point for the local community. The materials were all dug on site and handworked by local craftsmen under the direction of the carpenter, Alfred Wright. The kitchen court was built first and was on a smaller scale than the rest of the house with its hipped roofs, half-hipped dormers and tile-hangings. The main body of the house lies to the south and is built round a circular grassed courtyard, its western wing terminating in the small chapel. The multi-gabled north elevation is by far the most striking and was described in *The Builder* in 1917 as having the 'somewhat unfortunate skyline effect of an upturned and magnified saw'.[71] The south side is more conventional and dignified with a central recessed section set beneath three gables. However two first-floor loggias provide an unexpected Italianate note, merging the internal and external space and taking advantage of the scented formal garden below. The quality of the detail rewards close study, in particular the various chimney designs and the decoration of the leadwork by Norman Jewson. Internally the house is only a single room deep with a long north passageway providing access to the spacious rooms. The chapel interior is probably the most interesting feature. Its massive carved and cambered ceiling beams create a bold pattern that contrasts with the cool restraint of the whitewashed walls and Arts and Crafts furnishings. Ernest Barnsley also designed the garden which was laid out by William Scrubey, the head gardener. The garden takes the form of a series of rooms, each becoming gradually more informal away from the house. It also reflects the theories of Barnsley's former employer, J.D. Sedding, expounded in his book, *Garden Craft, Old and New,* of 1891. During the building of the house the local community was encouraged to become involved in the project and to attend classes on traditional handicrafts held in the drawing-room. The commitment to craftsmanship was absolute from start to finish. Ernest Barnsley received the ultimate tribute from Ashbee who, in 1914, wrote in his journal: 'The Eng. Arts and Crafts Movement at its best is here – so are the vanishing traditions of the Cotswolds'.[72]

Ashbee's commitment to craftsmanship was equally outstanding, but his diverse interests could never be confined to a single enterprise like Rodmarton. After the Guild of Handicraft moved to Chipping Campden in 1902, Ashbee became increasingly interested in the need to establish a standard of cottage design that was cheap to build, practical to live in and pleasant to look at. This was a popular subject at the time, fuelled by the enthusiasm for the cottage-style architecture of the Garden City Movement, the growing demand for weekend cottages and the need to provide labourers' cottages of a higher standard. Ashbee saw this as a means of preventing further rural depopulation, but warned that 'the little house will not serve us unless the man who lives in it is given a wage that makes life worth living'.[73] In 1906 he

5.3   *Izod's House, Chipping Campden, designed by C.R. Ashbee in 1902, using materials salvaged from a former pair of cottages on the site (Catherine Gordon)*

published *A Book of Cottages and Little Houses: for Landlords, Architects, Builders and Others* which, apart from its social and ethical overtones, was one of a number of books available on the subject. Others included Arthur Martin's *The Small House* and J.H. Elder-Duncan's *Country Cottages and Weekend Homes*. These were both published in the same year. Ashbee used several of his Campden buildings to illustrate his ideas. One of these was Izod's House in Park Street which he designed for William Nathan Izod in 1902 (Fig. 5.3). It is constructed from materials salvaged from a former pair of cottages on the site, and Ashbee noted that 'The stones were very carefully coursed so as to assist the rather subtle proportions aimed at & the roofing slates were similarly laid in gradation . . .'[74] The steep pitch and overhang of the roof, the tall chimneys, and the scale and position of the mullioned windows and doorway also contribute to the success of the design. Inside he incorporated the inglenook fireplaces from the former cottages into the hall and parlour, and provided space upstairs for four bedrooms. When compared with Daintree, a house of a similar size further down the road, it shows how important detail and proportion become within the context of a street frontage. Daintree was undertaken by a local builder, following general instructions from Ashbee to use the local stone and slates and to reuse the old door-head and window. According to Ashbee the result was unsatisfactory

66

because 'The plan is not considered in proper relation to the elevation, the dormers are too large and too high the timbers are too thin and what purport to be leaded lights are cast iron facsimiles'.[75] Yet Ashbee could ignore tradition completely and, like Voysey, he often chose to build in rough-cast irrespective of locality. This was partly for reasons of economy but also, as Ashbee's biographer Alan Crawford so rightly points out, because of its unpretentious neutrality and lack of regional identity that enables it to merge with any surroundings. Ashbee designed several blocks of rough-cast labourers' cottages at Catbrook, just outside Campden, between 1902 and 1906, only two of which were built. Although their modesty and balanced proportions appeal in his drawings, the completed buildings are disappointingly bland and subsequent alterations have finally eradicated Ashbee's good intentions.

The total restraint of Sidney Barnsley's architectural work is comparable to Ashbee's, but also reflects his own unassuming and ascetic nature. Beechanger, the cottage he built for himself in Sapperton in 1902/3, and the cottages he built in Miserden in 1923 for F.N.H. Wills are typical of his understated style. Similarly, the ten semi-detached almshouses he built in Painswick for the Gyde Trust in 1913 rely on their strong rooflines and sound proportions rather than detail for their impact (Fig. 5.4). They succeed in making a quiet but far more effective statement than P.R. Morley-Horder's vast Gyde Orphanage, also of 1913, which sprawls across the hillside beyond and is quite out of scale with the town.

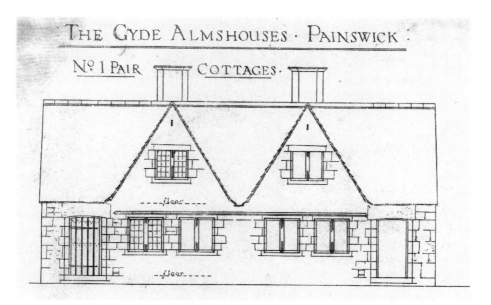

5.4   *Design by Sidney Barnsley for a pair of cottages, part of the Gyde Almhouses, Painswick (CAGM)*

Gimson's work speaks as much from the heart as from the intellect. Several of his buildings have an extraordinary affinity with their site, especially Stoneywell Cottage, Leicestershire of 1898. This merges with the granite outcrop due to the clever use of materials and its crooked dog-leg plan. The cottage was built by Blow and his team of itinerant craftsmen. This type of plan also features in the work of Blow and of Alfred Powell of a similar date. Gimson used it again in a modified form at The Leasowes, the cottage he built for himself in Sapperton between 1902 and 1903, and at Manor Cottages in Kelmscott, which he designed for May Morris in 1915 as a memorial to her father. At The Leasowes, as at Stoneywell, massive rubble walls of local stone support the apparent weight of the steep thatched roof (since replaced by slates), which swept over the wings and dormers giving an organic unity to the composition. The thatching was by John Fifield of Oxfordshire. The rest of the cottage was built by Sapperton craftsmen who worked on Alfred Powell's and the Barnsley brothers' cottages at the same time.

Alfred Powell's cottage at Tunley, Sherwood Hill (formerly The Thatched Cottage) is equally unusual. It was built around an earlier building in a combination of limestone rubble and heavy, vertical timber boarding. Its irregular plan is sunk into the steep hillside so that the walls are virtually obscured beneath the thatched roof. The interior also includes several interesting features such as a solid elm newel staircase, vertical panelling, a bedroom loft reached by a ladder and, in the room beneath, an oak and acorn plaster frieze by Gimson.

Upper Dorvel House, the Sapperton home of Ernest Barnsley, is probably the most accomplished design of the homes built by the four architect/craftsmen. Like Alfred Powell's cottage it was not an entirely new building but involved the conversion of a pair of existing cottages on the site. An L-shaped service wing was added at one end and a tower-like block, inspired by the seventeenth-century High Building at Daneway House nearby, was attached to the other. Ernest Barnsley also took advantage of the sloping site in his design, but here the plan seems uncontrived. The tall gabled tower is quite formidable when viewed from the lane, but descends to the intimate scale of the kitchen wing in an apparently natural transition that adds interest and variety to the original building. It encloses a semi-formal garden and gives the impression of a small country house rather than an extended cottage. This is reflected in the interior layout, in particular the large hall which was created from the original ground-floor rooms, and which has a fine plasterwork ceiling by Gimson (Fig. 2.6).

Two cottages to the north-west of the region are also notable for their distinctive, if less traditional, designs. The Palaces at Dumbleton are a neat pair of semi-detached cottages built between 1904 and 1905 for Miss Eyres of Dumbleton Hall. They are constructed entirely of ashlar, including the bay windows and pedimented dormers. This surprisingly lavish treatment is said to have provoked the comment from Miss

5.5   Thimble Cottage, Prescott, c. 1901, architect unknown (Catherine Gordon)

Eyres that 'she did not know she was building palaces for her tenants'. Thimble Cottage stands not far away at Middle Stanley Farm on Prescott Hill and is more unusual still (Fig. 5.5). It was built around 1901 for Reginald Hart Prentice and is a tiny, square, buttressed building. It has a pyramidal roof surmounted by a bulbous chimney and a large corner bay window with a three-sided dormer that looks like a small turret. The architect of these cottages is unknown, but since they are of such accomplished design it is possible that either Dawber or Ernest Newton were involved.

Newton was working nearby in Overbury for the Martins, the banking family, who were related by marriage to the Hollands of Dumbleton. Work began on Overbury village in 1875 when Robert Martin asked Norman Shaw to make some improvements, including a new school, post office and stores, and village hall. Newton was a pupil of Shaw's during 1873–6 and his assistant during 1876–9, and was probably involved in the Overbury project. This would explain why he was chosen, no doubt at Shaw's recommendation, to continue the improvements after Robert Martin was succeeded by Richard Biddulph Martin in 1897. Newton worked in Overbury until the outbreak of the First World War, altering and extending cottages and designing many new buildings. The handling of materials, proportion and detail are excellent throughout, and the appearance of a model village is avoided with skilful and sympathetic planning to give the impression of gradual development.

Although the Arts and Crafts architects were primarily concerned with the design of domestic architecture in the region, they also executed a substantial amount of community work that reflected the social conscience of the Movement. Many village halls were built at this time, including Ernest Barnsley's village hall in Sapperton, built in 1913 as a gift to the village from Lord Bathurst; Gimson's village hall in Kelmscott, which he designed in 1919 and which was built between 1928 and 1934 by May Morris; A.N. Prentice's Lifford Memorial Hall in Broadway of 1915–17, which dominates the western approach to the village with the bold articulation of its gabled bay windows; and Detmar Blow's Wemyss Memorial Hall at Stanway of 1939, a compact, formal building of classical inspiration. The Arts and Crafts architects also designed a number of schools, hospitals and war memorial crosses, including the cross at Fairford by Gimson; at Minchinhampton and Poulton by Sidney Barnsley (Fig. 5.6); and at least ten other crosses elsewhere in the region by F.L. Griggs.

The repair and alteration of buildings could produce equally interesting results, and often presented the greater challenge as the aspirations of the client could vary considerably from the principles of repair and maintenance recommended by the SPAB. Morris's manifesto had echoed Ruskin when it urged architects to stave off decay by daily care, to prop a perilous wall or mend a leaky roof by such means as are

5.6   *War memorial, Minchinhampton, designed by Sidney Barnsley, c. 1919*

obviously meant for support or covering and show no pretence of other art, and otherwise to resist all tampering with either the fabric or the ornament of the building as it stands. In general, the Arts and Crafts architects followed these recommendations closely and their work set a valuable example of sympathetic conservation and repair. Some of the alterations were executed on behalf of the SPAB as part of its role reporting on buildings under threat and supervising their repair. Between 1880 and 1930 the number of reported cases in the Gloucestershire Cotswolds amounted to over 120. This was largely due to the vigilance of members such as Gimson, the Barnsleys, Alfred Powell, Norman Jewson and A.S. Dixon.[76]

The problem of derelict cottages and farm buildings in rural areas was national, and one of the unfortunate effects of Britain's painful transition from an agricultural to an industrial society. Alfred Powell wrote a number of pamphlets and articles for the SPAB on the subject, notably his *Report on the Treatment of Old Cottages* of 1919. In this he appealed to all in a position to control or influence the fate of old cottages, '. . . to assist and be assisted in making a stand against the condemnation and demolition of these works of art . . .'[77] The situation in the Cotswolds reflected the nationwide problem and many cottages were in urgent need of upgrading. Quite apart from their aesthetic, historic and architectural value, this also provided a means of satisfying the current demand for small houses in the country. In Broadway, for example, although he was primarily involved in more prestigious commissions, C.E. Bateman also repaired and rebuilt a number of cottages. Notable among these was a group at Pye Corner, which he altered between 1924 and 1937 for T.L. Parke. Ashbee altered and converted numerous cottages in Chipping Campden, including Brooklyn, a thatched cottage in Park Lane which he altered for Rob Martin Holland, an influential director of the Guild; High House, Sheep Street which he virtually rebuilt in 1903 for Lord Gainsborough and which was occupied by Archie Ramage; and Woodroffe House, a cottage he extended in 1904 for Paul Woodroffe, the stained glass artist, which has a curious white matt-glazed brick finish to its street elevation. Newton's work in Overbury included the improvement and enlargement of many small cottages and houses, such as Sunnybank Cottage, altered in 1902 and 1908, and Northland House, also altered in 1902. Both of these were refitted with fine Chinese Chippendale staircases.

The repair and alteration of larger houses often presented more complex problems from both a technical and ideological point of view. This was certainly the case with the Norman chapel in Broad Campden which Ashbee repaired and altered between 1905 and 1907 for Ananda Coomaraswamy. The chancel had been demolished, a floor inserted in the nave and an addition built at the west end in the late fourteenth or early fifteenth century to convert it into a dwelling. Ashbee's initial scheme was to add a staircase, hall and south wing on the site of the former chancel. The final scheme was less ambitious. The walls of the nave were partly rebuilt and buttressed and it was converted into a music room, with a library and study above. The chancel arch was made into a large window at the east end. The later addition became the dining room and hall, with a new two-storey bay window to provide extra light, and a new service wing was built at its west end out of rough-cast brick. This provided a solution quite in keeping with the theories of SPAB in its honesty and lack of pretension. Coomaraswamy proved to be a very accommodating client. After he left Campden in 1911 he gave Ashbee the chance to lease the building for himself until 1919.

Gimson was less fortunate at Waterlane House, which he altered in 1907/8 for Maj. F.F. McMeekan. This seventeenth-century building had alrady been enlarged in 1845 by Thomas Baker. Gimson added an extension and a two-storey porch to the right of the south elevation which much improved its proportions. He also added a service wing at the rear and installed a new open-well staircase with animal finials inside. The work was a credit to Gimson's skill and tactful persuasion, for the client set him a modest budget of £1350 and disagreed with him on a number of points concerning the gabled roof and windows. He even criticized Gimson's decision to remove a coal and cistern excrescence at the rear to provide a view of the yew trees from the dining room. In a letter to McMeekan, Gimson argued that 'Life is commensurate with the number of beautiful impressions to be squeezed into it. Let us have as many as we can.' McMeekan could hardly disagree.[78]

Sidney Barnsley's alteration work was often more inventive than his new buildings, although he was always meticulous in his respect for tradition. In 1911 he made a number of alterations to Seynckley House for Henry Payne, the Birmingham stained glass artist (Fig. 5.7). Payne had acquired the medieval manor house on a twenty-one year repairing lease. The alterations to the north wing were most effective and included the removal of an inserted seventeenth-century floor and opening up the original fireplace. Also, the ground and upper floor windows were linked to form tall, elegant openings that expressed the interior alterations externally and gave an ecclesiastical feel to the building. One window was even designed without a transome to enable Payne to take large sections of glass through it. At Cotswold Farm, Duntisbourne Abbots in 1926, Sidney Barnsley added wings to the central seventeenth-century range to form a staggered H-plan for Major Birchall. These wings merged quite naturally with the original farmhouse, transforming it into a graceful and distinguished small country house. It is complemented by the formal terraced garden designed by Norman Jewson, who also created two splendid plaster ceilings inside.

There were some flagrant deviations from the principles laid down by SPAB. Despite the admirable achievements of Rodmarton and Upper Dorvel House, even Ernest Barnsley showed some lack of judgement when between 1919 and 1921, he altered Bledisloe Lodge (formerly Coates Manor) for Oswald Harrison, a shipping magnate. The former house of Bath stone was virtually rebuilt in white Warwickshire

5.7   *Seynckley House, Amberley, altered by Sidney Barnsley for the artist Henry Payne, 1911 (Catherine Gordon)*

stone that had been removed from Ham House in Warwickshire. The basement of Ham House was left behind and just the two upper floors and portico were grafted onto the surviving garden front of Coates Manor to produce a quite incongruous and disproportionate effect.

In Broadway, Dawber, C.E. Bateman and Andrew Prentice often took an equally liberal attitude to please their prosperous clientele. Bateman's first commission for Sydney Russell was the addition of the Great Hall to the Lygon Arms in 1910. Bateman was aware that the age and prominence of the building demanded a positive rather than a deferential response. His confident and flamboyant design succeeded as it read as a separate entity from the main building and also made an important contribution to the village street. At West End in 1910 he went so far as to rebuild a house at right angles to the road at the request of the owner, G.E. Sewell. Nearby in 1898, Dawber extended The Court House, a former sixteenth-century gatehouse, for Edgar Flower. The imaginative metalwork above the front entrance was a witty reflection of its former use, but the plate-glass windows in the new west wing which were installed so that Flower could admire the view are to be regretted. The most outrageous case occurred when A.N. Prentice moved an entire farmhouse up the hill from the centre of Willersley just outside Broadway in 1911–12. He refitted the interior in an extravagant seventeenth-century style. Fortunately such occurrences were rare, and the standard of repair and conservation work executed at this time set a valuable precedent, helping to protect the character and reputation of the region to this day.

The impressive amount of new building work was indicative of the new sense of vitality that surged within the Cotswold region early in the twentieth century. By the mid-1920s, once Ashbee had left and after the deaths of Gimson, the Barnsleys and Newton, a new injection of talent was needed to sustain this remarkable architectural revival. Norman Jewson played a key role in this respect. Jewson had originally come to Sapperton in 1907 as Gimson's architectural assistant and he soon became established as a prolific architect in his own right, collaborating with Gimson and the Barnsleys on a number of projects, several of which he completed for them after their deaths. His buildings share a similar unassuming and restrained manner, and certainly satisfy his wish that they would at least have good manners and be able to take their natural place in the surroundings without offence.[79] He continued to work in close association with the Sapperton craftsmen such as Alfred and Norman Bucknell, and his wide-ranging talents included plasterwork and leadwork which were embellished with a wealth of naturalistic detail inspired by Gimson's designs. His most notable works include Iles Green (formerly Iles Farm), Far Oakridge, which he altered for William Rothenstein in 1914 (Fig. 5.10); Warren's Gorse,

5.8   Norman Jewson, photographed by his father-in-law, Ernest Barnsley, outside Batchelor's Court, Sapperton
(CAGM)

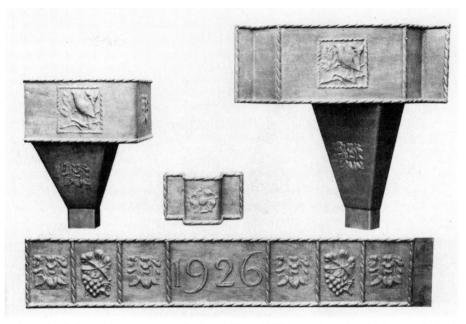

5.9   *Leadwork, designed by Norman Jewson for Cotswold Farm, 1926. Jewson designed similar decorative leadwork for many Cotswold houses, including Rodmarton Manor (CAGM)*

Daglingworth, a large house of 1922 built for Aubrey Price with elaborate plaster-work inside and an open-well staircase similar to Gimson's design at Waterlane House; Throughham Slad, near Bisley, altered for W.A. Cadbury in 1931 and refitted by Cotswold craftsmen; and, finally, Owlpen Manor, a superb medieval manor house which he bought and restored in 1925. Towards the end of his life, Gimson had formed an architectural partnership with his friend F.L. Griggs. Jewson maintained this friendship with Griggs and this helped to forge a link between the Chipping Campden and Sapperton communities. In 1929, Griggs instigated the formation of the Campden Trust, a small limited company to protect the town's historic buildings. He and Jewson supervised most of the restoration work, continuing the programme of conservation initiated by Ashbee.

Other architects who worked in the Arts and Crafts spirit in the Cotswolds included Thomas Falconer of Amberley and, to a lesser extent, V.A. Lawson and Maurice Chesterton. Thomas Falconer was a good friend of Jewson's and he used Bucknell ironmongery in much of his work. Between 1910 and 1930 he built and repaired numerous houses, mainly in the Amberley and Minchinhampton area, notably Upmead; The Park of 1925 for Miss Hartley, the jam heiress; and Great Rissington Manor which was remodelled for Major Marling in 1924. His smaller buildings

5.10   Iles Farm, Far Oakridge, altered and enlarged by Norman Jewson for the artist William Rothenstein, 1914
(Catherine Gordon)

include Marling Cottages, Amberley of 1925, a range of labourers' cottages in close keeping with Arts and Crafts aspirations. Three of his houses have a form of X or butterfly plan: Bowman's Green and Windrush in Minchinhampton, and Highstones (formerly Colaba) in Amberley, all dating from 1910/11. This was a popular Arts and Crafts sun-trap device developed by Gimson, Prior and Blow early in their careers. There seems to be only one other earlier example (1909/10) in the Cotswolds at Fox Hill Manor (formerly Furze Hill), Willersley by J.L. Ball, the Birmingham architect. However, Falconer's designs are possibly more successful, relying more on mass and proportion than excessive detail for their effect. His son, Peter, much extended the practice, but continues to design buildings in the area in close sympathy with the local tradition. A number of local builders and developers around Minchinhampton have also strived to follow the example of the Arts and Crafts architects with varying degrees of success.

The Arts and Crafts architects undoubtedly found the outstanding architectural heritage and lingering craft traditions of the Cotswolds a fertile environment for the demonstration and development of their ideas and beliefs. Despite their common interest in the building crafts, their work reflects their highly individual response to the issues of social responsibility and creativity versus professionalism that absorbed the architectural theorists of the Movement. They owed much to the enlightened patronage of influential and wealthy individuals and families such as W.A. Cadbury, Lord Bathurst, William Rothenstein, the Biddulphs, the Martin Hollands and the Russells. This close association with the wealthy and educated classes was typical of the unfortunate ironies that confounded the Movement's desire to establish what Morris had described as a 'Democracy of Art'. Yet the range of work executed in the Cotswold region proved that their architectural theories were applicable to all types of building, and to rural housing needs in particular. It also clearly demonstrated that the standards of fitness and propriety established by traditional building methods set an invaluable example to modern architects and builders that could not be ignored. Although Arts and Crafts buildings can appear contrived and self-conscious, as Ashbee explained, 'in these days the love of country is self-conscious. Alas that it should be so, but it is so; we have in these days to understand, to approach beauty again – the beauty of building through the avenue of the understanding.'[80]

The architectural ideals pursued by the Arts and Crafts architects in the Cotswolds may not have represented a progressive response to the contemporary problems that afflicted the architectural profession. However they did confront several important social and environmental issues that threatened the special character and identity of the Cotswold region. Within the space of twenty years their work had set new guide- lines for the design and repair of buildings, helping to revive the local crafts and the quarrying industry, and establishing a new respect among the local communities for the value and vulnerability of their built resources.

Chapter Six

The Simple Life in the Cotswolds

Slowly, but with no doubt or hesitation whatever, and in something of a solemn expectancy, the two animals passed through the broken, tumultous water and moored their boat at the flowery margin of the island. In silence they landed, and pushed through the blossom and scented herbage and undergrowth that led up to the level ground, till they stood on a lawn of a marvellous green, set round with Nature's own orchard trees – crab-apple, wild cherry, and sloe.

‘This is the place of my song-dream, the place the music played to me,’ whispered the Rat, as if in a trance. ‘Here, in this holy place, here if anywhere, surely we shall find him!’[81]

The late nineteenth-century nostalgia for rural life was closely linked with a search for moral values. This theme is reflected in literature of the period from Kenneth Grahame's *The Wind in the Willows*, quoted above, to E.M. Forster's *Howards End*. Early on in his career, C.R. Ashbee saw the excessive repression of Victorian society as a stumbling block to personal development. By the end of the nineteenth century he had come to believe that the simple life-style to which he aspired for his Guildsmen was attainable only in the countryside. The same feelings also found expression among the upper classes of society. For example, Lord and Lady Bathurst wanted their children to have a less trammelled upbringing in the country, so decided to make their family home for part of each year at Pinbury Park. In 1900, Philip Webb wrote to Sidney Barnsley describing the crafts settlement at Pinbury as ‘a sort of vision of the NEW Jerusalem’.[82] Ashbee had the same quasi-religious feelings towards Chipping Campden. For him ‘the little grey town with a majestic church tower’[83] epitomized ‘The City of the Sun’, or Camelot.

Despite the basic conservatism of the Cotswolds and the consequent survival of traditional skills, the ‘back to the land’ movement came just in time for the area: both the railways and tourism were encroaching on the old ways. Bricks and other manufactured building materials became cheaper and more readily available with the increasing numbers of lorries and other heavy goods vehicles on the roads. The agricultural depression in the second half of the nineteenth century meant that life in the country was no rural idyll and many farm workers were forced to leave the land. Yet

6.1   The yard outside Sidney Barnsley's cottage at Pinbury, c. 1896. Sidney Barnsley is looking out from one of
the first-floor windows while his nieces play outside (CAGM)

as the towns inexorably encroached on the countryside, there was a growing accep-
tance of the inherent 'goodness' of country life and country dwellers. The close links
between people's way of life and their livelihood which still survived in the countryside were seen as providing a moral framework for their existence. Ernest Gimson
wrote: 'If one's interest in the work were only that of design and utility, it would be
different but it is in the men themselves too and their ways of work and through that
to most things in life as you know.'[84]

The general appeal of the crafts was seen very much as a way of breaking down
divisions in society. Gimson and the Barnsleys, Ashbee and the other designer/crafts-
men who moved to the Cotswolds mixed socially with the main landowning families.
Their influence encouraged the local aristocracy to use their patronage to ensure the
survival of craft and building traditions. While the Arts and Crafts Movement never
abandoned the class structure – designers like Gimson always commanded the
authority of their position as well as the respect of their men – it did create channels
of communication between disparate groups of people. Ashbee tried to do this very
consciously within the Guild of Handicraft, while for others it was a more innate
respect for the dignity of labour. Some of the architects and designers of the Arts and
Crafts Movement managed to be quite at home in the countryside in all types of

6.2   Drawing of a shepherd wearing a smock, by Freda Derrick, 1941 (CAGM)

situation. Sidney Barnsley felt that both Philip Webb and Ernest Gimson fitted perfectly into the country scene because of their wide-ranging knowledge of nature, country traditions and the crafts. Theirs was the sort of knowledge that was not acquired from books but resulted from years of looking and listening.

In her book on the Guild of Handicraft in Chipping Campden, Fiona MacCarthy describes the local inhabitants of that town still wearing 'corduroy or rough natural-coloured cloth and black beaver hats in winter and white straw hats in summer, and broad old-fashioned birds-eye scarves in many shades of blue'.[85]

Among shepherds and other workers on the land, the smock-frock remained the principal garment until the early years of the twentieth century, utilizing the skills of the smocker to produce a uniquely individual yet practical item of clothing. From about 1900, smocks could be bought ready-made from linen-drapers or market stalls, and the quality of the materials and workmanship rapidly declined. The smock had been recognized as an item of English folk art as early as the 1850s and as the tradition declined, so the collection of old smocks grew. The stained glass artist, Paul Woodroffe, who moved to Chipping Campden in 1904, acquired a smock and occasionally wore it instead of an arist's smock while at work. Ernest Gimson, though he too acquired a smock possibly for theatricals or because of his wife's interest in embroidery, never wore it on a daily basis.

The relative informality of life in the Cotswolds is illustrated by differences of

6.3   Group photograph at Pinbury, c. 1896. Back row, left to right: Mr and Mrs Herbert Barnsley, E. Corfield, Ernest and Alice Barnsley. Seated: William Barnsley, Gertrude Corfield (neé Barnsley), Lucy Barnsley, Mrs William Barnsley. Sidney Barnsley is sitting cross-legged at the front (CAGM)

dress in a photograph of the Barnsley family, taken on a visit to Pinbury by the two elder brothers and their wives in about 1895 (Fig. 6.3). Herbert and William Barnsley, Birmingham businessmen, appear constrained in their stiff collars and heavy waistcoats, compared to the soft shirts and loose-fitting suits of their younger brothers. Ernest Gimson wrote ecstatically about the freedom of the countryside in a letter to his sister, Sarah:

> Today is a day for the country . . . A house is an encumbrance. Every hour indoors is an hour wasted. Clothes are almost an encumbrance too. This morning I spent at Francombe Wood with the dogs. This afternoon Pinbury went to gather watercresses in Dorval wood. We had tea in the garden hatless and waistcoatless.[86]

At Chipping Campden the Ashbees presided over the Guild of Handicraft and the ever-increasing circle of associates, with Ashbee in his Norfolk jacket and Janet in her artistic dress of peasant smock, sun hat and fisherman's jacket. Janet had discarded her stays on a beach at the start of her married life in 1898 and had never worn them again. Most of the Guildsmen were traditional in taste as far as clothing was concerned, but the jeweller, Fred Partridge, adopted what his fellow Guildsmen called the 'Jolly Art Style' of dress,[87] which included flannel shirts and sandals as prescribed by Ashbee's mentor, Edward Carpenter.

As early as the 1880s the north Cotswolds had attracted tourists and artistic visitors, such as John Singer Sargent, Henry James, C.R. Mackintosh and the actress, Mary Anderson, who settled at Broadway in 1895 and whose presence added an exotic element quite new to the area. Many visitors to the Cotswolds ended up staying and becoming part of the social scene. William Rothenstein was first introduced to the Cotswolds in 1910 by his friend and fellow painter, Charles Gere. Two years later, on a return visit with his wife and the Indian philosopher, Rabindranath Tagore, they came across an old semi-derelict farmhouse overlooking the Golden Valley. Rothenstein fell in love with the setting and bought the house with 55 acres of land for £1300 by borrowing from his father. He employed Norman Jewson to carry out repairs and extend the house. For the next fifteen years, Iles Farm was Rothenstein's country home whenever he was seized by the 'old Tolstoian mood'.[88] Even after he had given it up he described his home in the visitors book at Daneway House in 1930s as 'spiritually Cotswolds'.[89] Weekend visitors to Iles Farm included John Galsworthy, W.B. Yeats, W.H. Davies and Henry Newbolt. Rothenstein's literary visitors, 'the poets in the country', puzzled and amused him:

> I would take them to remote valleys, through flowering orchards and hanging beech woods, yet they never seemed to notice anything. Yeats would keep his

6.4   Janet Ashbee, painted by William Strang while on holiday in Brittany, 1910 (CAGM)

eyes on the ground, and while Davies was with us he would talk literary gossip and ask my opinion of this or that poet, whilst cuckoos sang and rainbows arched the valley.[90]

William Rothenstein's interest in Indian arts and crafts and music meant that Rabindranath Tagore was a regular visitor to the Cotswolds. This interest was shared by another semi-permanent resident, attracted by the Ashbees and the Guild of Handicraft to Chipping Campden. Ananda Coomaraswamy was an Anglo-Sinhalese who had been educated at Wycliffe College and London University. He married Ethel Partridge, sister of the Guildsman Fred Partridge, in 1902 and they made their home in the Norman Chapel at Broad Campden from 1908 to 1910. As well as adding significantly to the social, spiritual and philosophical life of Campden, they also played a major role in supporting the Guild in its last years. They achieved this as shareholders, and with commissions for the interior of the Norman Chapel which became a focal point for cultural life of the area.

The 'back to the land' movement catered for both mind and body. The tradition of an open-air existence which had been pursued by the Morris circle at Broadway Tower was continued. Henry James was shocked by the primitive conditions at Mary Anderson's seventeenth-century farmhouse, Court Farm: 'You, if I may say so, have made yourselves martyrs to the antique, the picturesque. You will freeze, you will suffer from damp. I pity you, my poor dears.'[91]

At Rodmarton Manor, Ernest Barnsley originally conceived the garden as becoming wilder and closer to nature as it moved away from the house. When it was first built, this Arts and Crafts country house boasted two loggias or bedrooms open to the elements; only one remains today. At Chipping Campden, healthy outdoor pursuits were very much the order of the day. In the East End of London the tradition of expeditions into the countryside had been well-established. After work finished at 5.30 p.m., rambles and cycle rides became popular summer evening pastimes at Chipping Campden. However, Guild outings were not confined to the evenings. The Guildsmen caused dismay among sections of the local community by their activities and outlandish dress on the Sabbath. Strenuous efforts were made to involve locals in the simple life. One of Ashbee's pet projects was the building of a bathing lake for the Guild and townfolk alike at Westington. The first Campden Aquatic Sports were held there in 1903.

The enthusiasm of craftspeople for traditional entertainment cut across class barriers. The folk-song and dance revival went hand in hand with the Arts and Crafts Movement. Like the crafts, the initial appeal was to writers and musicians rather than to ordinary countryfolk. Poets like Walter de la Mare and John Masefield, a friend of the Ashbees and a frequent visitor to Chipping Campden, were inspired to write in a traditional idiom.

The influence of folk tunes can be seen in the music of Ralph Vaughan Williams

6.5   The cast of As You Like It, *a play chosen by C.R. Ashbee for the aptness of its setting to the Cotswolds,* *performed by the Guild of Handicraft and friends, 1905. Back row: Ashbee/Jacques (fifth from left); Will* *Hart/Charles the wrestler (centre, arms folded); Cabinet-maker, Arthur Bunten (next to Hart); foreman of cabinet,* *W.A. White/the Duke (seventh from right); Alec Miller/Orlando (fifth from right); Gwendolen Bishop/Rosalind* *(next to Miller); Ashbee's secratary, Hilda Pook/Phoebe; Ron Haydon/shepherd; F.L. Griggs/shepherd. Front row:* *Charlie Downer/Touchstone (jester) (Guild of Handicraft Trust)*

and Gustav Holst. Between 1902 and 1903, Vaughan Williams lectured on folk music to adult education groups in Gloucester. The Australian-born composer, Percy Grainger, was particularly keen on collecting local tunes and songs, and built up close relationships with the country people who provided him with material. He was a frequent guest at fashionable house parties held by Lady Elcho at Stanway House, with Arthur Balfour being delegated to provide transport for the composer and his phonograph. Alfred Powell was particularly in demand in the social life of the Cotswolds because of his fine singing voice. In 1926, Sidney Barnsley wrote to his son, Edward, about an impending supper party at Rodmarton Manor to celebrate the visit of Ramsey MacDonald to the house: 'I expect Mrs Biddulph is to have an informal singing and dancing party. So no doubt AHP and Oliver Powell will be there!'[92] Parties were always informal when Alfred and Louise Powell were involved, as they refused to dress for dinner. Emily Gimson, as befitted an archdeacon's daughter, played the organ but also the piano for country dancing every week in the village hall and for the school at Sapperton. The village school had been the venue for plays and other village entertainments before the hall was built in 1911. They must have

6.6   *A page from* The Essex House Song-Book, *a collection of songs formed for the singers of the Guild of Handicraft by C.R. and Janet Ashbee, edited by Janet Ashbee and printed by the Essex House Press, 1903–5 (F.C. Scorey for CAGM)*

provided as much entertainment for the participants as for the audience with titles like *Mrs Jarley's Waxworks*, much involved Ernest Barnsley dressing up as Mrs Jarley. A more traditional note was struck by mummer's plays. A manuscript notebook from Sapperton has survived with the four-page text of a mummer's play ending with the note, 'Collected 1914'.[93]

The simple enthusiasm and good fellowship of the Arts and Crafts Movement could be irritating. At times, William Rothenstein found it too much of a good thing. He described the followers of William Morris as being inclined to say, '"No" to life. Perhaps amongst themselves, these men said "Yes", but they made me feel that we painters were doubtful characters, with second wives hidden away somewhere, and an absinthe bottle in the studio cupboard.'[94]

Eric Gill, a doubtful character himself, gave vent to his impatience and irritation with the theory and mood of the Arts and Crafts Movement in an even stronger fashion: 'You can SEE the boys don't drink – you can see they're not on speaking terms with the devil.'[95]

Despite Eric Gill's comments, teetotalism was not necessarily the order of the day. Norman Jewson recalled that, as with all his personal habits, Ernest Gimson's abstinence 'was never allowed to obtrude itself in any way in his association with other people'.[96] Drink was indeed an important part of daily life in the Cotswolds. Gimson and the Barnsleys fermented their own cider at Pinbury from local apples. Sidney Barnsley talked of having 1000 gallons in the Pinbury cellars at one point which was sold to locals as well as for their own consumption. It was common practice for farm labourers to take a stone jar of cider out into the fields to slake their thirst during the day's work. Norman Jewson was one of many to be regaled with Ernest Barnsley's sloe gin. He also wrote of the pleasure of sampling such unusual delicacies as cowslip wine, birch wine made from the sap of the birch tree, and the potent plum jerkum, a local treat of the north Cotswolds. The taste of the Arts and Crafts men and women was for staple but good-quality fare. The staff of life was home-made bread, usually taken with local cheese until the making of farmhouse cheeses became unprofitable in the 1930s. William Rothenstein wrote evocatively of Eve Simmonds's baking skills: 'A loaf from her is the kindest gift I can receive. Yet her bread, she declares, is baked in the usual way, only she gets her flour from a neighbouring flour mill. What a reflection on our age, when a good loaf of white bread is rarer than the finest delicacies of the table.'[97]

Many male designers and craftsmen took a great deal of support and encouragement from the women in their lives, but the traditional women's role was secondary. Lucy Barnsley's practical function in establishing the Pinbury community has already been related and her husband, Sidney, always acknowledged his debt to her unwavering support and encouragement. Her strength of character in the face of her hearing disability must have been quite tremendous. Janet Ashbee, too, made an immense practical and emotional contribution to the success of the Guild of Handicraft, particularly after the move to Chipping Campden when the day-to-day problems required all her tact and strong cheerful spirits. Yet she did not see herself as a supporter of women's rights. She was disparaging of her unmarried and highly educated sisters-in-law, Agnes and Elsa Ashbee, who were fervent supporters of the Suffragette cause. Within the Guild of Handicraft, Janet Ashbee built up much closer bonds with the male Guildsmen than with their wives or even the few female craftswomen involved. Indeed, the upset caused by the affair between the bookbinder, Statia Power, and the jeweller, Fred Partridge, was such that Janet felt it justified the avoidance of including women as Guild members. This state of affairs obviously left her in a unique position on which she thrived, despite the occasional hankering after a more settled existence and an increasing desire for children.

The Guild ideal was so strong that it was very difficult and almost disloyal for anyone to have a nuclear family life. This pull of loyalties inevitably caused strains on all concerned. In his *Journals*, Ashbee quoted a letter of 1909 received from Will Hart, one of his favourite Guildsmen, just before Will's marriage. Hart wrote:

You must remember, Mr Ashbee we live in a very conventional age and people like yourself who I always imagine have very little use for the conventions as far as living is concerned, look at things from a totally different standpoint. What I mean is this (and I am a little sorry) that Dora is the sort of girl whose idea of living is preferably in a modern house with modern conveniences and among modern goings-on. Of course this is naturally not to my taste but I am perfectly willing to submit my all if necessary for a happy life.[98]

The idea that women, because of their involvement with the daily business of life, home-making and above all children, hold men back from achieving their dreams is a pervasive one. Fiona MacCarthy describes Eric Gill's view of the 'active male and passive female: man providing the direction, intellectual and spiritual; women the emotional support and sustenance'.[99] In the more contemporary context of Arnold Wesker's play, *I'm talking about Jerusalem*, set in a fledgling craft community of the 1940s and 1950s, one of the characters says: 'I think I hate women because they have no vision . . . only a sense of self-preservation.'[100]

This blinkered attitude hides the way that many women's contributions to the Arts and Crafts Movement have been neglected over the years. The female element within many husband-and-wife teams has often been ignored. One instance of this is in the

6.7   *Ernest Gimson's living room at Pinbury, drawn by Alfred Powell. From the memorial volume,* Ernest Gimson, His Life and Work

work of Alfred and Louise Powell, two craftspeople working together on an equal footing. Until quite recently, the range and importance of Louise Powell's contribution was largely overlooked in favour of her husband's. Her work is particularly distinctive for its use of colour and bold rhythmic shapes, providing a welcome addition to the muted shades of oak, whitewash and stone which dominate the typical Arts and Crafts interior. She was in many ways a pioneer. She inspired many women to take up a craft and was responsible for attracting others, such as Phyllis Barron and Dorothy Larcher, to the Cotswolds. At a different level, groups such as the Rodmarton Women's Guild used their traditional needlework skills to produce craftwork, including an evocative series of appliqué embroideries of everyday village life.

The Ashbee household at Woolstaplers Hall espoused the mixed interior beloved of Morris and his generation. The austere Arts and Crafts style of oak floors and whitewashed walls was partly hidden by a rich mix of Eastern carpets, Morris textiles and a proliferation of ornaments. Ashbee himself felt it was important to get away from the individualism of the previous generation – that in order to succeed the Arts and Crafts Movement had to provide the crafts with a crucial role in everyday life. His social experiment was the crux of the Guild Idea. One of his greatest and most lasting achievements was the foundation of the Campden School of Arts and Crafts in 1904. In Elm Tree House on the High Street, Guildsmen and locals were able to mix together at a wide variety of classes aimed at fulfilling at least some of their practical and spiritual needs. The Ashbees were able, just, to steer clear of major political confrontations and even patronized the local landed gentry – the Redesdales at Batsford Park were particular favourites. Some of the Guildsmen, however, found themselves under fierce attack for their political views. Archie Ramage, a compositor at the Essex House Press, got into trouble for distributing Fabian pamphlets. At a public meeting at Mickleton, Lord Harrowby talked about a revolutionary element at Campden while waving the offending tracts. Ashbee described the occasion gleefully, writing:

> Better housing for the people, better schooling, common lands and sweeter conditions of life and independent life are all things we need, and need very badly here in Campden, but we shall get none of them if men like Lord Harrowby or the crew that applaud him on a public platform can help it. Meantime go ahead Archie![101]

Yet Ashbee found the reality of the Tolstoyan agricultural settlement at Whiteway depressing. After a bicycle expedition to Miserden near Stroud in 1904, he described the Whiteway Colony as 'all very uncouth and experimental'.[102] This idealistic and intrepid community had its roots in a group of Socialists from Croydon that had been inspired by accounts of the collective life on Leo Tolstoy's Russian country estate. An initial commune established in Purleigh, Essex had come close to collapse and a

6.8   A class at the Chipping Campden Summer School, 1914

breakaway group set off on bicycle to find pastures new. One of the founders, Nellie Shaw, had been a dressmaker specializing in artistic and rational dress for the artistic middle classes. In her search for a purposeful existence she went first to Croydon and then to Whiteway. She described her arrival in the area with Arnold Eiloart, who had turned his back on his career as a chemistry lecturer for the co-operative way of life:

> I was wearing what was then termed 'rational dress' consisting of knickers and a neat Norfolk jacket reaching to my knees. As the weather was very hot my companion gradually divested himself of various garments till all he wore was a short-sleeved vest, red braces, knickers and sandals. It is hard to say which of us attracted more attention.[103]

Malcolm Muggeridge, who knew the colony as a child through his father's Socialist links, described it as, 'a truly heroic enterprise; the more so as most of the participants were clerks and schoolmasters and shop assistants, with absolutely no experience of fending for themselves under primitive conditions'.[104]

The community purchased fifty acres of rough upland pasture and then publicly burned the title deeds in a ceremonious rejection of the idea of property. This led to the first of many crises of conscience at Whiteway, related by Malcolm Muggeridge:

> Unfortunately a neighbouring farmer heard of their noble gesture and began to encroach on their land. To resort to the police, even if it had been practicable,

was unthinkable. So, after much deliberation, they decided to use physical force to expel the intruder; which they did on the basis of a theory of detached action, whereby it is permissable to infringe a principle for the purpose of a single isolated act without thereby invalidating it. The intruding farmer was, in fact, thrown over the hedge in the presence of the assembled Colonists.[105]

The colonists suffered material deprivation and great hardship in the attempt to make themselves self-supporting. Almost worse were the petty jealousies, quarrels and scandals within the group. From the first, they attracted notoriety and prurient disapproval from the outside world. Talk of free love and nude bathing was too good a seller for the popular press to miss. The proponents of a whole spectrum of ideologies arrived at Whiteway as well as a number of eccentric opportunists ready to take advantage of the idealistic anarchists. Yet, against the odds, the Whiteway Colony did survive and continues in a much changed form today. One of the original colonists, Sudbury Protheroe, set up a bakery which still survives producing delicious wholemeal bread. Over the years the community has been enriched by several printers, the sandalmaker, S.L. Randolph, several weavers and the cabinet maker, Fred Foster, who trained with Sidney Barnsley and Peter Waals and designed many of the wooden houses at Whiteway.

A more moderate view of socialism was held by most of the designer/craftsmen working in the Cotswolds. As Alan Crawford wrote: '. . .[The Arts and Crafts Movement] did not take its stand on issues of political and social justice; in so far as it took a stand it was on questions for which politics had not yet found a language, questions of the value of work and of the effects of mechanised production.'[106]

As a young man, the stained glass artist, Edward Payne, was particularly struck by hearing the views of Alfred Powell and William Simmonds on money, 'so different from today' as he saw it. One of his persistent memories was of Alfred Powell's singing voice used in harmony with that of William Simmonds to express their contempt for money-making, greed and envy in 'The Angler's Song', composed by Isaac Walton:

> Man's life is but in vain
> For 'tis subject to pain and sorrow and trouble and money
> 'Tis a hotch potch of business and worry and care and worry and trouble and
>   money
> But let's not complain if the weather proves fair
> But angle and angle again[107]

It was this constant questioning about the value of craftsmanship, its relationship to daily life, and the importance of personal freedom to create and to enjoy creation that has ensured the continuing fascination for the lives and work of those involved with the Arts and Crafts Movement.

Chapter Seven

Alfred and Louise Powell

MAUREEN BATKIN

The Gist of all decorative design is in its hand and glove fitness for the material reception. The very invention of the subject and patterning depending on the facility and adeptness in the doing with pleasant effectiveness in the result.[108]

Although Alfred and Louise Powell were fluent in many areas of the Arts and Crafts, it is perhaps in the field of pottery design and decoration that they made their greatest impact. Philip Webb, author of the extract above, was one of the first to offer Alfred Powell words of encouragement at the start of his collaboration with the Staffordshire pottery manufacturers, Josiah Wedgwood & Sons Ltd.

Philip Webb, the architectural father-figure of the Arts and Crafts Movement, became a trusted adviser to the Sapperton group in the early years of the twentieth century and, at one time, it looked as though he would be joining Ernest Gimson and the two Barnsley brothers, Ernest and Sidney, in the Cotswolds. In April 1899 he even went to stay with the group with the sole intention of finding somewhere to live, and was still pursuing the idea in August 1900 when he wrote to Alfred Powell: 'There are still just hopes of the Gimson and Barnsley folk finding that the smallest of steadings, by Tunley Farm, may be had for me; and failing that coveted situation I may get housed in Sussex.'[109]

In the event, it was not Philip Webb but Alfred Powell who joined the 'little colony'. Alfred Hoare Powell was born in 1865 into a family with more than a passing interest in the Arts and Crafts. At least two of Alfred's brothers took up a craft. Malcolm Powell spent a year making furniture in the Cotswold tradition under Sidney Barnsley. He carried on the tradition at Reading where he established a workshop for making furniture items, some of which were painted by Alfred Powell. Malcolm also taught woodworking skills at Bedales School where another younger brother, Oswald, was Second Master. The other brother who took up a craft was Edgar Powell. He studied bookbinding under Douglas Cockerell. Later, Oswald's son Roger Powell, became a partner in the bookbinding firm of Douglas Cockerell and established his own bindery at The Slade, Froxfield in Hampshire.

The brothers' parents, Revd Thomas Powell and his wife, Emma Corrie, had thirteen children in all. Alfred was the sixth son. Although he may have attended school locally, it is possible that Alfred was educated at home by his sister, Margaret, who was sixteen years his senior. Margaret Powell was a classical scholar at Newnham College, Cambridge in 1884 and later headmistress of a girls' school in Staffordshire. Four of his brothers also became schoolmasters. At the age of fourteen, like his brothers before him, Alfred was enrolled at Uppingham, a progressive school with a history stretching back to the sixteenth century. By the early 1880s the school was enjoying something of a renaissance under the guidance of its headmaster, the Revd Edward Thring, who was linked with the Art Schools Association to which John Ruskin was elected president.

As a boy, Alfred obviously had his heart set on a career as an architect so, after leaving Uppingham, he broke with the family tradition by not going to Cambridge. Instead he was apprenticed to the architect, W.O. Milne, and enrolled at the Slade which was then under the influence of Alphonse Legros, an ardent follower of Gustave Courbet and one of the artists who had been associated with the Salon des Refuses. Legros believed in teaching by demonstration and, to inform and inspire his students, would make rapid portrait studies in their presence.

Alfred Powell made the most of what teaching he could get in drawing and sketching from nature, and he cultivated a passion for painting wildlife which remained constant. He held a number of one-man shows, including one at the Alpine Club in 1927 where seventy-three of his watercolour paintings were displayed, and for which William Lethaby wrote a foreword to the catalogue.

Alfred Powell spent three years with W.O. Milne, but his natural ability as a designer/craftsman appears to have blossomed after joining Sedding's practice in 1887. Sedding, a key figure in the Arts and Crafts Movement, was himself a designer for a number of media including embroidery, wallpaper, church metalwork and other traditional building crafts, and he had gathered around him some of the finest craftsmen of his day. The Arts and Crafts Movement represented a radical approach to design and pupils of Sedding were at the hub of activity. They came into contact with William Morris, Philip Webb, John Ruskin and other important figures within the Movement and it was in this atmosphere that the Sapperton craftsmen were drawn together. Under Sedding, they gained experience of working in many different crafts and had an overwhelming desire to capture the spirit of medieval craftsman in whose hands the techniques of weaving, embroidery and illumination achieved a perfection of their kind. These crafts were among the most successful to be revived and revitalized by Morris and his disciples, and were among the first subjects to be taught by practising craftsmen at Lethaby's Central School of Arts and Crafts where Louise Lessore, wife of Alfred Powell from 1906, was a pupil.

Although Ernest Gimson left Sedding's office shortly after Alfred Powell joined the practice, Powell would have followed with interest the founding and disbanding of the short-lived Kenton & Co. experiment. Alfred Powell was still at 447 Oxford

Street in 1891, the year of Sedding's death, and he continued to work with Henry Wilson, Sedding's chief assistant, before branching out on his own. Even though, for a time, his own career followed another direction, the group remained friends and Alfred Powell visited the craftsmen in the Cotswolds on more than one occasion.

By way of an experiment, Alfred Powell established an office in Guildford and is recorded as living and working there in 1899. The arrangement did not last after his move to Sapperton, nor did he believe in offices any more because most of his architectural commissions were coming through friends or the SPAB.

In his writings from this period, he came out strongly against speculative building which he believed encouraged the use of inferior materials and shoddy workmanship. Like William Morris, Alfred Powell had a passion for reviving and preserving craft skills; training others in excellence of workmanship was his guiding force. He abhorred commercialism in any form, and its effects on all aspects of design and more especially architecture: 'It is so dead and relieved of all variation that the workman, being no longer able to take any lively interest in it, is obliged to transfer what enthusiasm he has to the prospect of gain. And this condition is spreading.'[110]

Alfred Powell had been living and working in Yorkshire before joining the Sapperton group, but a persistent lung condition forced him to return to the family home and arrangements were made for him to take a long sea voyage, accompanied

7.1   *Interior of the Powells' studio cottage at Tarlton, 1920s. The ladderback chairs were probably made by Alfred Powell (Maureen Batkin)*

by his brother, to recuperate. Following his return, Alfred was invited to convalesce with the Gimsons at Pinbury. The craftsmen were kindred spirits; Alfred fell in love with the place and within months he had returned to stay. At first he rented part of a farmhouse from the squire at Edgeworth and, by early 1901, had established a small workshop in which he installed a pole-lathe, a primitive tool used for chair-leg turning. Once settled, Alfred began to share his time between chair-making and his architectural commissions, each day walking over to Pinbury workshops where he took instruction in turning.

Working at Sapperton gave Alfred Powell the opportunity to express the practical instincts of his temperament and develop his love of tools and materials. Long before he turned to ceramics, he gained a mastery of several handcrafts including chair-making, weaving, wood-engraving, and working in metals, wood and stone. He remained enthusiastic about all building-related crafts throughout his lifetime. He lived briefly at Oakridge Lynch before moving to Tunley, to a cottage he restored and extended for himself and his new wife.

Ada Louise Lessore, born in 1882, and her sister, Elaine Thérèse Lessore, two years younger than Louise, studied painting at the Slade. Louise was also an early pupil of the

7.2   *Group photograph, c. 1907. Left to right: Therese Lessore, Madame Lessore, Alfred Powell, Louise Powell (The Trustees of the Wedgwood Museum and Archive)*

calligrapher, Edward Johnston, at the Central School of Arts and Crafts where she came under the influence of Lethaby and Sydney Cockerell. Instructors at the Central School formed the link between Morris and the next generation and did much to raise the standard of crafts to an art form. Some of Louise's finest work was done in collaboration with the calligrapher, Graily Hewitt. They worked together on the decoration of William Morris's unfinished masterpiece, Virgil's *Aeneid*. The miniatures for this were executed by Charles Fairfax Murray after drawings by Edward Burne-Jones.

By the early years of the twentieth century, Louise Lessore had firmly established herself as a needlewomen. With her sister Thérèse, she studied embroidery at the Central School and was closely associated with May Morris and the Royal School of Needlework. Many of Louise's embroidery designs were worked on Morris silks. One such example is the altar frontal for St Andrew's church at Roker, Sunderland, worked on a Morris silk damask to Louise's design by Frances Channer and Louise herself (Fig. 7.4). This work was reviewed in the *Art Journal* for 1907:

> What she [Louise Powell] has done beautifully with her needle is part of a unity of design and execution in which the crafts of the weaver, the embroider-er, the wood-carver, metal-worker and artist in stained glass have been freely employed . . . In the work of the loom and of the needle, beauty and grace of the living flowers of the earth are translated into fair and happy art.

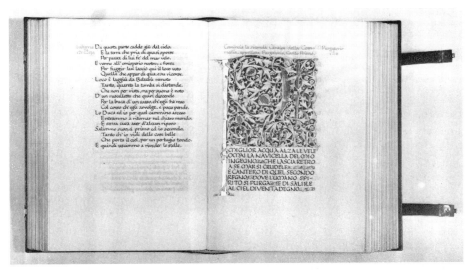

7.3   Dante's Divine Comedy, *written out and decorated by Louise Powell with the help of Graily Hewitt who drew and gilded the initial letters, and bound by Katharine Adams at Broadway, Worcestershire, for C.H. StJohn Hornby, 1906 (F.C. Scorey for CAGM)*

The work of Alfred and Louise Powell from this period reflects their commitment to Arts and Crafts ideals. Both painted furniture and ceramics either individually or in collaboration with each other, and in some early examples it is difficult to tell their work apart. As a general rule, however, Alfred's designs are the more formal and include buildings and landscapes, while Louise appears to have specialized in bold floral patterns which reflect her interest in medieval illuminated manuscripts.

It seems likely that it was through their association with the Central School, and William Lethaby in particular, that the Powells met. Lethaby and Alfred Powell were lifelong friends and shared many ideals on craft-training. Lethaby's aim in establishing the Central School was not only to raise the standard of the crafts but also to create a training ground for designers who were prepared to meet the demands of industry. Wedgwood was one of the companies that enjoyed a good working relationship with the School and, in September 1902, Cecil Wedgwood approached Lethaby for a designer/decorator and he was subsequently invited to the works. Shortly after this, Alfred Powell made the unusual step of approaching Wedgwood with designs.

There was considerable contact between Wedgwood and the Powells at the end of the nineteenth century, not least of all through Margaret Powell who was head-mistress of the Orme Girls' School, Newcastle-under-Lyme, which several of the Wedgwood children attended. In fact, the first mention of Alfred Powell's designs for Wedgwood appeared in a letter from the company sent to Margaret Powell dated 3 October 1903 and an invitation was extended for him to visit the works at Etruria. Following this visit he produced his first successful designs for the company and from that time on his career took on another dimension.

Louise does not appear to have submitted patterns at this stage although she came from a distinguished family of French artists, several of whom decorated Wedgwood pottery. For example her aunt, Thérèse Lessore, and her father, Jules A. Lessore, a well-known marine painter whose work was exhibited at the Royal Academy and the Paris Salon, worked for Wedgwood in the 1870s. Her grandfather, Emile Aubert Lessore, was employed by the firm as Artistic Director throughout the 1860s. In addition, her brother, Frederick Lessore, a successful portrait sculptor and instructor in Decorative Plasterwork at the Central School, decorated pottery which was shown at Arts and Crafts exhibitions in the first decade of the twentieth century. In 1923 he opened the Beaux Arts Gallery in London. Later, Louise's younger sister, Thérèse Lessore, who was on the fringe of the more avant-garde art movements, decorated Wedgwood pottery, although her pieces were usually sold at exhibitions or through friends and not marketed by the company.

Thérèse married the painter, Bernard Adeney, and was a founder member of the London Group which included several artists who formed the Bloomsbury circle. The Adeneys were close friends of the textile designer, Phyllis Barron, and they all spent summers together with the Powells at Tunley, Gloucestershire. Thérèse was

7.4   *Altar frontal for St Andrew's church, Roker, Sunderland, by Louise Powell, 1907 (F.C. Scorey for CAGM)*

married twice, the second time to the painter, Walter Sickert, in 1926. At least one item of Wedgwood pottery has been recorded bearing Walter Sickert's signature. For subject-matter they both drew heavily on carefully observed incidents from everyday life and their sketchy paintings on pottery have a delightful immediacy about them.

Alfred Powell probably had experience of pottery-making before the Wedgwood collaboration. Some of his early pieces were fired at Millwall and these bear no resemblance to the Wedgwood shapes. They are highly ornamental with high relief modelling and occasionally incised decoration. The association lasted until at least the 1920s when examples of Millwall ware, inspired by early Delft potters, were illustrated in the *Studio*.[111] These are of hard red clay covered in tin enamel and painted after glazing, often with lustre on a black or white ground. Pottery made at Millwall is usually numbered and marked with the letter 'M' as well as Alfred Powell's monogram.

In his writings, Alfred Powell was rather scathing about the state of the contemporary pottery industry. He looked back to the time of Josiah Wedgwood as an ideal period in English ceramic history. Until then, English pottery-making depended to some extent on knowledge coming from the Continent. Alfred Powell was especially interested in the development of English ceramics, and Creamware is of course traditionally English.

Josiah Wedgwood not only perfected the Creamware body but also established fundamental principles. More importantly, the greater potter was able to attract new patrons from royalty and the landed gentry and as a result, within his own lifetime, patronage reached new heights. This enabled Josiah Wedgwood to employ the finest modellers, decorators and craftsmen which inevitably raised the standard of all his products. In this sense, art was no longer just available for the few. The dexterity of his workers was also reflected in the quality and range of his utility wares.

Like William Morris, Powell's chief concern was with reviving and revitalizing the English traditional crafts and good working practices. Although many of the making processes within the pottery industry had been mechanized during the nineteenth century, some of the traditional handcrafts, such as throwing, turning, sprigging, fine painting and gilding, were still carried on to a lesser degree at Etruria in the early years of the twentieth century. It therefore seemed natural that Alfred Powell should make his way there.

On his second visit, Alfred stayed in Market Drayton and went into the works each day to see for himself some of the processes in operation. He was given the opportunity to practise ceramic painting sitting at the bench alongside established craftsmen. From the start he was sympathetic towards the painters and the conditions they worked under. For his own part, he found it hard to work for long stretches of time. A typical day spent painting pottery would be from about half past eight until five with a two-hour break, which he said was about as much as he could do! It must have been especially difficult for someone like Alfred Powell who loved the open air, as the following letter to his mother showed. Here he described work on a tea-set for Sidney Barnsley in February 1905: 'It is an unusual sort of drawing & I have to keep within a certain limit of error all the time, which becomes exhausting I suppose after a bit . . . I only wish I could do it running about instead of sitting like a monkey eating nuts!'[112]

The first fruits of the Powell/Wedgwood collaboration were well received when they were shown at W.B. Patterson's Gallery in Old Bond Street, London in 1905. Shortly afterwards, Alfred visited the Etruria Works with Louise Lessore who happened to discover some of Josiah Wedgwood's beautifully drawn and coloured early pattern books. The impact of seeing the eighteenth-century patterns painted free-hand had a lasting effect on their own work and they were more than ever convinced that, given the same conditions, simple patterns could be produced by hand.

Alfred Powell was also convinced that beauty of workmanship evident in eighteenth-century ware was related to surroundings and working conditions and, should these be improved, the 'beauty-in-work', or freshness and sponteneity, might somehow be recovered. The Wedgwood collaboration was an excellent opportunity to put theories into practice. Tableware patterns designed by the Powells were often small repeating flower and leaf designs, reminiscent of the eighteenth-century examples, which could be produced by paintresses trained in the traditional method of working with a loaded pencil.

In 1906 a whole range of revived eighteenth-century patterns modified to suit contemporary taste were shown at an exhibition of the Powells' work at the Adelphi Hotel, Liverpool. A number of the original border patterns were later produced exclusively for retail by Alfred Powell's cousin, James Powell of Whitefriars' glass-works. The Liverpool exhibition was a way of working more closely with the public

7.5   *Exhibition of Wedgwood pottery, decorated by Alfred Powell, Louise Powell and assistants, held at their studio in Red Lion Square, London, 1907 (Maureen Batkin)*

and an attempt to eliminate some of the worst trading practices. Also in 1906 the Powells' work in the Arts and Crafts Exhibition at the Grafton Galleries was favourably received, and Alfred Powell was invited by Lethaby to establish a painting-on-china class at the Central School.

It was probably a new-found confidence in their work that enabled Alfred Powell to persuade Wedgwood to establish a London studio, or *atelier*, in Red Lion Square. The studio was a platform for their ideals and it was hoped that they would attract new patronage for the firm from within the Arts and Crafts Movement and elsewhere. They held their first exhibition at the premises in 1907 (Fig. 7.5). The firm stipulated that lads and lassies from Gloucestershire should be taken on rather than those 'contaminated' by art school training. Alfred Powell's first assistant was a young boy with little or no training. He was later joined by Miss Margery Hindshaw who had some previous experience of 'brushwork' and was encouraged to produce her own designs. She later went on to teach at the Central School and designed furniture for Heal's.

Alfred and Louise Powell usually visited the works several times a year to supervise the production of new shapes and to place new orders. On these occasions, they had the use of a small studio where they gave instruction in the art of free-hand painting.

The Powells preferred to paint free-hand directly on to the ware before glazing. This is one of the most difficult methods of decorating pottery since, once applied, the colour is fixed and cannot be wiped clean as in on-glaze decoration. Large hampers of unglazed pottery, or 'blanks' as they were called, were sent either to London or Gloucestershire for decoration and then returned to Etruria for glazing and firing. Wedgwood paid Alfred and Louise Powell fixed sums as designers for their tableware designs and the most successful of these were put into general production.

As skilled young men were called into the armed forces during the First World War, more and more girls were engaged at Etruria and it was at this time that the Powells' true potential as teachers was fully realized. Young girls selected by the Powells were taught to appreciate nature in all its forms. They were guided into painting wild flowers, butterflies and birds by Alfred while Louise worked on commissions and supervised the free-hand painting of their patterns. To encourage 'happy thoughts', Alfred placed some of his own watercolours in the working area of the paintresses.

Louise Powell's work for Wedgwood increased considerably during the First World War. Although nearing fifty, Alfred himself was appointed Handicraft Adviser to the Society of Friends War Relief Committee and much of the work for the 1916 Arts and Crafts Society's exhibition at Burlington House fell on to Louise's shoulders. In addition to Powell/Wedgwood pottery on show, the Powells contributed an anteroom with massive painted panels representing an English copse wood in May. The panels were designed by Louise although the painting was undertaken by them both. Ernest Gimson executed the decorative plaster frieze for this scheme.

Alfred and Louise Powell were regular contributers to the Arts and Crafts exhibitions. These exhibitions were a good way of bringing in new commissions and gave them a platform for introducing new ideas. Examples of their painted furniture were usually shown on these occasions. In 1910, for example, the Powells exhibited several pieces, including a chest made by Sidney Barnsley and painted by Alfred and Louise Powell, and an ebony cabinet designed by Ernest Gimson, executed by Harry Davoll and painted by Louise Powell. A painted mahogany writing cabinet, also designed by Gimson and painted by Louise, was shown in 1916. The Cotswold craftsmen collaborated on a number of fine examples of painted furniture, ranging from simple chests to elaborate cabinets made from rich woods such as ebony, satinwood, walnut and veneered coromandel wood.

Among the pottery shown at Burlington House was a group of Wedgwood teawares designed and painted by Grace Barnsley, the daughter of Sidney Barnsley. Grace went to Bedales School and trained at the Birmingham School of Art, as well as taking instruction from the Powells. Alfred Powell taught pottery and watercolour painting to the daughters of several of their friends over many years and was still giving advice when he was well into his eighties. Some of their pupils, like Grace

7.6   *Gimson dresser with Wedgwood pottery decorated by Alfred Powell (W. Dennis Moss)*

7.7   *Detail of 'Woodpecker' cabinet, painted by Louise Powell on satinwood and made by Peter Waals, 1927*
(Richard Hookway)

7.8   Wedgwood earthenware, decorated by Grace Barnsley, 1920s (F.C. Scorey for CAGM)

Barnsley, were probably 'taught at the knee' and had their first experience of free-hand painting on pottery while quite young. Nina Griggs described seeing Grace, 'happily busy painting her "Wedgwood" pots. She evolved a pattern of her own – simplicity itself – the brush filled with paint "blobs" as we did as children worked into a pattern unique and lovely'.[113]

Grace Barnsley occasionally produced decorated pottery in collaboration with F.L. Griggs as well as her husband, Oscar Davies. Oscar took out a patent for the 'Duopour', a divided pot which dispensed hot milk and coffee at the same time which was introduced into Wedgwood's 'Veronese' range in 1938. About this time Grace and Oscar established the Roeginga Pottery at Rainham in Kent for the making and decorating of pottery.

Early pottery decorated by Grace was probably provided by Alfred and Louise Powell but, from at least September 1917, she purchased 'blanks' directly from the works on her own account. These were returned to the factory for firing. Grace Barnsley carried on the tradition of painting with a loaded pencil directly on to the unglazed ware and many of her own creations are clearly inspired by the Powells' freely-painted foliage and flower designs.

Among the young girls to join the hand-painting department in 1917 was the fifteen-year-old, Potteries-born 'Millie' Taplin. She was quick to learn and was soon working with the Powells. Millie Taplin acquired a gift for translating Powell designs in such a way that they could be executed by the handpaintresses trained by them. Wedgwood introduced a wide variety of Powell and Powell-inspired designs in this period, including the prestigious 'Persian' and 'Rhodian' ranges which are reminiscent of Louise Powell's work. In this way, by the mid-1920s, over fifty of their handcraft patterns had been put into production.

Gordon Forsyth, Superintendent of the Stoke-on-Trent Schools of Art, in his report on the Ceramic Section of the 1925 Paris International Exhibition, acknowledged the contribution made by the Powells in the field of ceramic design. Although their works were not in the strictest sense 'studio' pottery because they were made by Wedgwood, they appeared to him to be a very happy and sensible solution to the problem of producing fine pottery:

> Wedgwood's make excellent pottery and Mr and Mrs Powell are excellent artists. They no doubt design the shapes they decorate, and their work always shows a keen appreciation of suitable treatment of various articles of everyday use. Their best work is found in lordly bowls and plaques . . . They are based on the brave and honest pattern work of William Morris, and have a delightfully English style . . . English pottery would be very much poorer without their splendid contributions to the artistic side of the craft.[114]

Following the success of the Powells' ornamental wares at the exhibition, Wedgwood decided to establish a small handcraft studio and Millie Taplin was placed in charge of two young girls, fresh from the Burslem School of Art, who were invited to train as her assistants. At first there was some doubt whether the studio was really a practical proposition. It was feared that the girls might not be able to work fast enough to meet the demand for handcrafted patterns, but these doubts proved groundless.

By 1927, Alfred and Louise's teaching arrangement was put on a more solid footing. All the handcraft paintresses were encouraged to experiment freely and Millie Taplin began producing her own handcraft designs for studio production, thus making her one of the few working-class women to become a professional designer in the ceramic industry. She eventually went on to become one of Wedgwood's most prolific designers along with Victor Skellern.

Cecily Stella 'Star' Wedgwood was another important designer of Wedgwood ware who was trained by Alfred and Louise Powell. She was the daughter of Major Frank Wedgwood, Chairman and Managing Director of the company from 1916 until his death in 1930. Although she attended the Royal College, the Central School and a private drawing school in London all within a year, most of her ceramic design skills were acquired at the Burslem School of Art, and from Alfred and Louise Powell when they were at Etruria.

7.9   *The Handcraft Studio at Barlaston, Staffordshire, 1940s. Millie Taplin is standing at the back, and in front of her are watercolours by Alfred Powell (The Trustees of the Wedgwood Museum and Archive)*

After completing her training, Star Wedgwood was given a small studio of her own. She painted a number of individual pieces, which she signed on the base with a star and her initials, as well as creating patterns for the free-hand paintresses. Additionally, a number of her printed designs were put into general production, including 'Coronation', designed for the coronation of King George VI and Queen Elizabeth in 1937, and 'Play Box', a series of nursery wares introduced the same year. More surprisingly, in the 1930s both Alfred and Louise produced printed patterns for tablewares, including a delightful set of nursery rhymes for a range of children's ware and 'Rural England', a scene showing an old farmhouse and farmyard scene.

Perhaps as a result of the slump in trade in 1929, the Handcrafts Department was merged with the hand-painting section. Millie Taplin was placed in overall charge. It was at this time Alfred Powell's dictum came into operation and helped to stave off some of the worst effects of the depression. His dictum read: 'The very essence of pottery decoration lies in its continued rapid adaptability to form. It need not be more complex than can rapidly be managed with a loaded brush. It should be able to compel admiration by its quick wit, light handling and its almost inherent quality of surprise.[115] The simple free-hand patterns put into production gave work to hand-craft workers and helped to preserve their craft skills at a time when they were in real danger of being lost. Worthy of special mention are Millie Taplin's colourful 'Sun-lit' range, with bold floral and geometric designs that were free-painted onto a Caneware body, and 'Veronese' wares, a series of hand-thrown ornamental wares in which simplicity of form and colour were particularly important. The soft, subtle glazes were developed by Norman Wilson, the ceramicist who joined the firm as a works manager in 1927, while the painted decoration was either designed by Alfred and Louise Powell or adapted from their earlier patterns.

The Powells did not accumulate great wealth through their art. They continued to decorate Wedgwood pottery for many years and received commissions for illumination, painting and small architectural works, such as renovating old tithe barns, from a few enlightened individuals with an interest in the Arts and Crafts. They relied on their winter show to boost their income. In 1920, Alfred Powell designed and built the studio at Tarlton near Cirencester, where much of their work was carried out. It was very close to Rodmarton and they became closely involved in the furnishing of the Biddulphs' house. Alfred designed furniture, carved woodwork and metalwork, while Louise designed textiles, including curtains for the Chapel with appliqué decoration by the Rodmarton Women's Guild.

In the 1930s they concentrated their efforts on rekindling interest in the crafts and, in 1936, Alfred Powell was happy to report that the winter exhibition was going better than usual. People were:

> . . . more pleased and some signs of a reaction from the mad things people are showing under the name of 'art'! I saw a review of Clive Bell who is supposedly a sane critic of a show of pottery in Bond Street (Brygos Galery – or should it be 'By Gosh' Gallery!) where the pots were many of them in common brown glazes – some paler with rough scratched design – aiming at the work of C-slovakian peasants now to be signified by the Critics as 'great' and admirable . . . but oh me – they weren't lovely & their shapes were like nightmares. All of it expressively dull & with no pleasant mentality behind it & no beauty in the front of it.[116]

Alfred Powell found it increasingly difficult to come to terms with changing attitudes to building, believing that the old order was gone and the new order was simply 'assembling parts'. He was also frustrated at having to rely on local builders instead of having his own craftsmen to work for him. The firm he used for an extension to Nunwick Hall in 1937 is a typical example. He described them as being a 'hopelessly unsympathetic building firm – all seeped in cheap brickwork & the rest &

pretending to build in local stone'.[117] He added: 'However, I've done them some good I hope.'

The couple continued to work to a lesser degree into the 1950s, by which time Louise's eyesight was beginning to fade. She died in 1956 and Alfred Powell in 1960 when the Arts and Crafts were losing some of their popularity; it is only recently that their contribution has been reappraised. Alfred and Louise Powell never sought popularity through their work but their collaboration with the firm of Josiah Wedgwood & Sons brought them into the public eye. Their legacy at the firm was enormous and they are now recognized as protagonists of the revival of Staffordshire free-painting on pottery, but it would be wrong to overlook their other achievements. Together, Alfred and Louise Powell took Arts and Crafts principles further than many of their contemporaries and helped to raise the standard in all the various crafts in which they were involved. For them the crafts were the 'living arts' and, by going back to the roots, they did much to bridge the gap between the eighteenth and twentieth centuries and to eliminate some of the bad working practices that had affected design.

Chapter Eight

William and Eve Simmonds

William and Eve Simmonds are hardly known outside a small circle of devotees. Their work has been treasured by its original owners and their families, so that it has rarely escaped into the glare of the commercial art world. It is as if it carries with it some of the simple contentment and beauty of their lives. William Morris believed that art could be the visible expression of man's delight in his work and the world around him, 'a joy to the maker and the user'. [118] William and Eve Simmonds, living the simple life in the Cotswolds, brought Morris's words to fruition.

William George Simmonds was born in Istanbul on 3 March 1876, the son of Martha and John Simmonds. His father was an architect working in the Middle East at the time of his son's birth. His parents encouraged him to exercise his artistic talents from a young age. One of his earliest surviving sketches is a study of a guinea pig drawn when he was eight years old. In 1893, after spending four years in his father's architectural office and attending evening classes at Windsor School of Art, he began to study painting under Walter Crane at the Royal College of Art. He continued his training between 1899 and 1904 at the Royal Academy Schools where he took a number of practical classes, including one in scenery painting.

The influence of Walter Crane and the second generation of Pre-Raphaelite painters can be seen clearly in the few surviving examples of Simmonds's early paintings, such as *The Seeds of Love* of 1907.[119] The title and subject-matter of this watercolour was the first song collected by Cecil Sharp in 1903. Edward Payne remembered William Simmonds singing the song:

> I sowed the seeds of love
> I sowed them in the springtime
> And gathered them up in the morning
> When small birds so sweetly sing
> When small birds so sweetly sing.[120]

This romantic interpretation of literary and historical themes was a recurrent idiom much loved by the second generation of Pre-Raphaelite painters. Although the sentimental element was swept out of William Simmonds' work as he matured, he retained a lifelong interest in romance, legend, theatre and story-telling.

His enthusiasm for theatricals and painting on a large scale led him to work as an assistant to the American painter and illustrator, Edwin Austen Abbey, between 1906 and 1910. Abbey was an anglophile responsible, with a number of fellow-countrymen including Frank D. Millet, for discovering the natural beauty of the North Cotswolds and for publicizing its attractions in both Britain and America. In the mid-1880s they had rented houses for the summer months in the town of Broadway. This became the focal point for a flourishing artistic community visited by the novelists, Henry James and Edmund Gosse, and captured on canvas by John Singer Sargent in his famous painting, *Carnation, Lily, Lily, Rose*. In 1906, however, Abbey was based in Fairford, Gloucestershire, working on a commission for the production of mural paintings for the Pennsylvania State Capitol. As his assistant, William Simmonds was able to sketch in some of the background details. Edward Payne recalled a remark he made about 'the external quality in peoples' faces. When struck for a model for the "Mayflower" painting, he got an old lady from the village and dressed her in puritan costume and there was the face of the 17th century staring out from the 20th century.'[121]

It was during this period that William met Eveline, (Eve) Peart 'at the little dances we held every three weeks at the School of Arms in Knightsbridge'.[122] Eve Peart was born in 1884 in Walthamstow, London and studied art at the Slade under Walter Sickert. During her art school days she met two sisters (Thérèse Lessore and her elder sister, Louise, married to Alfred Powell) who were to become lifelong friends. Louise Powell, in particular, provided Eve with inspiration, support and encouragement. The Powells also introduced the young couple to Catherine (Casty) Cockerell, daughter of the bookbinder, Sydney Cockerell, and to the musician, Arnold Dolmetch. William and Eve Simmonds were married in 1912 at her brother's house in Fovant, Wiltshire. The couple lived in a nearby house for the first years of what was to be a long and happy married life. It was at this point that William Simmonds gave up thoughts of a career in painting and illustration, and began to think of himself as a carver and sculptor. In 1968 he referred to *The Singing Shepherd* as 'the second serious carving I ever did in about 1912'.[123]

Shortly after the outbreak of war in 1914, William and Eve Simmonds moved back to London to a flat on the top floor of Alfred and Louise Powell's house in Well Walk, Hampstead. Everyone had their own stories of wartime experiences and William and Eve were no exception. Eve Simmonds described them as living in a semi-detached house, 'the tenants of the other [house] had gone to Scotland. When the war was over and they returned, they found a bomb had fallen through their roof and had only failed to explode because it had lodged in the wire mattress of the bed. William and I were sleeping alongside!'[124]

During the First World War, William Simmonds' artistic skills brought him work as a precision draughtsman. He was involved in tank design with Colonel R.E.

Crompton and aircraft design with Captain Geoffrey de Havilland. He still found some time for his new interest in carving and it provided him with a release from the tensions of the period. Two strong characteristics began to emerge in his work during this period: a thorough knowledge of anatomical structure based on close observation, combined with an ability to reduce these observed details to their essentials. This is such a basic element in Japanese art that one suspects that his interest went beyond admiration for the traditional carved netsuke. These inspired a number of small ivory carvings which were done during the war through to the early 1920s. While away from home, William Simmonds got into the habit of carrying a piece of ivory and a small knife in his pocket. Whenever the opportunity arose, he would work on the intricate carving of the subject in hand, such as *Wood Nymph and Animals* (1917), *War Episode* (1919), showing a soldier on horseback arriving at a reclaimed village during the 1914–18 War as its inhabitants emerged from dug-outs, and *Kid Asleep* (1920). On completion, these tiny offerings were despatched by William Simmonds to his wife in matchboxes or other small containers.

The wartime years in and around the capital were not an easy period for William and Eve Simmonds, living with the constant fear of air raids and long periods of separation. In 1919 they decided to move out of London so that William could concentrate on his carving, and to continue in close touch with Alfred and Louise Powell who were full of their plans for a studio at Tarlton near Cirencester. They bought themselves an idyllic home in the village of Far Oakridge set in fields and surrounded by woods. It was a small house, almost derelict, originally a pair of adjoining two-roomed cottages knocked together, with a barn which William Simmonds converted

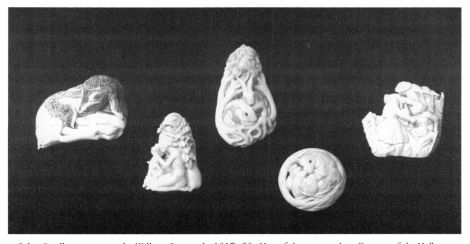

8.1   Small ivory carvings by William Simmonds, 1917–20. Most of these are in the collections of the Holburne Museum and Crafts Study Centre, Bath (F.C. Scorey for CAGM)

into a workshop. The house was sparsely but sensitively furnished and included some pieces of oak furniture bought from Sidney Barnsley which suited their simple good taste. Both husband and wife put a great deal of thought and effort into creating a home and garden of great character with very limited means. Much of the credit for this was due to Eve Simmonds, whom Nina Griggs described:

> Of all the women I have known . . . Eve is . . . the one with the most exacting and individual taste. Their house was a reflection of it. She liked quiet muted colours, creams, greys, honey unstained oak furniture, Baron [sic] and Larcher fabrics, a setting for old china lustre and gleaming glass. No pictures. The garden echoed her taste, one or two narrow borders round the lawn, filled with rare plants and rugosa. If a rosebush or two was permitted they would be of an unusual kind.[125]

Eve Simmonds had tried her hand at embroidery during the war, exhibiting a smock made for her sister-in-law's first baby at the Arts and Crafts Exhibtion of 1916. She wrote: 'everyone did [needlework] in those days',[126] but the initial impetus had come from Louise Powell. In about 1920, Eve Simmonds worked a silk hanging designed by Louise Powell showing a growing tree on hilly ground populated by squirrels and small birds. Her own designs range from delicate embroideries of flower and leaf forms, including a group of bags illustrated in *Modern Embroidery* [127] and a sampler made for the Cadbury family, to the gay and vivid *Flora* panel of 1916 (Fig. 8.2).

Their relatively isolated life in the Cotswolds gave William Simmonds the opportunity to become completely absorbed in his carvings and sculptures, and to extend his early artistic training with practical observation of nature. He developed a sure and confident eye for the general and the particular, which was noted by Edward Payne: 'He knows every horse in the neighbouring farms, which farmer has the finest goose, in which field there is a beautiful hare, or in his own garden, where the wren builds its nest, and how it lives and feels. This is the material which he uses for his wood carvings.' [128]

These qualities led William Rothenstein to describe him as 'a Little Master, in the old German sense'.[129] Wild creatures only give up their secrets after a great deal of patient and sometimes uncomfortable observation, and the background to some of the carvings, including *Three Leverets* (Fig. 8.3) carved out of a single block of oak in 1932, was related by John Gwynne:

> He went out on one occasion and found three leverets there together which is very, very rare indeed because the hare as a rule never produces more than two young ones. But he found three and spent a long time drawing, sketching

113

8.2   Flora, *embroidered panel in coloured worsteds by Eve Simmonds, 1916 (F.C. Scorey for CAGM)*

8.3   Three Leverets, *oak carving by William Simmonds, 1932 (Brian Donnan)*

them and getting them absolutely accurate in their positions . . . Then there is
the owl which . . . flew down the chimney in his house at The Frith at Far
Oakridge and he kept it in captivity for a day or two perhaps while he sketched
it and got that to perfection.[130]

It is easy to recognize, just by looking at the underside of one of his sculptures,
that William Simmonds was a perfectionist. One carving of a calf in marble (Fig. 8.4)
made in 1925 reveals the loving and painstaking detail of four little hoofs. His work
was never hurried at any point in its conception and completion. A great deal of
thought went into choosing exactly the right piece of wood or stone for each job. He
worked in many different materials relying, above all, on local woods such as oak,
elm, chestnut, pearwood and hawthorn, carefully chosen to suit the particular character of each carving. He occasionally used marble and alabaster to capture the deli-
cacy and ethereal quality of young animals. Like Eric Gill, Simmonds sometimes
chose to paint his carvings with oils giving a very rich, even surface to pieces such as
Autumn Calf of 1952 (Plate 8). Every piece was carefully finished off; the bases were
usually made for William Simmonds by Fred Gardiner of Waterlane, one of Peter
Waals's cabinet-makers.

Theatricals had played a part in William Simmonds' life from his youth and, as an
art student in London, he had painted stage scenery. According to Eve Simmonds:

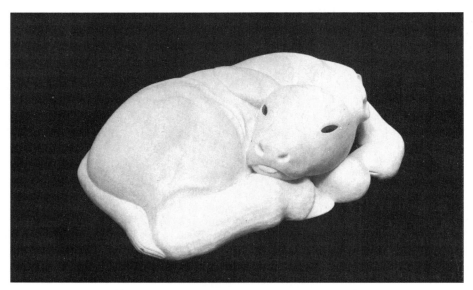

8.4   Calf, *marble carving by William Simmonds, 1925 (F.C. Scorey for CAGM)*

When his father was dying and William was spending long hours sitting with him he started making puppets for something to do. We used to have joint parties with my brother with puppet shows on the kitchen table. A favourite garden boy would play the trumpet or mouth organ, later I played the spinet having had lessons from Arnold Dolmetch, first on an early piano belonging to Alfred Powell, then on the spinet, and Catherine Cobb helped with stringing the puppets.[131]

Casty Cobb remembers that William Simmonds' first puppet was a clown which he made for a children's party – possibly the children of Eve's brother. He also made a Punch and Judy theatre for the children at Rodmarton Manor. Even out of context, they were full of life as one visitor to Simmonds' workshop described:

I always enjoyed seeing his tools, many of which he inherited from his father, hammers with long whippy handles – works of art in themselves. The puppets hang in a row, talking to themselves very happily, and now and again one of them is brought out to have a little massage for the joints, and all the others have the air of being much interested in this.[132]

In the 1920s and 1930s, puppet shows became an important part of the Simmonds's lives. They were also a well-remembered and much loved source of

I   *Marquetry cabinet in walnut, ebony and holly with whitebeam drawers and silver fittings, designed by Ernest Gimson, 1906 (CAGM/Bridgeman Art Library)*

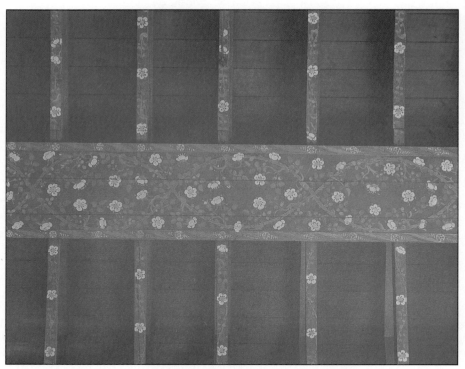

II   *Detail of the ceiling of the church of the Wisdom of God, Lower Kingswood, Surrey, designed and painted by Sidney Barnsley, c. 1890 (Jan Marsh/Margaret Dickinson)*

III Oak coffer, designed and made by Sidney Barnsley and painted in oils by Alfred Powell, c. 1907 (Design Council)

IV Ewer, Wedgwood earthenware with painted decoration by Louise Powell, c. 1920 (Michael Focard)

V   Cupboard, designed by Ernest Gimson and painted by Alfred Powell with local scenes for William Rothenstein, c. 1914. The initials refer to the Rothenstein children. The handles may be a later addition (Norman McBeath)

*VI   Guild of Handicraft silverwork, with enamelled decoration by Fleetwood Varley and William Mark. The pieces were designed by
C.R. Ashbee between 1901 and 1903, apart from the rectangular box which was probably designed and made by George Hart, 1913
(CAGM / Bridgeman Art Library)*

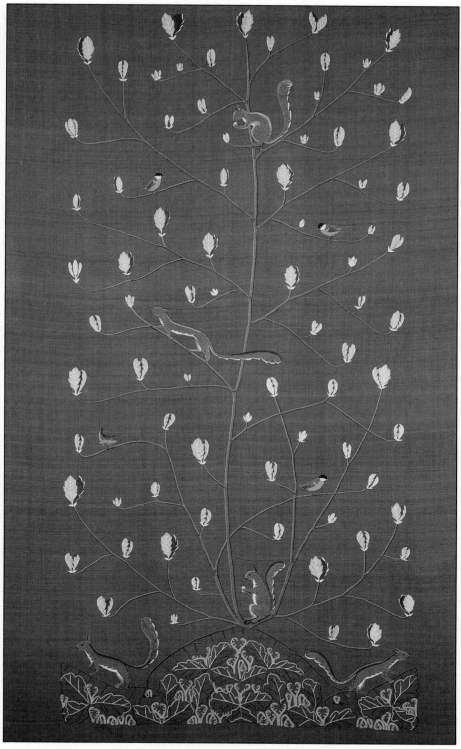

VII 'The Whitebeam Tree' hanging, designed by Louise Powell and embroidered by Eve Simmonds on hand-woven Assam silk dyed indigo by Ethel Mairet, c. 1920 (Whitworth Art Gallery, University of Manchester)

VIII Autumn Calf, *carved and painted oak inlaid with ebony on a base of ash by William Simmonds, 1952 (CAGM/Bridgeman Art Library)*

IX A Christmas party performance of puppets in the workshop of William Simmonds, a watercolour by Edward Payne. Henry Payne and Alfred Powell are seated in the foreground (CAGM)

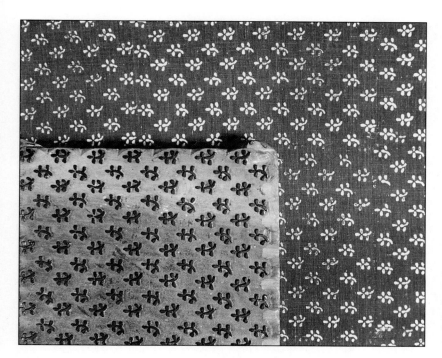

X Block and sample print of
'Lizard' in indigo discharge on
cotton. The block was originally
acquired by Phyllis Barron from
Fred Mayor in France, but
subsequently recut by Fred
Gardiner (Holburne Museum and
Crafts Study Centre, Bath)

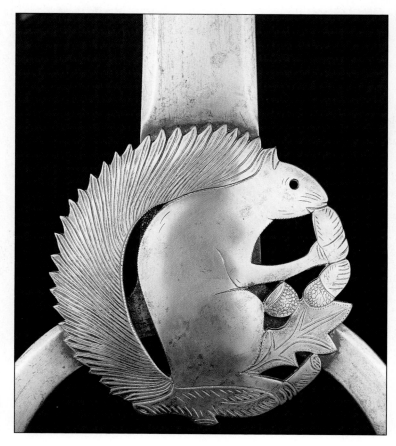

XI Detail of a firedog in polished
steel, designed by Ernest Gimson
(Jan Marsh / Margaret Dickinson)

XII *Detail of jacket and skirt belonging to Eve Simmonds made up from 'Peach' and printed in black on velvet. The design was named after Harry Peach of Dryad Handicrafts, Leicester (Holburne Museum and Crafts Study Centre, Bath)*

8.5 *William Simmonds with two hand*
puppets, probably 1920s

entertainment in the locality, both for children and adults. This was no amateur theatricals but a professional, if small-scale, venture. The Simmonds's puppet theatre
was one of three established in England at that time, playing an annual season of three
weeks at the Grafton Theatre in London and holding special performances at other
venues including the Art Workers' Guild. William and Eve Simmonds also took their
puppet theatre to country houses throughout the country to perform at private parties. These included Eaton Hall, Cheshire, home of the Duke of Westminster where,
on one occasion, the audience included Winston Churchill and the London and
Gloucestershire homes of William Rothenstein.

Casty Cobb acted as William Simmonds' assistant for many of the puppet shows in
the 1930s. Her main job was to prepare the puppets for the stage and hand each one
over as it was needed. She recalled that:

> Eve Simmonds made most of the costumes from her own scraps or pieces
> begged from friends. Every effort was made to ensure that the puppets were
> clothed in the lightest of material so that their movements were not impeded
> by their dress . . . The puppets were very well made including the controls,
> and the actions they were required to make were achieved with great accuracy.

William Simmonds worked on all the puppets single-handed above a unique stage designed by himself. It was portable so that it could be erected in an hour or so when needed. William himself stood in the middle of a semi-circular stage and the backdrops covered the convex part of the semi-circle and extended out at each side at right angles. They were painted by William Simmonds and could be peeled off very quickly between each scene to reveal the next setting.[133]

The puppet theatre was so designed that it could be dismantled for transportation in the boot of William Simmonds's car.

The same powers of observation and distillation that William Simmonds employed to such advantage in his sculpture were also used in the puppet theatricals. He was full of a gentle humour and quick to see it in the world around him. He brought into play not only his eyes but also his ears, and would record overheard conversations from everyday situations which filled a number of notebooks.[134] His stories and playlets were a mixture of traditional folk-tales, his own inventions and collected snippets of conversation, folk-song and dance. Musical accompaniment was provided by Eve on the spinet and virginals, sometimes with the artist, Barnet Friedman, on the fiddle, or occasionally by the gramophone. Casty Cobb described two particularly cunning theatrical devices that he employed:

> There was a circus with horse riders and even a pantomime horse made of two puppets. At the crucial moment the hook holding them together would be undone, briefly revealing the startled expression of the puppet playing the horse's back-end before they both scarpered off the stage. . .
>
> A surprising and unexpected happening occurred when the curtain was still down at the end of the interval. A door opened above the stage and two puppet workmen proceeded to clamber down, move props, and paint scenery, all the while conversing in broad Gloucestershire dialect as they discussed preparations for the next scene.[135]

The puppet shows made a lasting impression on young and old alike. The Christmas puppet shows held in the barn that was also William Simmonds's workshop were particularly evocative, with the audience seated on cushions and chairs (Plate 9). According to Nina Griggs, 'For an hour or more we entered into a Magic World of Make Believe Come True'.[136]

As well as puppet shows, William Simmonds was also given the task of staging amateur theatricals with the locals at Far Oakridge. This was a tradition begun by William Rothenstein when he first moved to the Cotswolds and carried on through the 1930s. One successful production was seen by the painter, Charles Gere:

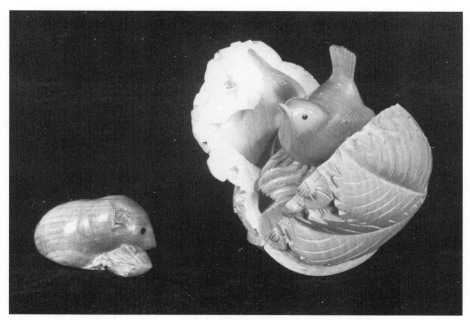

8.6   Mouse *in plumwood and* Wren on a beech leaf, *in English hawthorn by William Simmonds, 1935. The carving of the wren emerges from an oak case carved in the form of a strawberry leaf (F.C. Scorey for CAGM)*

'Everybody went to Oakridge last week to the Simmonds play. They did Yellow–Sands. Exactly the thing for those country players. Simmonds had trained them perfectly, had painted jolly little scenes and the result was a complete success. I enjoyed it thoroughly.'[137]

William Simmonds was prepared to make great efforts to entertain and entrance his friends. He would make intricate, individual birthday and Christmas cards for those who were closest to him, including the violinist, Violet Gordon Woodhouse, who provided him with a great deal of kindness and support. She lived at Nether Lypiatt Manor and was an expert in the authentic music and instruments of the six-teenth to eighteenth centuries. They were introduced by William Rothenstein in the early 1930s and it became customary for them to spend at least part of every Christmas Day together.

On their own, William and Eve Simmonds lived a very frugal existence. They relied on William selling one or two sculptures a year at the Royal Academy which he did without any trouble. He rarely worked on commissions. Both husband and wife gave freely of their time to help other artists and craftspeople. They were active and well-respected members of the local artistic community, exhibiting at Chipping Campden, Painswick and Cheltenham.

8.7   *Drawing of Norman Jewson and his daughter , Mary, by William Simmonds, 1931 (CAGM)*

In 1960 they gave up their home at Far Oakridge and moved to a small and more accessible cottage in Oakridge Lynch. Once again, Eve Simmonds put all her energies and creative ability into fashioning a picturesque garden. William Simmonds, in his eighties, learned to work in a new material. Unable to carve wood because of arthritic joints he took pottery classes at Stroud School of Art. He was taught to work with clay by Tony Davies who was impressed by William Simmonds's immediate grasp of new techniques and their inherent possibilities. He saw that his pupil 'was intrigued by the permanence of clay when fired and overjoyed at the speed by which models could be made and fired in contrast to the rather more laborious task of carving from a solid piece of wood'.[138] He continued working right up to his death which occurred tragically just after the opening of a major retrospective exhibition of his work in Cheltenham in 1968. His wife survived him for two years. John Gwynne described them as 'two of the happiest people one can ever imagine. So little money to live on but just enough; they wanted no more. They were entirely satisfied with themselves and their friends: a fairly wide circle, mostly living locally, and they were two of the most self-sufficient people I've ever come across.'[139]

Chapter Nine

Phyllis Barron
and Dorothy Larcher

B·ARLEY ROSCOE

In 1930 Phyllis Barron and Dorothy Larcher, both in their forties and two of the leading handblock printers of the inter-war years, left London to live in Gloucestershire. They had bought Hambutts House in Painswick and moved on 19 March – Barron's fortieth birthday – 'driving from Northleach in a terrific snow-storm with no chains'.[140] Their change of address card from 2 Parkhill Studios, Parkhill Road, announced:

9.1   *Hambutts House, Painswick, with the workshop beyond (Holburne Museum and Crafts Study Centre, Bath)*

We have much pleasure in inviting you to see our new workshop in the Cotswolds, where we are now living, and making our HAND BLOCK-PRINTED STUFFS. We have left Hampstead as there is more space in the country to carry on our work and to show it.

Furnishing and dress-stuffs can be chosen here under very pleasant conditions. Patterns and lengths of stuff can be posted to you on approval. Please say whether you wish to see silk, velvet, or cotton for dresses, or linen and cotton for furnishings. We have light coats of printed handwoven cotton, linen, silk, and velveteen which are very useful in the summertime and will wash or clean well.

Hambutts House was situated in Edge Road, a quiet lane leading off the main street in Painswick into beautiful open countryside. An elegant eighteenth-century house built of Cotswold stone, it had a garden either side of the lane and, most importantly, a separate stable block adjacent to the house which they converted into a spacious workshop complete with indigo vat. Later to become a great friend, Robin Tanner, etcher and educationist, recalled vividly his first visit to them there in 1938:

Round the doorway and along the walls of that beautiful Georgian house, on that cold spring morning, there were wonderful blooming plants: Daphne odora, Iris reticulata, sweet-scented sarcococca, Lenten hellebores – mostly greenish-white ones with dark spotted hearts – and up the wall the fragrant flowers of Wintersweet. Barron [as she was called by her friends] . . . was a tall, large, handsome, commanding figure, with fine eyes and brow, cropped silver hair, a beautiful outgoing expression, and a warm lovely voice. She wore clothes superbly made of her own printed stuffs. That morning she was dressed in a long linen garment, printed in one of her favourite designs which she called 'Guinea', in the galled iron black she was so fond of . . . . And all down the front were old silver Dutch buttons. She was wearing men's brogues . . . .

Dorothy Larcher, in contrast, was small yet of equally strong personality. She had a rather sad, quiet voice and a serious manner, though her sense of humour was every bit as keen as Barron's. She too was most beautifully dressed. She wore cotton printed in iron rust in her own design called 'Old Flower' the very first she ever cut . . . . [She] was a most distinguished embroideress. I observed at once the immaculate stitchery and the embroidered collar and cuffs of her dress, and the amber glass buttons chosen with perfect appropriateness . . .

[Coffee was] served in fragile old French cups, and we sat talking and laughing . . . in a room that seemed to me more harmoniously and subtly beautiful

9.2   Dorothy Larcher and Eve Simmonds at Hambutts House, drawn by William Simmonds, May 1934 (Holburne Museum and Crafts Study Centre, Bath)

than any I had ever seen. Curtains, covers, cushions were all their own, and each was printed in a scale exactly right for its purpose and with a character exactly appropriate to the setting. Every small detail of every object in that room seemed right. There was an old silver lustre jug filled with firstlings of Spring that Barron had brought from her walled garden across the lane, and Dorothy kept turning it about as if studying it. Barron was the gardener and Larcher was the painter and draughtsman . . . I thought, if ever there was a marriage of true minds it was here in this room.[141]

The two women had first met and formed a partnership in the early 1920s. Of the two, Barron was the more accessible, an exuberant and forceful personality. As creative and standard-conscious as Barron, Larcher's attitude to life was more deeply hidden behind a veil of reserve and a retiring nature. Their work was a complete contrast to what was generally being produced at the time and, by 1930 when they moved to Painswick, their distinctive designs, printed in subtle colours on quality materials, had earned them a considerable reputation in the craft world and among a discerning clientele.

9.3   Phyllis Barron and Dorothy Larcher at Hambutts House, probably late 1930s (Holburne Museum and Crafts Study Centre, Bath)

In contemplating a move out of London they had first briefly toyed with the idea of moving to Dartington. However, Painswick seemed a more obvious choice since they already had friends living in the area and were familiar with the Cotswolds from previous visits. Barron's first introductisn to this part of the world had been some fourteen years earlier when London friends – the painter Bernard Adeney and his first wife Thérèse Lessore – had invited her to stay with them in their cottage in Tunley where the Powells also had a cottage. A couple of years later Bernard met and subsequently remarried Barron's great friend the dress designer and painter, Noël Gilford, so visits to Tunley continued.

The first record of a visit to the Cotswolds by Dorothy Larcher was in 1909. Philippe Mairet, formerly a fellow art student with her at Hornsey School of Art (where she later taught), invited her together with another student and her flatmate Alice Richardson[142] to spend a week at Chipping Campden where he was working with C.R. Ashbee. While there they visited Ananda and Ethel Coomaraswamy at Norman Chapel and Alice, a music teacher gifted with a lovely voice, was persuaded to sing to the company. It was to prove a fateful evening, for it led to the breakdown of the Coomaraswamys' marriage; Alice subsequently joined Ananda in India, and

Ethel married Philippe in 1913. A year later Dorothy Larcher was also to go out to India when she accompanied Lady Herringham to help make a record of the Buddhist frescoes in the Ajanta caves. Later she taught and lived with an Indian family in Calcutta, since the outbreak of war prevented her return to England until 1921. No doubt it was in India that she first saw textiles being printed by hand. Following her return, Dorothy visited her friends, Eve and William Simmonds, in Far Oakridge. Eve recalled:

> while looking through a drawer we came across this piece of early Barron print. Dorothy became instantly very excited and interested about it, having never seen anything quite like it before, nor I think having heard of Barron or her work. It was not very long after that they met in London and began to work together. This piece of cotton print was therefore their first introduction to each other.[143]

The material Dorothy so admired was dyed in indigo blue and had been printed in nitric acid to discharge the design with a block called 'Lizard' (Plate 10). This was one of a collection of old French blocks which had first inspired Barron to find out about textile printing at the age of fifteen, while on a sketching holiday with her elder sister Muriel in Montreuil-sur-Mer, Normandy. Their tutor, Fred Mayor, had bought the blocks in a junk shop proposing to use them as a wall decoration, but Barron persuaded him to let her experiment with them. Concluding that they must have been used for printing on material, she eagerly tried to discover what dyes could be used but found it very difficult to obtain information. Even as a fine art student at the Slade, studying under Tonks and Steer, she was unable to get any practical help about dyeing and printing. Undeterred, she went back to primary sources searching the British Museum and Victoria & Albert Museum Libraries for any books on the subject. She found 'the most marvellous book' which she recommended 'everybody should read as a novel',[144] called *Experimental Researches concerning the Philosophy of Permanent colours and the best means of producing them by dyeing, calico printing etc.* by Edward Bancroft, (published in 1794), which became her Bible. She also discovered that *A practical hand book of dyeing and calico printing*, by William Crookes (published in 1874), was invaluable. Another useful source of information proved to be the Patent Office, as before a dye can be patented a full description of ingredients and processes has to be given. Alongside her reading, Barron was experimenting avidly with the French blocks printing on a lovely handwoven indigo-dyed cotton which she obtained from The Friends of Armenia in Victoria Street.

Soon Barron wanted to try to make her own indigo vat, but initial experiments were doomed to failure. An attempt to keep the vat warm by wrapping it in blankets and placing it near an old anthracite stove led to disaster when she was out at a party.

9.4   'Large Feather', indigo resist on organdie (Holburne Museum and Crafts Study Centre, Bath)

The blankets caught fire as well as the wooden bung to the pottery barrel which contained the indigo vat. This released the liquid which extinguished the fire but she 'had dyed practically nothing in it and there was a great mess to clear up'.[145] However she determined to try again, but this time using urine as a substitute for lime copperas:

> This vat had to be a little warmer than the other, so I put it on the gas cooker. I had a friend, Noël Gilford, coming to lunch and had everything ready when I realised I'd forgotten the bread, and ran out to get it. When I came back I found my urine vat flowing down the stairs to meet me – and a very furious friend saying 'what a disgusting smell. Whatever have you been doing now?'[146]

Later, in Painswick, Barron continued to use urine as an important feature of the indigo vat. Parties were not merely social occasions but an opportunity to obtain a supply of pure male urine and became known as 'Barron's Piddle Parties'.[147]

The failure of her second indigo vat and the outbreak of war temporarily put a stop to Barron's experiments and she went to work in a hospital in Belgium. Returning to London in 1915 she resumed her experiments, this time with cutch which gave her a brown, and then achieving a black by printing with pyrolignite of iron on grey linen prison sheeting from the Caledonian market or on wartime balloon cotton steeped in powdered oak galls. She also cut her first block in wood using the graining on it as the inspiration for her 'Log' design, spending many hours trying to get the pattern to repeat. A lecture given at the Victoria and Albert Museum by G.P. Baker, owner of the printing firm at Crayford in Essex, taught her how to make a steamer using a dustbin and gas ring which enabled her to fix the dyes and extend her repertoire. Ethel Mairet's book, *Vegetable Dyeing*, was published in 1916 and from this Barron discovered about dyeing with rust (ferrous acetate). Ethel's interest in dyeing was directly related to her weaving which she had begun at Norman Chapel and led to her setting up her influential weaving workshop at Gospels in Ditchling, Sussex. Barron decided to send Ethel Mairet samples of her work to comment on. Ethel 'wrote back at once, bubbling with excitement, to say she'd not seen anything so interesting for years . . .',[148] and encouraging Barron to exhibit and sell her work.

Towards the end of 1917, Barron had her first exhibition together with Noël Gilford, who often used Barron's materials for clothes' designing and dress-making. The exhibition was held in a drawing-room in Hampstead belonging to Boris Anrep, a mosaicist and Russian royalist emigré, and it was from here that Eve Simmonds bought Barron's print, 'Lizard'. Barron and Ethel Mairet also shared several exhibitions at the Brook Street Gallery, where Dorothy Larcher first sought Barron out. Detmar Blow, an architect friend and contemporary of Gimson and the Barnsleys currently engaged in work for the Duke of Westminster, saw Barron's prints at one of these exhibitions and wanted to commission Barron to print all the materials for the Duke's Elizabethan-style yacht, 'The Flying Cloud', which he was furnishing. The yacht had '40 cabins, each with divans, bunks and curtains, and an enormous saloon in the middle'.[149] This was the largest commission she had ever received and enlisting the help of a friend, Frances Woollard, she finished the job in three months, 'even to the cushions'.[150]

For a time, Barron, Frances and Dorothy, who had now joined them, worked together moving to rather a damp studio in 'a conservatory belonging to the Health Food shop in Hampstead High Street'.[151] The basement studio in Haverstock Hill in the house that Barron was sharing with the Adeneys was really too cramped for three. However, Barron and Frances Woollard had a final quarrel in 1923 and Frances left. Barron and Larcher then moved again, this time to 2 Parkhill Studios, accommodated in 'an enormously high mid-Victorian house in Park Hill Road, Hampstead, the most hideous studios in the world . . . But . . . quite convenient because [they] had a flat almost next door, and there was a garden all round with plenty of room for hoses'.[152] This was to remain their base until they moved to the Cotswolds. Recognition came quickly. 'The Flying Cloud' was but the first of a number of commissions received from Detmar Blow and the Duke, which were an important factor in helping to make Barron and Larcher's textiles fashionable among a wealthy clientele. As orders from private clients increased, more help was needed and the workshop expanded.

London galleries that exhibited Barron and Larcher's textiles included The Mayor Gallery, The Three Shields Gallery, The New Handworkers Gallery and The Little Gallery. The last two kept a range of their work in stock and The Little Gallery maintained very high standards. When Barron and Larcher moved to the Cotswolds their change of address leaflet was careful to mention on the bottom: 'In London a large and ever-changing selection of our stuffs can always be seen at The Little Gallery, 5 Ellis St., Sloane St., where we can also meet customers by appointment.'

Muriel Rose who ran the gallery became a good friend of both women and personally did much to promote them, taking their work out to the United States, first with Mrs Paul Watson, then later with the British Council during the Second World War. In general, Rose stocked their work on a sale or return basis and took a commission of 33%. Apart from keeping a varied selection of their materials available, Muriel Rose also kept sample books of their work in the gallery for prospective clients to choose from. A good postal service between London and Painswick enabled them to keep up a brisk business correspondence of orders and instructions as needed, interspersed with friendly chat. In addition, special exhibitions of their work were held at The Little Gallery on a regular basis throughout the 1930s. These received favourable reviews in *The Times*. On more than one occasion, Rose held a small exhibition of Barron and Larcher's historical collection of block-printed textiles to provide a

9.5 *'Elizabethan', designed by Phyllis Barron for the daughter of the Duke of Westminster's coming-out dance held at the Estate Office in Davies Street, London W.1., 1925 (Holburne Museum and Crafts Study Centre, Bath)*

9.6 *'Basket', the third block Dorothy Larcher designed, printed in iron on ungalled linen (Holburne Museum and Crafts Study Centre, Bath)*

9.7   *Dorothy Larcher and Phyllis Barron at a market on holiday in France (Holburne Museum and Crafts Study Centre, Bath)*

context for their work and show the rich historical source they had to draw on. The earliest pieces were two Indian examples, one of which had the device of the East India Company stamped on the sleeve and must have been bought by Dorothy when she was living out there. A wonderful selection of eighteenth- and nineteenth-century French materials was also included. Barron loved France and had often gone to the Pas-de-Calais region as a student. Later, she, Dorothy and other friends sometimes stayed in Muriel Barron's cottage in France and explored further afield. On these visits they had bought early printed stuffs very cheaply at Rouen, Arles and Marseilles, visited the *Musée de L'Impression sur étoffes* at Mulhouse in Alsace, and acquired Provençal cottons printed in madder and indigo as well as examples of the famous *Toile de Jouy*.

Notes such as 'Visitors to the Cotswolds are always welcomed at Hambutts House' and 'Visitors to Painswick can also see the printing and dyeing being done; working hours 10 to 5, Saturdays 10 to 1' began to appear on the invitations and the general leaflets they distributed. Special exhibitions were also held at Hambutts, usually in the summer, and visitors were encouraged to see the printing room and dye vats.

The workshop had been converted from the stable block next to the house. Barron's greatest wish on moving out of London had been to have enough space 'for a

9.8   The workshop at Hambutts House with Peggy Birt and Daisy Ryland, 1936 (Holburne Museum and Crafts Study Centre, Bath)

really big lovely indigo vat', because she regarded indigo as the 'greatest thrill'[153] of her printing life. With typical thoroughness she wrote to Sir Thomas Barlow, the head of the Manchester Cotton Board whom she had met at the Red Rose Guild, and asked him if he could put her in touch with any firms doing indigo dyeing in order to see how to proceed. He was most helpful, inviting them to stay for a couple of nights and arranging a visit to the Rosebank works, Accrington, which belonged to Turnbull & Stockdale. They were given a guided tour of the firm and a kindly manager could not have been more helpful, writing down exact instructions as to how the vat should be sunk into the floor and also getting special star frames made for them to help with the dyeing. On her return to Painswick, Barron got the local builder to dig out a pit for the vat in the stables where the stalls had been, and had tracking and

9.9   A sofa upholstered in 'Diagonal' and a cushion printed with 'Chanel' (Holburne Museum and Crafts Study Centre, Bath)

pulleys installed overhead. This meant they were able to lower and raise the material on the frames in and out of the vat without having to touch the wet dyed cloth. Often the gardener would have to be called into help with this procedure as up to 30 yards of sodden linen could be very heavy.

The floor above was given over to the printing room with several long tables for printing on. Here Peggy Birt, whom Dorothy had taught to print very well, could be watched working, sometimes helped by Daisy Ryland who sewed beautifully as well. Daisy made up the smaller articles, hemming the scarves with tiny stitches, while Emily Edsall was responsible for making up the loose covers, curtains, pelmets and cushions. All three women lived in the village and worked for Barron and Larcher on a regular basis.

Certainly extra help was much needed in the workshop for there were numerous associated tasks to the designing and printing:

> . . . dye mixing, dyeing and all the preparations for this, such as mordanting and even in some instances collecting the dyestuffs, walnut husks for example; steaming and washing, an onerous job before the days of the washing machine, when everything had to be washed and rinsed a number of times by hand, much of it hosed down out of doors. Then there was ironing galore . . .'[154]

In addition, there was all the administrative side of the business which mainly fell to Barron who had a particular flair for it. She was also especially good at dye mixing. Both women designed and cut blocks, although Dorothy was mainly responsible for the latter. Most of their wood blocks were 'made of mahogany, supplied by a local builder, who would cut them to a paper template'.[155] When his supply ran out, Barron bought the mahogany seating from an old boat to use. Their wonderful garden of rare plants was a great pleasure to them both, as well as a rich source of inspiration for the colour, form and texture of many designs. Designs were either cut direct into the wood, or into lino and then mounted on wood. Often they printed their blocks in unusual combinations, perhaps using one of the old Russian blocks Barron had bought in London at Madame Pagowski's shop in Bond Street or a French block to overprint one of their own designs. Barron herself had a lovely, quilted, cotton jacket, carefully stitched and with pierced pearl buttons, printed first with 'Eagle' (her own design) and then one of the early French blocks. They were always very inventive with what they would use to print with: the design called 'Motor' was simply a rubber car mat mounted on wood; sometimes lengths were embellished with a pastry cutter; and occasionally a rubber nailbrush was used for spotting.

Barron had arrived in the Cotswolds 'thirsting for more colours'.[156] Now she and Larcher began to experiment with new dyestuffs from Europe and found that Painswick 'was a luckier place than we had known, because Stroud, nearby, had the West of England Cloth Mills, and water especially good for dyeing madder, though they themselves used German red.'[157] They also exported dyes to primitive countries and offered to let Barron and Larcher have some in exchange for seeing their methods: 'So the chemists dropped in when passing and welcomed reciprocal calls.'[158] This showed the same generous spirit that Bard & Wishart, the English agents for the Swiss firm of Durand and Huguenin, had shown in the 1920s in sending personal representatives round to the workshop to advise on the use of the new chrome colours. Warners, Morton Sundour and Donald Brothers, who had supplied them with cotton and linen, had been similarly helpful, and recognized that because the workshop was on a relatively small scale they 'were in a position to break new ground in a way that they with their factories and huge overheads could not afford to risk'.[159]

Inevitably, sometimes there were failures, but not usually lasting ones. It was incredible how often a seemingly unsuccessful length could be resuscitated by redyeing or overprinting with another block, and curiously rich effects could be achieved. Important commissions in the early 1930s included indigo linen curtains for the choir stalls of Winchester Cathedral. The Dean was 'very surprised and relieved'[160] when he saw them in situ, as he had originally thought velvet would be more appropriate. In 1933 they were working on a big geometrical design for the curtains for the Fellows Senior Common Room, Girton College, Cambridge, for which Fred Gardiner made the tables and chairs. Barron also persuaded him to re-cut some of their French blocks which had been damaged by nitric acid. Sometimes the names of the blocks derived from the commission, as did 'Winchester' and 'Girton', but the names were not always so obvious; for example 'Clifford' was after the name of the hairdresser where Barron had thought of it and 'Carnac' after the designs on the standing stones in France.

Prices varied depending on the type of material used and the number of times it had been printed. In 1938 a selection of their work was shown as part of the Red Rose Guild of Art Workers Exhibition at the Whitworth Art Gallery in Manchester (7 May–18 June). All their work was for sale and ranged from 12s. 6d. (63p) per yard for 'Holly' printed in rust on linen (no. 95) to £2.15s. (£2.75) per yard for a grey printed velvet (no. 131a). Barron had become a member of the Red Rose Guild in 1927, although she had shown in their first exhibition in 1921. Quite apart from the occasional show in a special venue, Guild exhibitions were held annually in the autumn up to the outbreak of the Second World War in Manchester in the Houldsworth Hall, Deangate. Barron and Larcher exhibited there on a fairly regular basis and, as their work was of such a good standard, they were sometimes pursued if they failed to apply. For example, it was noted at a meeting on 20 April 1936 that one or two stalls should be left 'vacant . . . until the Hon. Secretary made enquiries of Miss Barron'. At a further luncheon meeting in October after Barron had written regretting she would not be taking a stall that year, Ethel Mairet countered that 'Barron and Larcher <u>must</u> be got to show, every effort to facilitate their sending should be made'.[161]

Nearer to home, Barron was also a member of the Gloucestershire Guild of Craftsmen from 1933 onwards, becoming Chairman from 1958 to 1964, so they showed regularly at Guild exhibitions. Their order book for 1938–45 included commissions taken by The Little Gallery, often pinned in with a sample scrap of material to indicate exactly what was wanted, quite apart from orders taken direct. Purchasers ranged from the Queen and titled patrons such as Lady Alice Reyntiens and Lady Debenham, to notable figures in the craft world such as Gordon Russell, and Ernest Gimson's widow.

The outbreak of the Second World War brought a virtual end to production. They stopped having a regular London sales outlet as The Little Gallery was forced to close; materials were scarce and, although some orders trickled in, there was no longer the same demand for their work. Later Barron was to write:

> When we had to stop because of the War it was at first a relief. It had been such a struggle. When things began to slump we sold so little and still had wages and all the expenses going on as well as feeling that people were no longer interested. We had to let the house and camp out in . . . [the] workshop.[162]

It was to be the end of an era. Subsequently they were to sell Hambutts House and have the money to convert the workshops into a more compact but equally comfortable home which was called, simply, Hambutts. Susan Bosence, who was first inspired to start hand-block printing after seeing Barron & Larcher's work at Dartington, remembered her first visit there in the late 1940s:

> I was overwhelmed by the beauty of their house and garden. Every square inch was a delight to the eye: no nasty advertisement-covered packages, cleaners or plastic containers were visible. Interesting and well-formed kitchen utensils were hung in convenient places all round the room, and the uglier ones shut away. There was a lovely dresser with flowers, glass, china and collections of small enchanting objects: very inspiring.[163]

This period also coincided with the start of a long illness for Dorothy, and throughout the forties she devoted much of her time to her flower painting, Barron bringing her her favourite flowers from the garden, such as 'black pansies, gold laced polyanthuses, indigo-coloured clematis and trails of ivy; and she would compose her picture with these around her, usually seeing them placed in one of the many treasured pots, glasses or baskets she and Barron had collected'.[164]

By the time of her death in 1952 she had completed some forty of these small distinctive paintings which so beautifully complemented her designs for hand-block printed textiles.

After a partnership of nearly thirty years, Barron felt the loss of her friend very keenly, but with characteristic energy and resilience threw herself into local projects and new ventures. Her own obituary in a local paper in 1964 gave an indication of the wide range of her interests and activities:

> She took a leading – although never obtrusive – part in the life of Painswick, giving valued help as the chairman of the horticultural section of the Painswick show, as a member of the Painswick Food Production Society, as a member and for a while chairman of the Painswick Parish Council, as a member of the

Gyde Home Committee and in other ways, while in a wider sphere she was for 22 years a member of the Stroud R.D.C.

She served for a considerable time as the chairman of the Council's Building Plans Committee and was the vice chairman of the Area Planning Committee. In addition she represented the Council on the Stroud Museum Committee, the Stroud Educational Foundation and other bodies.[165]

She involved herself wholeheartedly in this work and did not take her responsibilities lightly. Her death deprived many meetings of her clear-sighted wisdom and forthright commonsense.

A new field that brought her much pleasure was education, something she had boldly professed to dislike when she first met Robin Tanner. Now it was to prove a new interest and win her many friends. She was a born teacher and could not have been more generous in sharing her experience and advice, both on an individual basis and when sought out by various schools of art. As a governor of the Stroud School of Art, she made regular visits there to help with classes in the mid-1950s, and was invited to Corsham in 1956 for a three-day course to talk about block printing and to demonstrate making an indigo vat.

Between 1960 and 1964, Robin Tanner asked her to take part in some of the Ministry of Education Courses he ran at Dartington Hall. These focused on art and craft, and their place in Primary and Secondary education. These courses, for some forty to fifty teachers, lasted ten days from a Tuesday to a Thursday, and Barron was billed to address the group on the Saturday morning with 'My life as a Block-Printer'. At first she was not sure that she could do it, but Robin managed to persuade her to try:

> . . . and she was greeted in the Round Room by such a powerful display of her printed cottons, linens, silks and velvets that she felt at ease and at home immediately. And she told her story so vividly and with so much wit that at the end of the session she was positively beseiged, and instead of returning home to Painswick next day as planned, she became part of the course and stayed till the end.[166]

Responding to an appreciative letter Robin sent her after another of these courses in 1962, she wrote:

> It is yourself who has given so much to my life, you have made it possible for me to take part in this Dartington project; to speak a little and to learn so much from your ways and your friends. This has made more difference to my life than anything that has happened to me for many years. And I do thank you with all my heart.[167]

Robin and Heather Tanner could not have been more warm or sustaining friends, and equally she relished their company. The previous year they had their first touring holiday in France together, planning their route to embrace 'as many Romanesque churches and as great a range of wild plants as possible',[168] savouring the food and the wine and delighting in the bargains they were able to pick up along the way. Shortly before his retirement in December 1964, Robin planned a series of meetings with her to complete the great record of Barron and Larcher's work that he was compiling in duplicate. He had made good headway with it and looked forward to his retirement to finish it. Sadly, Barron died before it could be completed. Two days before her death, Barron wrote to Heather on 21 November 1964 saying she had had eight days in bed with influenza, but soon hoped to shake it off. Her death was a terrible shock to her many friends who, while grateful that she had not had to suffer a long illness, had had no time to prepare themselves.

In her will she left Robin her wonderful collection of textiles and blocks. With care and dedication, Heather sorted and listed them, and Robin completed the record of their work and bound it in two vast volumes. Three memorial exhibitions were arranged; the first in Painswick in 1965, the second at the Royal West of England Academy, Bristol the following year; the third at Cheltenham Art Gallery and Museum in 1967. Many people visited these exhibitions and were inspired and enthused by the beautiful materials they saw.

Chapter Ten

The Craft Workshops
between the Wars

The old buoyancy is broken – Strang is dead, Gimson is dead. Roger Fry's
Omega Workshops are closed down. The Private Presses have stopped work.
Rothenstein has given up his Gloucestershire home. The Daneway colony, like
our Guild, is no more, except in each case for a few stragglers.[169]

C.R. Ashbee's personal obituary on the Arts and Crafts Movement, made during a
brief visit to London from Jerusalem in 1921, was a comment on the impact of the
First World War and his bitter reassessment of the Movement's purpose and future in
a changing world. By 1915 the wider aims of the Arts and Crafts Movement had
shrunk. It was no longer driven by an evangelical or socialist impulse to change society or people's daily lives. It had all boiled down to individual expression and creativity with a tacit hope that its influence would spread by example. Ashbee once again
revealed his own disappointment by writing: 'We have made of a great social movement, a narrow and tiresome little aristocracy working with great skill for the very
rich.'[170]

Yet in 1916, in the middle of the war, the Arts and Crafts Exhibition Society
mounted its largest show ever. It was impressive not only for its sheer size, but
because the Society had finally achieved a measure of public recognition by being
given an exhibition in the Royal Academy. Rather than the usual serried ranks of furniture with smaller items crammed in, there was an attempt to put objects into an
appropriate setting. Artists, designers and craftspeople were allocated spaces to decorate and furnish as they wished following the model of the 1908 exhibition of
German decorative art at Munich. Louise Powell designed a room around twelve
panels painted in tempera which was furnished by Ernest Gimson and Sidney
Barnsley. A set of furniture designed by Gimson and painted vermilion by May
Morris was exhibited in a bedroom setting for which they were both responsible. It
also included a bedstead made at Daneway and elaborately decorated by May Morris,
Alfred Powell, Ethel Everett and A.E. Swinney, the cost of which – £170 – made a
reviewer from the *News Chronicle* bristle with horror.

The 1916 exhibition also contained a display mounted by the Design and Industries

Association (DIA), founded a year earlier by a group of craftsmen, designers, architects and retailers to encourage good design in mass-produced goods. They were motivated by the growing elitism of the Arts and Crafts Movement in the face of increasing competition from continental and particularly German designs. The argument that the DIA raised – whether it was right to sacrifice high standards of craftsmanship for a wider market – was never properly resolved. Those who clung to quality handwork suffered a loss of confidence, particularly as their former mentor, William Lethaby, because such a spirited convert to the work of the DIA. Life for the handcrafters went on but became more marginalized and tinged with the arty-craftyness that was caricatured by many writers, such as E.F. Benson in his Mapp and Lucia novels.

Although the Cotswolds were often used as the setting for such caricatures, it was an undeserved characterization. In Gloucestershire, the Movement had taken a firm root over a wide spectrum of society and the quality of work produced remained high. In Chipping Campden, the Guild of Handicraft survived after 1908 as a much less formal arrangement, but remained a potent force in the town. The majority of Guildsmen left the community that had come to mean so much to them: a poignantly short yet affecting experience. After C.R. Ashbee himself finally left in 1919, a small

10.1   Silver cup and cover by George Hart, 1925 (F.C. Scorey for CAGM)

nucleus remained. Two years earlier, Jim Pyment, the builder and cabinet-maker, had bought the silk mill in which the Guild of Handicraft had established itself and rented out work space to the remaining craftsmen. The firm of Pyment & Co. described itself in 1908 as 'Joiners, Cabinet-makers and Repairers of old buildings'. Jim Pyment, joined in 1910 by his two sons, Harold and Arthur, worked on a number of important local commissions including the building of Dover's Court for Fred Griggs. Gradually the building and joinery side took over from cabinet-making. Renting workshops in the silk mill were Charley Downer and Bill Thornton who ran the smithy, Will Hart and Alec Miller working as woodcarvers, and George Hart as the only remaining silversmith. He was also the only Guildsman with any farming experience. The farm at Broad Campden became a more and more important part of his life, particularly during and immediately after the First World War.

However, craftwork continued to play a significant role in the life of the town. In 1926, a survey of rural industries[171] noted that towns like Broadway and Chipping Campden attracted enough tourists to provide a market for craft products. George Hart was one of several craftspeople that became involved with the Gloucestershire Rural Industries Committee in the 1920s in its effort to support local craftsmen and women. He returned to silversmithing once again in the late 1920s with the help of two assistants: his step-brother, Reynell Huyshe, and a local youth inspired by School of Handicraft classes, Harry Warmington. All three designed and made pieces, and their work brought them important commissions. Particularly significant was George Hart's success in the competition organized by the Worshipful Company of Goldsmiths for the Royal Ascot Hunt Cup in 1926. In 1929 he was admitted to the Company of Goldsmiths of the City of London and also elected a member of the Art Workers Guild. The Hart workshop was, and still is, very much a family concern with both sons, George and Henry Hart, completing apprenticeships with their father and joining him as fully-fledged silversmiths in the 1930s. They continued to work in the style established by Ashbee and the Guild of Handicraft, producing elaborate silver trophies, ecclesiastical and other ceremonial items. Their domestic wares relied on the simple rounded forms that had become the hallmark of the Guild's work. These wares were sold in London through the retail outlets of the Goldsmiths' and Silversmiths' Company and of Omar Ramsden's workshops.

Locally, the Hart workshop produced work for Russell & Sons which was featured in their catalogue and sold in their Broadway shop, while the Harts also opened their own retail outlet: Ancient and Modern Hand-Crafts. The front room of Ivy House, a small property on Campden High Street, was run as an antiques shop and showcase for the work of local craftsmen and women by George Hart's wife, Edith, and his brother, Fred. Although the Campden School of Arts and Crafts was closed down in 1916, the Hart workshop maintained its traditions by running classes in silversmithing and jewellery for locals. These were held under the auspices of the

10.2   Bill Thornton in his smithy, 1908 (Mrs J. Wilgress)

Gloucestershire Education Authority up to the 1950s. They brought together a wide range of poeple with very mixed abilities, with the result that Campden is now overflowing with hand-made silver.

Like the Harts, Bill Thornton and Charley Downer also sold their work through Russell and Sons as part of the 'Lygon' range and continued to work as blacksmiths until the 1940s. They were very skilled at their craft, making deceptively simple-looking domestic fire-tools in wrought iron and polished steel, with twisted handles and a scattering of stamped decoration.

On the first floor of the Silk Mill, Alec Miller concentrated on architectural carving including a larger than life-size statue of St Michael for Coventry Cathedral in 1922. The photograph of him in his workshop hints at the thoughtful and sensitive side of his personality which so appealed to Ashbee (Fig. 4.9). This characteristic also found expression in the small intimate portrait carvings which became an increasingly important part of his work. From 1910 he made a number of visits to the United States for exhibitions of his work and lecture tours. He finally settled in California in 1939 and continued to work until his death in 1961. Will Hart also continued carving at Chipping Campden but, as a result of injuries sustained during active service, he was only able to work on a small scale as a hobby after the First World War.

On the other side of the Cotswolds, the First World War had made a major impact on the Daneway workshops. Edward Gardiner had already moved the chair-making business to Warwickshire where it still flourishes in the hands of his former pupil, Neville Neal. Ernest Gimson managed to keep the furniture workshop going for a couple of years but, by 1917, the majority of craftsmen had left Sapperton either for the Front or to take up war work like Fred Orton, who repaired ships in Bristol Docks, or Fred Gardiner, who worked on aircraft construction in Ipswich. Stocks of wood were in short supply and clients scarce. After the war, many of the craftsmen returned briefly to Daneway until Gimson's death in 1919. He had no children but his foreman, Peter Waals, wanted to carry on the furniture workshop in some form. There was no question of continuing at Daneway, partly because the Gimson family wanted to make a clean break. It also suited Waals to move to Chalford where he could take advantage of the railway service.

Peter van der Waals was a solid, strong figure whom many of his craftsmen nicknamed 'Dutchy' as he had never lost that slight awkwardness of a foreigner. Those

10.3   Chestnut roaster in wrought iron by Charlie Downer, probably 1930s (F.C. Scorey for CAGM)

10.4   Dick, *a relief portrait in pear-wood of Dick Russell as a boy by Alec Miller, 1916 (F.C. Scorey for CAGM)*

10.5   *Peter Waals, c. 1910 (Leicestershire Museums, Arts and Records Services)*

who knew him have commented on his deep voice and occasional gruffness. The writer John Gloag described Peter Waals as 'a first class craftsman and a very nice chap. He was an enormous bulky great Dutchman with shoulders like a gorilla and a deep voice. He loved to contradict people which he did all the time. He was very articulate.'[172]

Among his craftsmen and the locals, Waals made a deep impression by owning a car instead of the more usual bike or motorbike. It was obviously difficult for him to step into Gimson's shoes and make that transition from being foreman to running the workshop. Ernest Smith, appointed foreman at Chalford, felt his was a nominal position only coming into service when Waals was absent.

Similar adjustments were being made elsewhere. In 1919, Edward Barnsley, Sidney Barnsley's son, had considered the possibility of training with Ernest Gimson but instead had gone to Froxfield, Hampshire, where one of Gimson's pupils, Geoffrey Lupton, an architect, builder and craftsman, had set up a workshop. Both men had been pupils at the progressive Bedales School in the nearby village of Steep. For nearly two years they worked together on the building and furnishing of the Memorial Library at Bedales. It had been designed by Gimson before his death and the work was subsequently supervised by Sidney Barnsley. Edward Barnsley spent a

year at the Central School studying furniture under Charles Spooner before returning to Froxfield. The sudden departure of Geoffrey Lupton for South Africa had left
him, at the age of twenty-three, with a workshop of his own to run as he thought fit.
He was given many of his father's commissions to execute as Sidney Barnsley was
finding it increasingly hard to work at the bench. Inevitably his first influences came
from the Sapperton workshops in which he had grown up and he maintained close
links with the Cotswolds throughout his career.

Peter Waals set up at Chalford in Halliday's Mill at the bottom of Cowcombe Hill.
The building had been used as a silk mill until 1902 when the business moved to
Nailsworth. Waals and his family moved into the living accommodation attached to
the mill and the workshops took over the two floors of the mill. On the ground floor
was the woodworking machinery. Initially this involved only a saw bench and a
petrol-driven treadle saw. On the first floor were the craftsmen's benches. Each man
had his own bench and brought his own tools. Ernest Smith had his treasured set of
tools, some of which had belonged to his father who had worked for Queen Victoria
at Windsor. Waals continued to work at the bench occasionally or in a drawing office
next to the workshop.

Waals designed furniture very much in the style that he had helped to develop at
the Daneway Workshops. He used Gimson's designs occasionally, as in the burr elm
bureau made at Chalford in 1921 after a design of 1917. Waals and the majority of
his craftsmen had worked so closely with Gimson in a way that they appreciated and
understood that it was almost second nature to them. They continued to work with

10.6   The workshop at Chalford, c. 1924. Among the craftsmen in the photograph are Ernest Smith (right
foreground) and Harry Davoll (at the next bench) (Leicestershire Museums, Arts and Records Service)

Alfred Bucknell who had moved the smithy to the hamlet of Waterlane near Tunley. Peter Waals did introduce distinctive features into his work: the greater use of wooden handles, the heavy, carved feet and the emphasis on panelling. In a letter to one of his most regular clients, Mr Goddard of Leicester, he wrote: 'I am particularly pleased about the attention given to the ebony wardrobe. I made this as a protest against the dull flat surfaces in modern furniture. Mass made furniture could be enlivened by the play of light on simple fielding of small panels.'[173]

Peter Waals was basically self-conscious and unsure of his own capabilities as a designer. This lack of confidence was present throughout his life. Despite this he maintained good working relationships with colleagues such as Sidney and Ernest Barnsley and, in particular, with the younger Norman Jewson who worked extensively as an architect and designer. He shared with Waals the same tentative approach to design but produced fine, sensitive examples of furniture, plasterwork and metalwork. Waals's work was also appreciated by other architect/designers such as C.F.A. Voysey and Edwin Lutyens, who commissioned a bedroom suite in English cherry for Queen Mary's Doll's House which was exhibited at the Wembley Exhibition of 1925. Percy Burchett was the craftsman entrusted with the execution of this commission. He adapted a table knife in order to saw the tiny yet perfect tenon joints and the completed suite fitted into a size 7 shoe box.

There were about ten men working at Chalford at any one time. They included five experienced cabinet-makers from Daneway: Ernest Smith, who was appointed foreman, Harry Davoll, Percy Burchett, Fred Orton and Fred Gardiner. Bert Hunt had also served his apprenticeship with Gimson and at Chalford acted as a journeyman, helping to set up work already made and specializing in screens and staircases. Waals continued the principle established at Daneway that one man should be responsible for one job. Each craftsman filled in a time-sheet recording the hours spent on a particular piece and Waals kept a record book as Gimson had done.

Percy Tanner, Frank Rust, Norman Bucknell, Rowland Young and William Taylor were all apprentices, the first two having begun their training at Daneway. Apprentices usually came with some recommendation or family connection. Frank Rust was the son of the gamekeeper at Edgeworth Manor and wanted to follow in his father's footsteps. The lack of work after the First World War and the enthusiasm of Squire James of Edgeworth, something of a craftsman himself who subsequently gave Peter Waals many a helping hand in hard times, encouraged the gamekeeper to apprentice his son to Ernest Gimson. Alfred Bucknell apprenticed his son, Norman, somewhat against his son's wishes. Norman Bucknell maintains that he would have preferred to have gone into industry as an engineer. In 1930 he gave up woodworking for his family craft of metalworking. He set up a smithy in the village of Bisley and produced a range of items which rivalled those of his father in quality. Another apprentice at Chalford, Owen Scrubey, was the son of William Scrubey, the gardener

10.7   *Drop-front writing cabinet in English walnut, designed by Peter Waals and made for the Wembley Exhibition of 1924 (F. C. Scorey for CAGM)*

at Rodmarton Manor. It was Mrs Biddulph's influence that led him to work for Peter Waals. Apprentices were normally taken on trial for three months without pay. Pay started at 2s. 6d. (12p) rising to 5s. (25p) in 1932 when Derek Gardiner began to qualify for 'appearance pay'. Apprentices were entrusted with basic tasks such as making up the holly and ebony inlay on a treadle saw or preparing pieces of panelling.

At Chalford, the craftsmen worked a 49-hour week: from 7.30 a.m. to 5.00 p.m. with 45 minutes for lunch on weekdays and from 7.30 a.m. to 12.00 p.m. on Saturdays. Waals ran the workshop quite strictly as he had done at Daneway. There was no general talking; questions could be asked only of the foreman. This well-disciplined atmosphere was occasionally enlivened, particularly by the mischevous Derek Gardiner who was notorious for his practical jokes. He related one incident, the butt of which was Harry Davoll, nicknamed after that seriously well-meaning character, Mr Pooter, devised by George and Weedon Grossmith:

> Harry Davoll always brought his lunch to work in a wickerwork basket and always put a block of wood in it to take home at night. Someone nailed through the block into the bench one day and when Harry (Pooter) grabbed the handle and went to dash out and catch his bus at 5 o'clock, he of course left the bottom of his basket nailed to the bench. I got the blame for that, but was innocent that time.[174]

The craftsmen took great pride in their work: this gave them a sense of comradeship and a certain status among their peers. Quite a few of them came from the villages of Oakridge and Waterlane and would walk together down to Chalford and back. One such was Percy Tanner, whose sister commented that the villagers felt proud of their craftsmen despite the fact that none of them could afford to buy the work produced at Chalford. She also noted that the men would exchange knowing looks when some of the visitors to the workshops 'pretended to know all about furniture, joints etc. when they clearly didn't'.[175] One outsider who was accepted because of his skill and obvious appreciation and understanding of the work at hand was George Trevelyan. A Cambridge history graduate, undecided as to his future apart from a need to work with his hands, he went to Waals's workshop at Chalford for tuition in 1931. His time there, intructed in the craft of cabinet-making by Peter Waals, Percy Burchett and the other craftsmen, was to be a formative experience. He felt that he had become part of a great tradition and in 1969 he wrote movingly of the 'cohesion of the team' at Chalford:

> Never was that let down by any hint of skimping work or 'making do' with anything less than the best, even in the quality of unseen back panels in cupboards . . . Each man of the group knew himself to be engaged in something

far greater than himself which he might not let down by any carelessness. The nature of the work, individual yet responsible to the group standard, built into them a human quality which made those men a veritable rural aristocracy.[176]

George Trevelyan was well served by Percy Burchett who developed into a gifted and inspiring teacher as well as a craftsman. He often accompanied Peter Waals on lecturing assignments, and became technical instructor in cabinet-making at Brimscombe College and Cheltenham School of Art. The skills and approach of the Chalford workshop were disseminated widely over the years from classes held for locals at Rodmarton Manor in the 1920s to the craft teaching course at the East Midlands Training College in Loughborough where Peter Waals was appointed Design Adviser in 1935. This was a new post which was offered to Waals at the suggestion of Frank Pick, then Chairman of the Design and Industries Association. Peter Waals taught students in a despotic fashion; they worked on his designs under his supervision and were not encouraged to comment on the work. The process gradually became more relaxed and two-way under Edward Barnsley who took over from Waals in 1938. From the start, however, this teaching post was tremendously influential and several generations of craft teachers began work instilled with the principles of Cotswold Arts and Crafts.

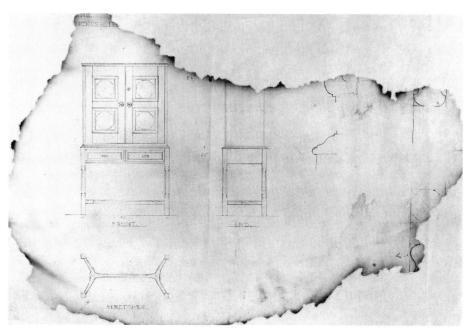

10.8 Design by Peter Waals for a cabinet, one of the few drawings to have survived the fire at the Chalford workshop (CAGM)

Peter Waals was in an anomalous position as far as the Chalford workshop was concerned, for he was running it on the same terms as Ernest Gimson at Daneway, taking only a small percentage for himself without having a private income to fall back on. Prices had been kept low at Daneway and as the majority of clients remained the same it would have been impossible to raise them to a more realistic level. Times were very hard for all craftsmen in the 1930s because of the Depression. Work was increasingly hard to come by and Peter Waals was forced to lay off men including Bert Hunt and Frank Rust. Harry Davoll also left the Chalford workshop in 1933 and set up as a cabinet-maker on his own account at Oakridge. Peter Waals did have a number of clients such as the brewer, Arthur Mitchell, and W.A. Cadbury whose patronage helped the workshop survive through difficult times. However, the strains of money problems took their toll and Peter Waals died on 30 May 1937. His wife and son tried to carry on, but a devastating fire at the workshop in 1938 followed by Leo Waals's call-up to war in 1939 put an end to their efforts. The fire was a heartbreaking blow for all concerned. A great deal of fine work was lost, including choir stalls for Cam Church. Almost all of Peter Waals's drawings and designs were destroyed, as were the precious tools that were the livelihood of each individual craftsman. Despite this blow, many of the craftsmen were able to carry on making furniture as part of their livelihood in garden sheds and outhouses. George Trevelyan wrote movingly of one such craftsman, Ernest Smith, who:

> . . . established a tiny workshop in his garden and for some ten years executed pieces to my design until he suddenly went blind. Calling on him I found to my surprise, a new little garden gate to his terraced Chalford house, with the

10.9   Box in walnut with an ivory lock-plate, designed by George Trevelyan and made by Ernest Smith, 1937 (F.C. Scorey for CAGM)

fielded panels and champered edges typical of the tradition. In gallant defiance of his fate Ernest had made this gate, blind, as the closing act of his great career of craftsmanship.[177]

The contribution of many such individuals, including Harry Davoll, Owen Scrubey and Norman Bucknell, have ensured that the traditions of handwork and fine craftsmanship survived in the Cotswolds.

Chapter Eleven

Gordon Russell

The Cotswold craft revival in the 1920s and 1930s was profoundly shaken by the efforts of one man, Gordon Russell, who gave it a new vision and vigour which had been lacking since the First World War. The craftsmen and women, almost overwhelmed by the struggle to make a living from their work, largely regarded the phoenix in their midst as a cuckoo. Russell himself was conscious of being an outsider. In his autobiography he wrote:

> I landed myself in trouble, not for the first time. On the one hand, many handworkers regarded me as a traitor to the cause, although we continued to produce a good deal of fine handwork, and on the other, many manufacturers in the furniture trade regarded me as a crazy crank full of strange and unworkable ideas.[178]

The centenary of Gordon Russell's birth, celebrated in 1992 by exhibitions and a new biography, marked a watershed in the reputation of a man who was such a wideranging and powerful force in twentieth-century design and craftsmanship that he has seemed beyond criticism. Although, more recently, he has been used by some commentators as the scapegoat for endemic problems of British design while being ignored by other sections of the design history establishment, the range of his achievements is remarkable. To find a parallel to Gordon Russell and to help understand his 'peculiarly English' character, one has to go back to the eighteenth century, to the Industrial Revolution, when '. . . the course of events was dominated by a small group of manufacturers who saw clearly the links between industry and culture. Men such as Abraham Darby, Josiah Wedgwood and Matthew Boulton founded businesses that were inspired by a search for excellence as well as a capacity for making profits. These then were autocratic dynasts with a sense of purpose. They were paternalistic, but they were also passionately idealistic, forward looking and involved in public affairs. Self-made, they were seldom specialists.'[179]

Russell's contribution to design and the crafts remains to be fully appreciated. This particular account is necessarily limited to those sections of his career relevant to the main theme.

The two most powerful and persistent influences on Gordon Russell were his family, particularly his father, and the Cotswold countryside. In fact, he was born in Cricklewood, North London, in 1892, but his formative years, from the age of twelve, were spent in Broadway and Chipping Campden. His father, Sydney Bolton Russell, was an agency manager with the Midlands brewers, Samuel Allsopp and Sons. On one of his tours of inspection he was captivated by the beauty and commercial potential of the delapidated Lygon Arms, a partly sixteenth-century coaching inn on the main street of Broadway. In a characteristically bold gesture and with a loan from a former business contact, he bought the inn from the brewery in 1904. It became the mainstay of the family's existence and efforts. S.B. Russell was a man who combined great charm and a receptive mind with a forcefulness and domineering tendency illustrated by his nickname, 'Rock' Russell, exacerbated by hard work, financial insecurity and chronic indigestion. Running through all that he did was a deep respect for craftsmanship and a striving for quality rather than quantity or profits; these remained powerful influences on Gordon Russell throughout his life. They also typified the spirit in which his father approached the renovation of the Lygon Arms. Having recognized the potential of the inn as a hotel rather than a public house, he set about restoring it to its former glory. He removed Victorian windows, boarding and layers of wallpaper and paintwork, and took great pains with the decoration and furnishing. Having seen the possibilities of tourism inherent in the advent of the motor car, he set about providing comfort and good English food and drink, 'not the bastard-French hotel tradition',[180] in a visually pleasing setting, combining good antiques with the best craftwork. He was also ahead of his time in the forcefulness of his advertising. Broadway had its tradition of American visitors and the American actress, Mary Anderson, a long-time resident in the town, continued to attract the rich and famous from both sides of the Atlantic adding a cosmopolitan atmosphere to the small community. S.B. Russell capitalized on the American links by advertising the Lygon Arms on Cunard liners. Among his visitors were the actor, Charles Laughton, his wife Elsa Lanchester, and Henry Ford.

The Lygon Arms absorbed both Sydney Russell and his wife, Elizabeth, who was thrust into the supervision of the kitchens almost by default. It provided a heady atmosphere for the young Russell children, three boys called Gordon, Don and Dick. Gordon Russell attended the Grammar School at Chipping Campden with his brother, Don, and children from many different backgrounds. Pupils included sons of Guildsmen and the links with C.R. Ashbee's 'Cockney invasion' were emphasized by the woodwork classes which took place in the same building which housed the Guild of Handicraft's museum. Although there was very little visual education to be derived from school, Gordon Russell always acknowledged the influence of the rich mix of craft traditions around him. As well as his familiarity with the work of designer/craftsmen at Chipping Campden and further afield at Sapperton, he also felt an instinctive admiration for traditional craftsmen: masons, tilers and hedgers and the like whose skills added a restrained and easy beauty to the Cotswolds villages and lanes. Above all it was the stone of the Cotswolds and the skills of the men who worked it that inspired him. Working with stone, whether building drystone walls or carving inscriptions, remained a potent source of pleasure throughout his life.

In 1908 Gordon Russell began working alongside his father in the Lygon Arms. Its restoration to a flourishing concern was capped by the architect, C.E. Bateman, whose bold extension was completed in 1910. He spent the first six years of his working life as a Jack of all trades. His father, known to him as 'the Guvnor', was not the easiest of employers; he could be authoritarian, demanding and pernickety. Gordon Russell worked in the Lygon office preparing bills and doing basic shorthand and typing for his father, he roasted coffee, set up barrels of beer and bottled fruit, he designed lettering for letterheads and wrote advertisements. He was also in day-to-day charge of the family antiques business next door to the Lygon, keeping the books and marking the stock, showing visitors around and sketching items for customers all over the country and in America. He rapidly developed a good eye for antiques and a respect for the traditions of English craftsmanship over the centuries. He subsequently tried to pass this on to a wider audience through a clearly-written publication, *The things we see – Furniture*, produced in 1948.[181] S.B. Russell had also set up a workshop where three or four men repaired old furniture from the Lygon or the antiques shop and did other odd jobs. Under the direction of the foreman, Jim Turner, this little workshop began making up some of Gordon Russell's furniture designs as a sideline.

At this time, he attended a life class at Campden. It must have been awe-inspiring for a young man in his late teens to take his place alongside some of the mainstays of the Campden Arts and Crafts community, including Paul Woodroffe, Alec Miller, George Hart and Will Hart. It was the contact with so many different craftsmen to which Gordon Russell attributed his confidence in trying his hand at whatever activity fired his imagination. He wrote about some of his more successful attempts: 'Among such I remember one or two oak beds, a napkin ring in silver, a few letterheadings and some buttons for the head porter at the Lygon.'[182]

He also made a number of leather blackjacks, traditional seventeenth-century drinking vessels, preparing the wooden moulds and in some cases decorating them with brass dies and silver mounts made for him by George Hart. In 1911 he acquired a copy of Edward Johnston's *Writing and Illuminating and Lettering*, and found it so clearly written that he was able to use it as a manual for the crafts of the pen. He undertook a number of calligraphic projects including a collection of poems by Keats bound for him at Katie Adams's St Eadburgha Bindery. The bookbinder provided him with a great deal of encouragement and boosted his confidence by introducing him and his work to Sydney Cockerell and Robert Bridges. The whole atmosphere at Broadway was one conducive to broadening the mind, both in the crafts and in the wider world of painting, music and literature. He appreciated the richness of his own upbringing; it was the narrowness of people's lives and the lack of visual awareness that Gordon Russell always saw as the main enemy.

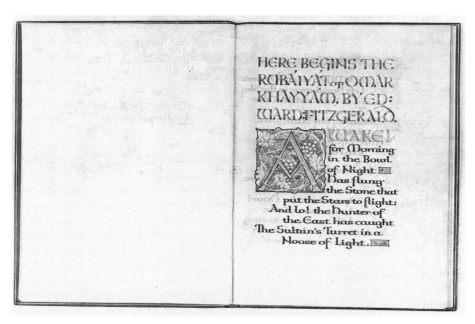

11.1   'The Rubaiyat of Omar Khayyam', by Edward Fitzgerald, written and illuminated on vellum by Gordon Russell and bound by Katharine Adams, 1914 (F.C. Scorey)

Gordon Russell's life was totally disrupted by the First World War. He enlisted and fought in France, winning the Military Cross for his bravery. Like so many young men, he had gone into active service with rather romantic notions of patriotism and heroism which were rapidly dispersed by the horrors of trench warfare. He was profoundly shaken by his experiences, but not shattered. He returned to Broadway determined to make his mark on the world: 'I felt very strongly that my generation, which had destroyed so much lovely work, had a constructive duty to perform; somehow or other we had to hand on to those coming after us good things of our own creation.'[183]

S.B. Russell took a hand in matters by making his two elder sons his partners, dividing the business between them and renaming it Russell & Sons. Although he retained overall and sometimes even day-to-day control, he apportioned the Lygon Arms to Don and the antiques business to Gordon. Having described himself as a 'Designer of Furniture' in his army record book of 1917, Gordon Russell set about making this a reality. He expanded the established antiques business to provide the funds for his own designs. An old farmhouse near the Lygon was bought to serve as extended showrooms, and the business gained the assistance of the youngest brother, Dick, and Toni Denning who answered an advertisement for a general dogsbody because 'it seemed an unusual job'. Toni had sterling qualities and immediately fitted in to a tightly-knit family group. In August 1921, she and Gordon Russell were married; they remained a devoted couple throughout their lives together.

Gordon Russell wanted to celebrate their marriage by designing a 'fitting double bed'. It was completed in some haste by Edgar Turner, the son of the foreman, and inspired Russell to more designs. The quality of the end-products, however, was not what he had envisaged. He saw that 'the men in the workshop were really joiners, used to repairing seventeenth-century oak furniture – solid, honestly-made pieces with none of the cabinet-maker's delicate skill which developed in the eighteenth century'.[184] Gordon Russell, always a self-publicist as Ashbee had been, was able to exploit this situation. He had recently joined the Design and Industries Association and hoped to find assistance from within its ranks. He took photographs of his work to London to a fellow member, John Gloag, the architectural historian and writer. Gloag was encouraging and became a fervent supporter of Russell's work. Practical help also came from Percy Wells, head of the cabinet-making section of the London County Council Shoreditch Training College. Wells advised him to train his own foreman rather than employ a trained outsider, and Edgar Turner, who had more or less grown up in the Russell workshop, was sent to Shoreditch.

This move paid off and, in March 1923,[185] Gordon Russell was invited to show some of his work at Cheltenham Art Gallery and Museum. A mutual interest in craftsmanship linked the curator, D.W. Herdman, and S.B. Russell, and this was the first of a succession of Cotswold Arts and Crafts exhibitions at Cheltenham in which the Russell family was involved. The display by Russell and Sons consisted mainly of metalwork with an oak stool, and some examples of calligraphy by both Sydney and Gordon Russell. It was shown alongside the work of well-established Cheltenham art manufacturers, such as H.H. Martyn and Co., and R.E. and C. Marshall Ltd; Alec Miller and Paul Woodroffe from Chipping Campden, Cotswold Co-operative Handicrafts from Whiteway, and an assortment of mainly amateur artists, embroiderers and lace-makers. The show at Cheltenham led to an invitation later that year from the British Institute of Industrial Art to exhibit a room setting alongside the established firm of Heal's at the Victoria and Albert Museum in London (Fig. 11.2). Sir Ambrose Heal became a personal friend of the Russell family and close links were maintained between the two enterprises.

Like Ashbee, Gordon Russell showed a genuine concern for his employees which did not cease at the end of the working day. He held talks at Broadway to provide inspiration and enlightenment; speakers included Russell himself, local luminaries, such as George Hart and Paul Woodroffe, and newer London-based contacts such as Harry Trethowan, one of the managing directors at Heal's, the architect/designer, C.F.A. Voysey, and Percy Wells. There were also evening classes in cabinet-work which were attended by showroom and office staff as well as the workshops. Even

11.2   *'A Model Cafe', designed by Gordon Russell and made by Russell and Sons for an exhibition at the Victoria and Albert Museum, 1923 (Corinium Museum, Cirencester)*

amateur theatricals were organized, reminiscent of the heyday of the Guild of Handicraft.

Gordon Russell's furniture designs were closely modelled on the work of Gimson and the Barnsleys. Large numbers of turned ladderback chairs were made in the tradition of Philip Clissett, Ernest Gimson and Edward Gardiner. There seemed to be a constant demand for these chairs from schools, colleges and other public buildings. The design of the craft furniture was based on simple lines, solid construction and decorative details such as chamfering, panelling, inlaid stringing and integral wooden handles. Like the Sapperton craftsmen, the Broadway workshop left its furniture unstained to show off the grain of the wood. The level of craftsmanship was high, but occasionally the showmanship and historical details sit uneasily with the Cotswold Arts and Crafts tradition. One of the most prestigious pieces, a cabinet in English walnut inlaid with box, ebony and yew, is known as the Paris cabinet in honour of the gold medal awarded in the Paris Exhibition in 1925 (Fig. 11.3). Although a spectacular piece, some of its detailing, such as the curved corners on the octagonally panelled doors, looks fussy and mannered.

The connection with the Sapperton tradition was increased when Harry Gardiner, whose father had worked at Gimson's smithy, began making up Gordon Russell's metalwork designs. Like Gimson, Russell had been forced to set up his own smithy at

11.3   Cabinet in English walnut inlaid with ebony, yew and box, designed by Gordon Russell. It won a gold medal at the Paris International Exhibition of 1925 (F.C. Scorey for CAGM)

11.4   Glassware, designed by Gordon Russell, 1920s (Corinium Museum, Cirencester)

Broadway as he could not get work made to his standards elsewhere. By employing Harry Gardiner he ensured that the standard of workmanship was of the highest. Gordon Russell also designed a series of glasswares, including pieces based on the seventeenth-century wrythen technique which were produced by the Stourbridge firm of Stevens and Williams. These items and many others featured in a publicity leaflet put out by Russell and Sons. It was written, drawn and designed by Gordon Russell, with a unique concern for layout and typography which makes it stand out from other commercial publications of the period.

Gordon Russell was a great publicist and a firm believer in the powers of advertisement, not just for himself but to ensure the survival of the family business and the jobs of his workforce. Within the trade, the idea of a furniture-making business thriving in the backwaters of the North Cotswolds aroused astonishment. Gordon Russell was happy to play on this by emphasizing the rural craft links with the slogan 'Made by Hand on the Cotswold Hills', and the tree and cottage logo used until 1929. The workshop was changing however; new machinery suitable for small-scale serial production was available in the 1920s and was gradually introduced at Broadway. Gordon Russell desired either 'good handwork or good machine work'.[186] However the line between the two is never clear-cut; the craftsmen at Chalford and elsewhere saw their prices undercut by the Broadway workshop and the public was unable to distinguish between the range of handmade furniture they were offered.

By 1925 the business had become known as the Russell Workshops and Gordon Russell was finding himself more and more torn between running the workshops and producing new designs. He had temporarily lost the assistance of his younger brother. He and Dick Russell had decided that some additional design input would soon be

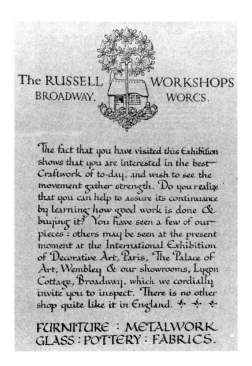

The RUSSELL WORKSHOPS
BROADWAY. WORCS.

The fact that you have visited this Exhibition shows that you are interested in the best Craftwork of to-day, and wish to see the movement gather strength. Do you realize that you can help to assure its continuance by learning how good work is done & buying it? You have seen a few of our pieces : others may be seen at the present moment at the International Exhibition of Decorative Art, Paris, The Palace of Art, Wembley & our showrooms, Lygon Cottage, Broadway, which we cordially invite you to inspect. There is no other shop quite like it in England. ✦ ✦ ✦

FURNITURE : METALWORK
GLASS : POTTERY : FABRICS.

*11.5 Advertisement, designed by Gordon Russell
for the Russell Workshops, 1925 (CAGM)*

needed and it was acquired in a characteristic way. Gordon Russell felt that the majority of good furniture designers in the recent past, such as Mackintosh, Voysey and Gimson, had been trained as architects. This seemed to be the course to pursue. Dick Russell was keen to acquire some professional training and began a four-year course at the Architectural Association's school in 1924. He came back to Broadway in 1928 as a director and amply repaid his brother's faith in him. He had come into contact with a whole range of new ideas and new people, including fellow students Eden Minns, David Booth and Marian Pepler, who became his wife in 1933.

With Dick Russell running the drawing office from 1929 and a new financial manager, R.H. Bee, the whole character of the enterprise and Gordon Russell's role within it began to shift. The popularity of the simple modern furniture designed by Dick Russell and financial constraints on handwork persuaded Gordon Russell to give up designing. Yet although his heart lay with the decorative craftwork of the earlier years, he had made his own contribution to the new style. A boot cupboard in Cuban mahogany with veneered blockboard doors from 1925 has caused much speculation for its simple design and flush surfaces. It has been described as a 'radical departure in style' and 'the mystery of the futuristic boot cupboard'[187] and cited as a precedent for furniture design in the fifties.[188] Gordon Russell himself saw it as a logical

11.6   The cabinet-making workshop at Broadway, 1927 (Corinium Museum, Cirencester)

progression from 'the Gimson tradition'[189] and it does relate very closely to Gimson's designs (Fig. 3.11).

The move towards machine production was acknowledged by the adoption of the circular saw symbol and a new name, Gordon Russell Ltd. Both Gordon and Dick Russell became aware of developments on the Continent, particularly in Sweden where:

> . . . it was possible to design in a Bauhaus manner and yet still retain a national character; in the Swedish case a 'joyful personality and lightness of touch' which strongly appealed to the British designers. The Swedes had managed to integrate their existing craft traditions with machine production in a way that greatly impressed Dick Russell.[190]

The Swedish model remained a source of inspiration for Gordon Russell. As well as admiring its approach to design and craftsmanship, he welcomed the generally high level of visual awareness.

In the late 1920s, Gordon Russell was able to devote more time to overseeing the company and visiting customers. However, the concern was still small enough for them to do 'a bit of everything, packing crates of glass, writing address labels,

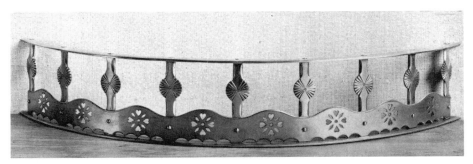

11.7   Polished steel fender, typical of the metalwork designed by Gordon Russell in the 1920s (Corinium Museum, Cirencester)

sending off catalogues and information, choosing timber, and selling furniture'.[191] Gordon Russell had more opportunities to publicize his ideas about furniture-making and design, writing pamphlets and articles and lecturing widely. He also expanded into new areas by opening a showroom and retail outlet in Wigmore Street, London. This was managed by Ted Ould, a former Broadway employee who was a staunch supporter of modern design. The new venture was almost killed off by the catastrophic repercussions of the Wall Street Crash, a matter of weeks after the opening in September 1929.

The Russell family business was particularly badly hit by the financial collapse of 1929. The demand for antiques in the American market disappeared, as did the wealthy American tourists who had patronized the Lygon Arms. An increasing emphasis on machine production seemed to be the only response Gordon Russell Ltd could make to the economic situation. It was in these desperate conditions that Gordon and Dick Russell were approached by Frank Murphy to design the cabinets for his new business, Murphy Radios. The revolutionary approach of the two brothers completely altered the appearance of wirelesses at a time when sets were becoming a standard feature in many households. Dick Russell designed a series of cabinets between 1931 and 1939 which provided the firm with constant work during the lean 1930s. A new factory was opened in Park Royal, West London, set up specifically to cope with the needs of mass production. Friendly rivalry existed between the Broadway and London workshops fuelled by football matches and the staff magazine, *The Circular Saw*. This publication, as well as all the company's brochures and advertising material, maintained the same high standards of graphics and typography that Gordon Russell had established in the 1920s. However the economic situation was such that some of the workforce had to be laid off during this period.

Despite these problems, both Gordon and Dick Russell remained committed to the retail side of the business. They saw it as an attempt to bring the image of the company and an awareness of good design to a wider market. Toni Russell and later Marian Pepler acted as buyers for the London and Broadway showrooms. In

11.8   Garden seat, designed by Gordon Russell for the Russell Workshops, late 1920s (Corinium Museum, Cirencester)

Broadway, antiques were sold alongside some of the best industrial ceramics and glass from firms like Wedgwood, Carter, Stabler and Adams, and Powells' of Whitefriars, and of course furniture and metalwork from Gordon Russell Ltd. During the 1930s the London showroom moved to larger premises in Wigmore Street designed for Gordon Russell Ltd in an elegant, modern idiom by Geoffrey Jellicoe. It represented a major innovation in the development of retailing, laid out in room settings without a counter, and became known for its modernist rugs and fabrics by Marion Dorn and Marian Pepler and some avant-garde designs from the Continent – fabrics from Germany, Thonet's bentwood chairs and furniture by the Finnish architect, Alvar Aalto.

According to Sir Nikolaus Pevsner, Gordon Russell was 'a very useful manufacturer and retailer, more concerned with the quality of products in general than with the selling of his own projects.'[192]

He was also a good judge of character, able to pick out talented newcomers including Marian Pepler, Ted Ould and later Ray Leigh, and he gave them the support and space to develop their full potential. In return he won their devotion and undying loyalty. Nikolaus Pevsner was another such protegé; Gordon Russell appointed this emigré from Nazi Germany, who was to become one of the first twentieth-century design gurus, his chief buyer in 1936.

The outbreak of the Second World War caused a crisis for Gordon Russell. The scarcity of materials and the uncertainties of wartime led to financial problems and he was forced to resign as executive director of Gordon Russell Ltd. He made the transition to the public stage and found new satisfying work away from the Cotswolds. The first step came in 1942 when he was invited to join the Utility Furniture Advisory Committee, and his belief that good contemporary design should be available for all was realized through the Utility Furniture scheme. He went on to become Chairman of the Council for Industrial Design, an organizer of the Festival of Britain in 1951, and founder of the Design Centre in London in 1956. Gordon Russell was knighted for his services to design in 1955.

Although his new role kept him in London for much of the time, he retained his affinity for the Cotswolds. He had begun work on the family home, Kingcombe, near Chipping Campden, in 1925. The house was designed for Gordon and Toni Russell by Leslie Mansfield, but the garden, with its stone-walled terraces, carved stonework and small canal, partly lined with empty wine bottles on end, set in concrete, was Gordon Russell's creation over more than fifty years. He also returned to furniture design towards the end of his life with a series of yew pieces made for him by Adriaan Hermsen, also retired from Gordon Russell Ltd. This furniture reflects his enduring interest in decoration, craftwork and the role of machinery. He wanted modern design with a human face and often cited the Scandinavian approach as a model. In an interview with Roderick Gradidge, published in July 1979, he said:

> I always wanted to make furniture for ordinary people who wanted something better than the kind of stuff that I had seen in shop windows . . . I had always wanted to develop the English tradition. I never went over to a passion for flat roofs and the Bauhaus and all that, though I thought some of it very good. But obviously it made it too easy for someone who was purely a businessman to build a block of offices without any trouble, just putting one unit on top of the other. It was money for jam.[193]

Gordon Russell never took money for jam, he preferred hard physical graft. In this he resembled his contemporary, Edward Barnsley,[194] yet the difference in approach between the two was so great that it caused them mutual distrust and antagonism. Despite his enthusiasm for the Arts and Crafts style, Gordon Russell was dismissive of its underlying philosophy and often ungenerous of its achievements. This is not to decry his own outstanding achievements in the history of British design. He was, above all, a businessman and a propagandist; he had a self-centred determination quite foreign to the Arts and Crafts Movement which enabled him to succeed in very different fields. His last years were marred by the wasting effects of a muscular disease and he died at Kingcombe in October 1980.

Chapter Twelve

A Living Tradition

Craftsmanship in twentieth-century Britain was badly affected by two world wars and the intervening depression. After 1918, in the Cotswolds, traditional craftsmen whose skills had been acquired over generations, such as wheelwrights, blacksmiths, saddlers, basket-makers and charcoal burners, found it hard to settle back into civilian life. At the same time, the craft communities which had been the Cotswolds' contribution to the Arts and Crafts Movement were forced to face up to new realities in the post-war climate. The crafts had become the domain of the state with civic and ecclesiastical patronage playing a major role. The end of the First World War saw a brief flurry of public building as war memorials were erected in almost every town and village as a symbol of hope and renewal. In the 1920s and 1930s many Arts and Crafts designers followed into the public sector, moving into education and administration. William Rothenstein wrote and lectured about the force of the universities. For many designers and craftspeople, teaching became an important source of funding, enabling them to survive while practising their craft and to disseminate their skills and ideas. Over the years the wide range of skills of Arts and Crafts men and women was lost as each area became more specialized and technical.

The importance of preserving the past assumed greater significance in the context of political upheavals and insecurities of the first half of the twentieth century. The last decades of the nineteenth century had seen the formation of a number of societies and pressure groups working in the field of preservation, such as the Society for the Protection of Ancient Buildings, the National Trust and the Council for the Preservation of Rural England. Their concerns and support strengthened and widened over the ensuing years. Preservation also became an important local issue. The most effective pressure group in the Cotswolds was the Campden Trust, set up in 1929 by the architect and artist, Fred Griggs. He had come to Chipping Campden in 1904 and remained for the rest of his life, captivated by the pastoral setting of the stone-built town. Under his guidance, the Campden Trust bought up and restored local properties, and monitored new building and details such as shop signs, often with Griggs and friends, such as Norman Jewson, providing architectural expertise free of charge. Griggs also bought Dover's Hill, subsequently given to the National Trust, for the community and it still serves as the site for the traditional Cotswold Games. His own home, Dover's House in Campden, was begun in 1927 as a craft exercise to make a twentieth-century contribution to the traditions of Chipping Campden.

It is significant that the only major craft community to emerge after 1918 was that dominated by a woman: the weaver, Ethel Mairet, who set up workshops at Ditchling in Sussex. She was the sister of Fred Partridge, jeweller with the Guild of Handicraft, and had come to Chipping Campden in 1902 with her first husband, Ananda Coomaraswamy. In 1914 she married another associate of the Ashbees, Philippe Mairet, and became a powerful and inspiring figure in the crafts between the wars. The first decades of the twentieth century saw a great increase in the number of women designers: almost as many women as men were credited as such in the 1910 Arts and Crafts Exhibition, representing a fivefold increase on 1888.[195] At the same time the interest of women in interior design was growing and giving home-making a creative edge:

> It was an immense excitement, shoping to make a home . . . There should be simplicity indeed . . . but no bareness, no harshness, never an ugliness nor a discord. She had always loved colour in the skies, in the landscape, in the texture of stuffs and garments; now out of the chaotic skein of countless shops she could choose and pick and mingle her threads in a glow of feminine self-expression.[196]

There was also a revival of interest in country crafts. The Rural Industries Bureau was set up in 1922 to nurture and revitalize traditional communities. It attempted to ensure the survival of the crafts by encouraging the apprentice system and improving standards of design and production. However the local market for the traditional rural occupations of blacksmith, potter and wheelwright was rapidly disappearing and handicrafts were increasingly becoming luxury items for sections of the upper middle classes. As a result, two crafts – weaving and pottery – became dominant in the 1920s and 1930s. They were crafts that could be practised on a relatively small scale and whose end-products were geared towards the domestic setting. Both areas saw the emergence of major figures, Ethel Mairet and Bernard Leach, who dominated developments in the first half of the twentieth century. In St Ives, Cornwall, Bernard Leach and Shoji Hamada had set up a pottery in 1921, on the scale of a traditional English country pottery but inspired by the aesthetics of Far Eastern ceramics. Through his creative work, whether pottery or writing, Bernard Leach had a tremendous influence on the development of the crafts.

It was S.B. Russell, father of Gordon Russell, whose interest in traditional handcrafts was responsible for introducing one of Bernard Leach's pupils, Michael Cardew, to the Cotswolds. This initial introduction took the form of an expedition with heroic overtones. Michael Cardew described how Bernard Leach and Gordon Russell had planned to mount:

> . . . a grand demonstration of the country crafts at the Russell workshops at
> Broadway in Worcestershire. This was to last for a whole week during Easter
> 1926. Bernard and I set out from St Ives on his motor-bike. The sidecar was
> full of our tools and gear, and I rode behind on the carrier. It was a three-day
> journey . . . Towards the end of our journey we passed through Winchcombe,
> a small but handsome town all built of severe dark grey Cotswold stones.[197]

Despite the almost inevitable unreliability of Bernard Leach's motor-bike, the
week was a great success. Michael Cardew found that the malleability of the local
clay inspired him to turn different shapes and his days were spent throwing pots. The
evenings were just as inspirational: full of conversation and argument between the
two potters, Gordon Russell and an unidentified architect-friend and fellow member
of the DIA. According to Michael Cardew:

> . . . the four of us used to have great arguments about handcraft and manufac-
> ture. Gordon Russell and his friend advocated the use of machinery to do the
> bulk of the heavy work. They spoke from the point of view of an architect and
> a furniture-maker . . . Bernard and I spoke as potters, both of us insisting that
> in clay-work – or at least in making pots – it was necessary for the human hand
> to have control at every stage. We forgot to mention pugmills, blungers,
> crushers and ball mills.[198]

Despite these disagreements, the Russell family encouraged Michael Cardew in his
desire to set up his own workshop and suggested a move to the Cotswolds. The most
momentous event of the week came when S.B. Russell took him to see the Greet
Pottery, also known as Beckett's Pottery, just beyond Winchcombe. Since the early
nineteenth century, this pottery had used the local red clay and the traditional lead
glaze to make flower pots, chimney pots, milk pans, washing pans and such like for
the surrounding villages. The last potter, Alan Beckett, had died in 1915, possibly of
lead poisoning. Since then the pottery had been abandoned and absorbed into a small-
holding, with the kiln serving 'as a nice, quiet cool place for broody hens'. For
Michael Cardew 'the whole pottery gave out a feeling of generosity and good old-
fashioned country ways of working'.[199] It also recalled his formative childhood memories of the pottery at Fremington in Devon run by Edwin Beer Fishley.

Later that year, Michael Cardew moved to Winchcombe to fulfill his ambition to
make slipware in the manner and on the scale of a traditional country pottery. He
rented the former Greet Pottery for 10s. [50p] a week and, having cleared the kiln of
debris left by the hens, his first move was to trace the last thrower to have worked
there, Elijah Comfort. He persuaded him to return on the same wages – about £2 a
week – that he was earning locally as an agricultural labourer. The two men and a

local boy, Sidney Tustin, got the pottery working again with Elijah Comfort turning out traditional useful wares and Michael Cardew concentrating on making:

> . . . pots which could be used for the purposes of daily life and to make them cheap enough for ordinary people, as I mentally called them – that is, obscure middle class people like me and my friends and relations – to be able to use them and not mind too much when they got broken. I also wanted to make them in a modern style, though by this I did not mean using modern manufacturing techniques.'[200]

Michael Cardew made large, round-bodied jars, pots and bowls with slip-trailed designs or sgraffito decoration, the pattern incised into the clay or slip. The designs were distilled from his interest in English slipware and Chinese T'zu-chou stonewares. His enthusiasm grew for bigger and bigger pots, struggling with 24 pound narrow-necked cider jars, turned on a power wheel. 'The struggle to make the neck narrow without damaging the form below' while working on this scale was 'a sort of magic' and 'an excruciating kind of fun'.[201] In 1931 he took some of these large pots to a mixed exhibition in London and to his astonishment found himself an overnight success, selling all his twelve exhibits – the most expensive was priced at seven guineas [£7.35] – and being singled out for favourable mention by a review in *The Times*. He was briefly fêted by the London art world, including the painter Maresco Pearce who, over lunch at his Chelsea house, described Michael Cardew as 'a Fauve (but he had to explain what that meant), and said my pots were like Gauguin's painting, the same kind of animal outburst.'[202]

This was only a fleeting dalliance with the art world. For Michael Cardew, reality lay in the hard graft of his wood-fired kiln and the simple life with his painter-wife, Mariel, and their children. They seem to have lived an unfettered existence, not

12.1   Jug in slip-decorated earthenware, made by Michael Cardew, Winchcombe Pottery, c. 1930 (F.C. Scorey for CAGM)

always able to provide support for each other when it was required but accepting the needs of each partner.

Despite the fact that he derived such physical and intellectual pleasure from making pots, Michael Cardew was continually troubled by the role of a craft pottery in an industrial society. His friend, the American scholar, craftsman and Marxist, Henry Bergen, made a strong case for the survival of the crafts within a communist system. Michael Cardew, however, was sceptical, writing perceptively of both systems: 'But I suspected that the crafts [in Russia] were being fostered only on the periphery, just as in capitalist societies crafts are tolerated and even encouraged as ornamental adjuncts of the "real" civilization.'[203]

Cardew made a very conscious effort to work with industry. Through his contacts with the Wedgwood family and Gordon Forsyth at the School of Art in Stoke he came to the firm of Copelands. He was able over several weeks to produce turned teawares as prototypes, although they were never put into production. He was impressed by the craft skills of all those, men and women, working within the industrial pottery system. The end-products of his efforts, however, 'looked very cold compared with what we made and used at home' and were not pursued by Copelands.

Michael Cardew was only able to take part in this experiment at Stoke-on-Trent because of the reliable team that he had built up at Winchcombe. In 1936 he was joined by Ray Finch, a young man whose early taste of factory conditions had con-

12.2   The Winchcombe Pottery, c. 1934. Left to right: Elijah Comfort, Charlie Tustin, Michael Cardew, Trigger the horse who powered the pugmill, Sidney Tustin (Ray Finch)

vinced him of the need to find work on a more human scale. Finch had admired pots by Michael Cardew in the house of a friend and, with no experience as a potter, asked to be taken on as a pupil. Not surprisingly, Michael Cardew turned him down, but, after a year at the Central School, Ray Finch was taken on at Winchcombe. The five men, Michael Cardew, Ray Finch, Elijah Comfort, Sidney Tustin and his brother, Charlie, worked closely together until 1936 when Michael Cardew returned to Cornwall to set up a second pottery at Wenford Bridge. He left Winchcombe in the capable hands of Ray Finch.

One of Cardew's sources of encouragement and practical assistance, like many of the craftsmen and women struggling to make a living in the Cotswolds, was the librarian/curator at Cheltenham, D.W. Herdman. Herdman came to Cheltenham in 1922 and spent the remainder of his working life devoting himself to the support of the rich craft tradition of the Cotswolds. He was responsible for establishing a tradition of Cotswold Arts and Crafts exhibitions at Cheltenham from 1923 onwards, and Gordon Russell was only one of many to acknowledge the significance of his support. Herdman also began buying contemporary craft items for the Art Gallery and Museum, sometimes as exhibits but also for use, laying the basis for the unique Arts and Crafts collection. Above all his constant interest in the crafts and his willingness to make time for individuals must have been a tremendous moral boost for the craft community.

Local craftsmen and women also began to organize themselves, partly through government bodies such as the Gloucestershire Rural Community Council set up in 1923 and partly through independent bodies such as Cotswold Co-operative Handicrafts founded by a group from the Whiteway Colony. In 1933, various groupings were brought together as the Guild of Gloucestershire Craftsmen and exhibitions were held throughout the county and further afield. The intention was for established craftsmen and women to provide standards and inspiration for younger, less-experienced members. In 1968 a second professional craft body was formed, taking the name of the Craftsmen of Gloucestershire.

A new attitude to craftsmanship can be seen in many books of the 1930s and 1940s. The work of twentieth-century craftsmen and women was seen in the perspective of pre-industrial traditions, with much Victorian design providing a hiccup in the nineteenth century. John Gloag's *The English Tradition in Design*, published as a King Penguin in 1947, was a formative example of this approach. Others include *The things we see – Furniture*, by Gordon Russell in 1948, reprinted as *Looking at Furniture* in 1964, and Arthur Lane's *Style in Pottery*. Possibly the most influential writer of the period was Sir Nikolaus Pevsner, friend and colleague of Sir Gordon Russell and tireless propagandist for good design. In *The Pioneers of the Modern Movement*, first published in 1936 but probably best known as the Penguin reprint, *The Pioneers of Modern Design*, he singled out C.R. Ashbee and Ernest Gimson for special praise describing the latter as 'the greatest of the English artist-craftsmen'.[204]

12.3   Folding table in English walnut, made by Fred Foster, c. 1940 (F.C. Scorey for CAGM)

After the horrors of the Second World War and faced with the increasing tensions of the cold-war period, many people saw the antidote as a return to a less complicated way of life. The Festival of Britain, the country's effort to raise spirits after the war, dwelt on the inherent 'goodness' of craft products. The South Bank exhibition included a Country Pavilion where crafts such as weaving, straw-work, saddle-making and appliqué-work were included. Two major shows took place in the Cotswolds, each quite unique in its scale and impact. In the old museum in Cirencester Park, the architect, Oliver Hill, then living at Daneway House in Sapperton, staged a dramatic and well-designed exhibition, 'The Cotswold Tradition'. It included captions written by John Betjeman and inscribed by Ruth Raymond. Oliver Hill, through his love of 'stunts', bedecked the streets of Cirencester with life-size horses' heads above Venetian poles. They had been made by a school for sub-normal children at Fairford from moulds lent by a London film studio. The exhibition itself concentrated on the three main areas of Cotswold life: Church, Wool and Agriculture. It was described by Christopher Hussey in the accompanying booklet as 'successful because it is designed round a living theme and because it is a notable instance of the modern art of display'.[205]

12.4   A view of 'The Cotswold Tradition'
exhibition held at Cirencester, 1951 (The
Royal Commission on Historic Monuments,
(England))

Cotswold craftsmanship was also the theme of Cheltenham's contribution to the Festival of Britain and the 1951 Festival of British Contemporary Music. At the Montpellier Rotunda, an overwhelming collection, over three hundred exhibits 'of over half-a-century's effort by eminent designers and craftsmen',[206] working in the Cotswolds was gathered together. The inspiration came from the museum curator, D.W. Herdman, with the assistance of local craftspeople including George Hart, Norman Jewson, Dorothy Larcher, and William and Eve Simmonds.

Although this exhibition concentrated on past achievements, there were some exhibitors who carried on working and expanding into the 1950s and 1960s. Ray Finch described how the Winchcombe Pottery re-emerged from the ravages of the Second World War:

> In 1946, Sid and myself were demobbed and returned to make a fresh start, soon to be joined by Charlie. Though the world had changed irrevocably in those five years, the pottery stood there just as we had left it, wrapped in a sort of time warp which I suppose enveloped us too because we carried on exactly as we had left off.[207]

12.5   Sideboard in English walnut, designed and made by Harry Davoll, c. 1946 (F.C. Scorey for CAGM)

Ray Finch bought the equipment and good will from Michael Cardew and continued to rent the land until 1952 when he had the opportunity to acquire it outright. He began making domestic wares once again although changes were introduced. In 1953 he abandoned slipware and then, in 1959, he changed from using an earthenware to a stoneware body which was more suitable for tablewares. The Winchcombe Pottery was able to take advantage of the explosion of interest in craft pottery in the 1960s. Concurrent with this was an enthusiasm for healthy eating and wholefood, epitomized by the Cranks restaurants which have always used the distinctive yet serviceable Winchcombe Pottery in their establishments. The oil crisis of the 1970s gave Ray Finch an excuse to return to a pottery tradition:

> I had never really liked oil which though easy and convenient was noisy and smelly and had yearned often for the more aesthetically satisfying qualities of

12.6   Christchurch, Chalford. Numerous craftspeople, including Norman Jewson, Peter Waals, George Hart, William Simmonds and Edward Payne, were involved in the renovation of the interior of this church in the twentieth century (CAGM)

wood: gentle, quiet and requiring complete involvement in the final stages of a potter's work. Better for the pots too, giving an added extra quality to clay and glazes.[208]

The wood-fired kiln at the Winchcombe Pottery continues to produce domestic stonewares with a limited range of basic glazes. Ray Finch and his son, Mike, work there with a small team which seems the most appropriate for the manufacture of domestic ware, and also gives the chance of a satisfying job to a few individuals.

Despite a lean time in the 1960s, the crafts emerged strengthened in the 1970s. The whole tenor of existence was moving in their favour. The political activism, inspired partly by the continuing Cold War and the anti-Vietnam War protests, saw a massive increase in membership for organizations such as the Campaign for Nuclear Disarmament which questioned the nature and priorities of society. There was also a search for new, spiritual values, typified by sections of the hippy movement and the vegetarian/wholefood ethos which found expression in the craft revival of the 1970s and 1980s. Examples of the changing mood range from the stripped pine furniture and homespun appeal of Habitat, to the folk music revival and the nostalgia purveyed by the media in, for example, the Hovis advertisements. Because of these superficial trappings, the crafts are sometimes seen as escapism: safe, secure and cocooned in a rosy past. More often, however, they function at the cutting edge of economic survival, constantly having to redefine their position in a rapidly changing society.

Support for the crafts has come from new national bodies including the Crafts Advisory Committee, now the Crafts Council, and the British Crafts Centre, now Contemporary Applied Arts, as well as from professional groups, such as the Craftsman Potters Association, and from the education system through the art colleges. Locally the crafts have been fostered by the Crafts Study Centre at the Holburne Museum, Bath, established by the efforts primarily of Robin and Heather Tanner under the auspices of the University of Bath. The original spur came from the records of Barron and Larcher's work, bequeathed to Robin Tanner by Phyllis Barron in 1964. The Tanners wanted to create 'not a museum of objects untouchable behind glass but a living, expanding Study Centre whose work could be held in the hand and enjoyed, and a whole archive consulted.'[209] With the help of other educationalists and craftspeople, including Bernard Leach, Katherine Pleydell Bouverie and Rita Beales, the Crafts Study Centre opened in June 1977 'on a beautiful evening when the cuckoo was still calling, clear, loud and long'.[210] A second major craft development in the Cotswolds was the Cirencester Workshops, now part of Brewery Arts, which have provided workshops, exhibition and retail space for craftspeople since 1980.

These developments have ensured the survival of the crafts in the Cotswolds, despite rapidly rising house prices exacerbated by the encroaching commuter belt from Birmingham, London and the Thames Valley. Particularly successful are workshops making small domestic items: jewellery, wearable textiles and pottery. The Winchcombe Pottery still thrives with a workforce of five or six, taking on occasional students and trainees. The same site includes the workshop of the woodworker and furniture-maker, Will Hall, who is able to use modern power tools to make pieces that are still finished by hand. Paul Spriggs in Dursley has continued the turned chair tradition established in the Cotswolds by Ernest Gimson, while the metalworker, Alan Evans, has revived the blacksmith's art from his workshop at Whiteway. He has received many prestigious commissions including the gates for St Paul's Cathedral Treasury in 1981, and a major scheme of railings for the Broadgate Development in the City of London between 1988 and 1989. In 1990 he completed a metal grille for the extension at the Art Gallery and Museum, Cheltenham, which includes as a mark of respect and point of reference, the squirrel motif originally used by Ernest Gimson in a pair of firedogs.

The Arts and Crafts Movement in the Cotswolds was the true inheritor of the tradition of Ruskin and Morris containing dual strands of 'nostalgia and a pioneering

12.7   Metal screen, designed by Alan Evans for the Art Gallery and Museum, Cheltenham, 1989 (Alan Evans)

sometimes revolutionary exploration of modern avant-garde ideas'.[211] It is still a powerful inspirational force today for craftsmen and women throughout the country and even further afield. Oscar Wilde captured the earnest, questioning spirit of the Movement when he wrote: 'A map of the world that does not include Utopia is not worth even glancing at, for it leaves out the one country at which humanity is always landing. And when humanity lands there, it looks out, and seeing a better country, it sets sail. Progress is the realisation of Utopias.'[212]

Notes

Chapter One

1. Osbert Lancaster, *Homes Sweet Homes* (London, John Murray, 1939), p. 52.
2. Robert Schmutzler, *Art Nouveau* (London, Thames and Hudson, 1978), p. 97.
3. C.R. Ashbee, *Craftsmanship in Competitive Industry* (London, Essex House Press, 1908), p.10.
4. Quoted by Gillian Naylor, *The Arts and Crafts Movement* (London, Studio Vista, 1971), p. 12.
5. Lionel Lambourne, *Utopian Craftsmen* (London, Astragel Books, 1980), p. 3.
6. John Ruskin, 'The Nature of Gothic', *The Stones of Venice* vol. II (London, 1853).
7. Annette Carruthers, 'Like Incubi and Succubi', *Craft History Two* (April 1989), p. 59.
8. *The Collected Works of William Morris*, May Morris (ed.) (London, Longmans, Green & Co., 1910–15), XXII, p. 77.
9. Jan Marsh, *Jane and May Morris* (London, Pandora 1986), p. 97.
10. *Ibid.*, p. 146.
11. William Morris, *Collected Works* (London, 1915), p. 202. First published as *News From Nowhere* (1890).
12. William Morris, 'Textiles', *Arts and Crafts Essays* (London, Longmans, Green & Co.,1893), p. 36.
13. W.R. Lethaby, Alfred H. Powell, F.L. Griggs, *Ernest Gimson: His Life and Work* (Shakespeare Head Press, 1924), p. 15.
14. Freda Derrick, 'The Face of the Countryside', *The Illustrated Carpenter and Builder* (November 7, 1952), p. 1874.
15. J.W. Mackail, *The Life of William Morris* vol. I (London, Longmans, Green & Co., 1899), p. 231.
16. Unpublished letter, Philip Webb to Alfred Powell (19 July, 1902).
17. Unpublished letter, Edward Barnsley to Humphrey Gimson (10 October, 1969), Edward Barnsley Educational Trust archive (EBETA).

Chapter Two

18. Unpublished letter, Ernest Gimson to Ernest Barnsley, Leicestershire Museums, Arts and Records Service, 19 February 1988.
19. Lethaby, *Ernest Gimson,* p. 5.
20. *Ernest Gimson*, an exhibition catalogue (Leicester Museums, 1969), p. 34.
21. Alan Crawford, *C.R. Ashbee* (New Haven, Yale University Press, 1985), p. 15.
22. *Ibid.*, p. 10.
23. *Ibid.*, p. 20.
24. Reginald Blomfield, *Memoirs of an Architect* (London, Macmillan, 1932), p. 76.
25. *Ibid.*
26. C.R. Ashbee, *Craftsmanship in Competitive Industry* (Essex House Press, 1908), p. 104.
27. Blomfield, *Memoirs* p. 77.
28. Lethaby, *Ernest Gimson*, p. 6.

Chapter Three

29.   Lethaby, *Ernest Gimson,* p. 15.
30.   Eric Sharpe, *Fifteen Craftsmen on their Craft,* John Farleigh (ed.), (London, Sylvan Press, 1945), p. 102.
31.   Unpublished letter, Sidney Barnsley to Philip Webb (30 June, 1901).
32.   Freda Derrick, 'Sapperton Today' *The Illustrated Carpenter and Builder* (10 October, 1952), p. 1690.
33.   Unpublished letter, Sidney Barnsley to Philip Webb (19 December, 1900).
34.   Unpublished letter, Edward Barnsley to Olga Barnsley (25 November, 1968), EBETA.
35.   Unpublished letter, Sidney Barnsley to Philip Webb (30 June, 1901).
36.   Norman Jewson, *By Chance I Did Rove* (Roundwood Press, 1973), p. 79.
37.   Unpublished letter, Sidney Barnsley to Philip Webb (1 May, 1904), EBETA.
38.   Unpublished letter, Sidney Barnsley to Philip Webb (6 July, 1902), EBETA.
39.   Unpublished letter, Sidney Barnsley to Edward Barnsley (25 August, 1926), EBETA.
40.   Unpublished letter, Sidney Barnsley to Philip Webb (1 May, 1904).
41.   Jewson, *By Chance*, p. 14.
42.   Sir George Trevelyan, in *Ernest Gimson*, an exhibition catalogue (Leicester Museums, 1969), p. 43.
43.   *Ibid.*, p. 33.
44.   Jewson, *By Chance*, p. 25.
45.   *Ibid.*, p. 26.
46.   Victor J. Taylor, in *Fine Woodworking* (September/October, 1984).
47.   Lethaby, *Ernest Gimson*, p. 20.
48.   Unpublished letter, Edward Barnsley to Humphrey Gimson (10 October, 1969), EBETA.
49.   Quoted by F.L. Griggs.
50.   Jewson, *By Chance*, p. 12.
51.   Lethaby, *Ernest Gimson*, p. 11.

Chapter Four

52.   This account is heavily indebted to the indispensible books on Ashbee and the Guild of Handicraft by Alan Crawford and Fiona MacCarthy. I am very grateful to Alan Crawford and MaryGreensted for their helpful comments on a draft of this chapter.
53.   Crawford, *C.R. Ashbee*, p. 116.
54.   *Ibid.*, p. 75.
55.   Fiona MacCarthy, *The Simple Life: C.R. Ashbee in the Cotswolds* (Lund Humphries 1981), p. 48.
56.   1894.
57.   *Modern Design in Jewellery and Fans*, C. Holme (ed.) (London, 1902), p. 4 .
58.   Gloucestershire Records Office, D2909/5.
59.   H.A. Evans, (Macmillan, London, 1905).
60.   Craig Fees has explored the background politics and local personalities of Campden in his unpublished Ph.D. thesis, *Christmas Mumming in a North Cotswold Town* (Leeds Univ., 1985).
61.   Crawford, *Ashbee*, p. 366.
62.   Essex House Press, Broad Campden.

63. Unpublished letter, Edward Barnsley to B.G. Burrough (November, 1970), EBETA.
64. Crawford, *Ashbee*, p. 104.

Chapter Five

65. Guy Dawber, 'The Stone Buildings of the Cotswolds', *The Builder* (1893), CXIV, p. 387. Dawber read this paper before the Architectural Association on 12 May 1893.
66. Campden School of Arts and Crafts, Report for 1904–5, (Victoria and Albert Museum Library), p. 32.
67. A.W.N. Pugin, *An Apology for the Revival of Christian Architecture* (London, 1843), p. 21.
68. W.R. Lethaby, *Philip Webb and his Work* (1935, republ. London, 1987), p. 119.
69. *Country Life* (26 November, 1910), p. 758.
70. Quoted by Alan Crawford, *A Tour of Broadway and Chipping Campden* (The Victorian Society, September 1978), p. 14.
71. *The Builder* (1917), CXIII, p. 3.
72. Quoted by Clive Aslet, *Country Life* (19 November, 1978), p. 1181.
73. C.R. Ashbee, *A Book of Cottages and Little Houses: for Landlords, Architects, Builders and others* (Batsford, 1906), p. 110.
74. Ibid., p. 9.
75. Ibid., p. 103.
76. SPAB case files.
77. A.H. Powell, F.W. Troup, Charles C. Winmill, A.R. Powys, *Report on Treatment of Old Cottages* (SPAB, 1919), p. 8.
78. Unpublished letter, Ernest Gimson to F.F. McMeekan, Arlington Mill Museum, Bibury, Gloucestershire (23 October 1907).
79. Jewson, *By Chance*, p. 14.
80. Ashbee, *Book of Cottages*, p. 6.

Chapter Six

81. Kenneth Grahame, *The Wind in The Willows* (Methuen, London, 1981), p. 150. First published 1908.
82. Letter, Philip Webb to Sidney Barnsley (10 August, 1900), quoted by William Lethaby in *The Builder* (4 December, 1925), p. 814.
83. MacCarthy, *The Simple Life,* p. 33.
84. Unpublished letter, Ernest Gimson to William Lethaby, B.G. Burrough archive, Cheltenham Art Gallery and Museums (CAGM).
85. MacCarthy, *The Simple Life*, p. 53.
86. Letter, Ernest Gimson to Sarah Gimson (17 March, 1895), quoted by Miss Pinnell in *Village Camera* (Alan Sutton, 1990).
87. MacCarthy, *The Simple Life*, p. 71.
88. William Rothenstein, *Men and Memories*, (London, Faber and Faber, 1932), II, p. 273.
89. Daneway House Visitor's Book, Emery Walker Library, CAGM.
90. Rothenstein, *Men and Memories*, II, p. 341.
91. Alan Crawford, *A Tour of Broadway and Chipping Campden*, (The Victorian Society, 1978), p. 5.
92. Unpublished letter, Sidney Barnsley to Edward Barnsley (1926), EBETA.

93. In the collections of Arlington Mill, Bibury, Gloucestershire.
94. Rothenstein, *Men and Memories*, II, p. 191.
95. Fiona MacCarthy, *Eric Gill* (London, Faber and Faber, 1989), p. 93.
96. Jewson, *By Chance*, p. 32.
97. Rothenstein, *Men and Memories*, III, p. 3.
98. MacCarthy, *The Simple Life*, p. 180.
99. McCarthy, *Eric Gill*, p. 18.
100. Arnold Wesker, *I'm Talking About Jerusalem* (Evans, 1961), p. 30.
101. MacCarthy, *The Simple Life*, p. 97.
102. *Ibid.*, p. 100.
103. Nellie Shaw, *The Whiteway Colony* (C.B. Daniels, 1933), p. 39.
104. Malcolm Muggeridge, *Chronicles of Wasted Time I: The Green Stick* (Collins, 1972), p. 42.
105. *bid.*
106. *By Hammer and Hand*, Alan Crawford (ed) (Birmingham Museums and Art Gallery, 1984), p. 12.
107. Unpublished letter, Edward Payne to Mary Comino (3 February 1980), CAGM.

Chapter Seven

108. Letter, Philip Webb to Alfred Powell (April, 1904), quoted by W.R. Lethaby in *Philip Webb and his Work* (Oxford, 1935).
109. Letter, Philip Webb to Alfred Powell (7 August, 1900), *Ibid.*
110. *Architectural Review*, (June–December 1899), 6.
111. *The Studio*, Year Book, 83.
112. Unpublished letter, Alfred Powell to his mother (21 February, 1903).
113. Unpublished letter, Nina Griggs to Max Burrough (28 March, 1984).
114. Gordon Forsyth's contribution to the official report on 'The Position & Tendencies of the Industrial Arts' following the 1925 Paris Exhibition.
115. Alfred Powell, 'New Wedgwood Pottery', *Studio*, 98.
116. Unpublished letter, Alfred Powell to Geoffrey Lupton (20 December, 1936).
117. Unpublished letter, Alfred Powell to Geoffrey Lupton (27 February, 1937).

Chapter Eight

118. William Morris, 'The Beauty of Life', quoted by Gillian Naylor in *The Arts and Crafts Movement* (London, Studio Vista, 1971), p. 108.
119. Part of the Chantry Bequest at the Tate Gallery, London.
120. Unpublished letter, Edward Payne to Mary Comino (3 February, 1980), CAGM.
121. *Ibid.*
122. 'Eve Simmonds, a personal account', compiled from conversations and letters to Heather and Robin Tanner (1971), in *William and Eve Simmonds*, an exhibition catalogue (CAGM, 1980), p. 23.
123. Quoted by Gerry Carter in his introduction to the 1968 exhibition of William Simmond's work, CAGM.
124. *William and Eve Simmonds*, p. 23.
125. Unpublished letter, Nina Griggs to Max Burrough (3 May, 1984).
126. *William and Eve Simmonds*, p. 24.

127. *Modern Embroidery* (1933).
128. Edward Payne, 'William Simmonds: Sculptor and Craftsman', *Gloucestershire Countryside* (October 1933–July 1937), 2, pp. 218–220.
129. Rothenstein, *Men and Memories*, III, p. 3.
130. Taped conversation, John Gwynne and Mary Greensted (11 September, 1980), CAGM.
131. *William and Eve Simmonds*, p. 23.
132. Unpublished letter, Charles Gere to Francis Dodd (12 August, 1934), CAGM.
133. Casty Cobb, unpublished notes (January, 1980), CAGM.
134. These notebooks are now in the collections of the Museum of English Rural Life, Reading.
135. Casty Cobb, unpublished notes.
136. Unpublished letter, Nina Griggs to Max Burrough (3 May, 1984).
137. Unpublished letter, Charles Gere to Francis Dodd (3 April, 1932), CAGM.
138. Tony Davies, in *William and Eve Simmonds*, an exhibition catalogue, p. 30.
139. Taped conversation, Gwynne and Greensted.

Chapter Nine

140. Phyllis Barron, *My Life as a Block Printer*, transcript of a talk given at Dartington Hall, Devon (22 February 1964), on a Ministry of Education Course organized by Robin Tanner on 'Art and Craft: Their Place in Secondary Education'.
141. Robin Tanner, *Phyllis Barron 1890–1964*, transcript of a talk given at The Holburne Museum and Crafts Study Centre, Bath (1 June, 1978).
142. Philip Mairet, *Autobiographical and other papers*, C.H. Sisson (ed.) (Carcanet, Manchester, 1981) pp. 42–51. Here referred to as Ethel Richardson, but called Alice by Dorothy Larcher and Phyllis Barron.
143. Unpublished letter, Eve Simmonds to Robin Tanner (17 March 1965).
144. Barron, *Block Printer*.
145. *Ibid.*
146. *Ibid.*
147. Stuart Robinson, *A Fertile Field* (Guild of Gloucestershire Craftsmen and CAGM, 1983), p. 19.
148. Barron, *Block Printer*.
149. *Ibid.*
150. *Ibid.*
151. *Ibid.*
152. *Ibid.*
153. *Ibid.*
154. Enid Marx, 'Working with Barron & Larcher in the 1920s', *Hand Block Printed Textiles: Phyllis Barron & Dorothy Larcher* (1978), Crafts Study Centre, Holburne Museum, Bath.
155. Barron, *Block Printer*.
156. *Ibid.*
157. *Ibid.*
158. *Ibid.*
159. *Ibid.*
160. *Ibid.*
161. Notes taken from luncheon meetings of the Red Rose Guild between 26 and 30 October, 1936.
162. Letter, Phyllis Barron to Susan Bosence, in Susan Bosence, *Hand Block Printing and Resist Dyeing* (David and Charles, Newton Abbot, 1985), p. 48.

163. Susan Bosence, 'Barron', in *Hand Block Printed Textiles: Phyllis Barron and Dorothy Larcher* (1978), Crafts Study Centre, Holburne Museum, Bath.
164. Tanner, *Phyllis Barron*.
165. 'Painswick Artist Dies '(25 November, 1964), *Gloucestershire Echo*.
166. Robin Tanner, *Double Harness* (Impact Books, 1987), p. 165.
167. Unpublished letter, Phyllis Barron to Robin Tanner (2 May, 1962).
168. Tanner, *Phyllis Barron*.

Chapter Ten

169. C.R. Ashbee in an unpublished address to the Art Workers' Guild (June, 1921), quoted by Fiona MacCarthy in *Craft History One* (Combined Arts, 1988), p. 31.
170. C.R. Ashbee, unpublished journals (early June, 1915), *Ibid.*, p. 34.
171. Helen E. FitzRandolph, M. Doriel Hay, *The Rural Industries of England and Wales 1. Timber and Underwood Industries and some Village Workshops* (Oxford, 1926).
172. Quoted by Bevis Hillier, *The Times* (9 September, 1978).
173. Unpublished letter, Peter Waals to Mr Goddard (16 August, 1934), Leicestershire Museums, Arts and Records Service.
174. Unpublished notes, 'Local Craftsmen who worked with Peter Waals', compiled by Kay Rhodes (1988), copy lodged with CAGM.
175. Kay Rhodes.
176. Sir George Trevelyan, in *Ernest Gimson* an exhibition catalogue (Leicester Museums, 1969), p. 44.
177. *Ibid.*, p. 45.

Chapter Eleven

178. Gordon Russell, *Designer's Trade* (London, Allen & Unwin, 1968), p. 140.
179. Ken Baynes, Kate Baynes, *Gordon Russell* (London, Design Council, 1980), p. 7.
180. Russell, *Designer's Trade*, p. 65.
181. Gordon Russell, *The things we see – Furniture* (Penguin, 1948), reprinted by Lund Humphries as *Looking at Furniture* (1964).
182. *Ibid.*, p. 62.
183. *Ibid.*, p. 117.
184. *Ibid.*, p. 121.
185. In *Designer's Trade*, Gordon Russell dates his first exhibition as 1922. This date has been accepted by other commentators but records at Cheltenham show that the exhibition took place in 1923.
186. Russell, *Furniture*, p. 77.
187. Jeremy Myerson, *Gordon Russell* (London, Design Council, 1992) pp. 38, 44.
188. Gillian Naylor, *A History of Gordon Russell Ltd 1904–76* (published privately, 1976).
189. Russell, *Furniture*, p. 35.
190. Rosamund Allwood, Kedrun Laurie, *R.D. Russell Marian Pepler*, an exhibition catalogue (Geffrye Museum, 1983), p. 3.
191. Allwood, Laurie, *Russell Pepler*, p. 4.
192. Nikolaus Pevsner, 'Roots and Branches' in *Design* (13 December, 1959), p. 32.

193. *The Guardian* (28 July, 1979).
194. See Annette Carruthers' biography of *Edward Barnsley and his workshop* (White Cockade Publishing, 1992).

Chapter Twelve

195. Lynne Walker, 'The Arts and Crafts alternative', *A View from the Interior* Judy Attfield, Pat Kirkham (eds), (London, The Women's Press, 1989).
196. H.G. Wells, *Marriage* (London, 1912) Book 2, Ch. 1.
197. Michael Cardew, *A Pioneer Potter* (London, William Collins, 1988), p. 55.
198. *Ibid.*, p. 56.
199. *bid.*, p. 57.
200. *Ibid.*, p. 61.
201. *Ibid.*, p. 81.
202. *Ibid.*, p. 84.
203. *Ibid.*, p. 95.
204. Nikolaus Pevsner, *Pioneers of Modern Design* (London, Penguin, 1960), p. 152.
205. Christopher Hussey, *Cotswold Heritage* (1951), booklet for The Cotswold Tradition exhibition, Introduction.
206. D.W. Herdman, (1951) catalogue of an exhibition of Cotswold Craftsmanship held at the Montpellier Rotunda, Introduction.
207. Ray Finch, transcript of a talk given at CAGM (14 July, 1990).
208. *Ibid.*
209. Tanner, *Double Harness*, p. 179.
210. *Ibid.*, p. 180.
211. Rosemary Hill, 'Nostalgia or New Wave', in *Crafts* (July/August, 1992), p. 16.
212. Oscar Wilde, 'The Soul of Man under Socialism', (1891) *De Profundis and Other Writings* (Penguin, 1986) p. 34.

Select Bibliography

Books and Catalogues

Alexander, R., *The Furniture and Joinery of Peter Waals*. Campden, Alcuin Press, 1930.

Ashbee, C.R., *A Book of Cottages and Little Houses*. London, Batsford, 1906.

Ashbee, C.R., *Craftsmanship in Competitve Industry*. London and Campden, Essex House Press, 1908.

Backemeyer, S. & Gronberg, T., *W.R. Lethaby 1857–1931*. London, Lund Humphries, 1984.

Batkin, M., *Wedgwood Ceramics 1846–1959*. London, Richard Dennis, 1982.

Batkin, M. & Greensted, M., *Good Workmanship with Happy Thought: the Work of Alfred and Louise Powell*. Cheltenham Art Gallery and Museums (CAGM), 1992.

Baynes, K. & Baynes, K., *Gordon Russell*. Design Council, 1980.

Blomfield, R., *Memoirs of an Architect*. London, Macmillan, 1932.

Bradshaw, A.E., *Handmade Woodwork of the Twentieth Century*. London, John Murray, 1962.

Brill, E., *Cotswold Crafts*. London, Batsford, 1977.

Cardew, M., *A Pioneer Potter*. London, William Collins, 1988.

Carruthers, A., *Ernest Gimson and the Cotswold Group of Craftsmen*. Leicestershire Arts, Museums and Records Service, 1978.

Carruthers, A., *Edward Barnsley and his Workshop*. White Cockade Publishing, 1992.

Carruthers, A. & Johnson, F., *The Guild of Handicraft 1888–1988*, CAGM, 1988.

Cheltenham Art Gallery and Museums, *Good Citizen's Furniture: the Work of Ernest and Sidney Barnsley*. 1976.

Cheltenham Art Gallery and Museums, *William and Eve Simmonds*, 1980.

Crafts Study Centre, *Hand Block Printed Textiles: Phyllis Barron and Dorothy Larcher*. Holburne Museum, Bath, 1978.

Crawford, A., Greensted, M. & MacCarthy, F., *C.R. Ashbee and the Guild of Handicraft*, CAGM, 1981.

Crawford, A., *A Tour of Broadway and Chipping Campden*. Victorian Society, 1978.

Crawford, A. (ed.), *By Hammer and Hand*. Birmingham Museums and Art Gallery, 1984.

Crawford, A., *C.R. Ashbee: Architect, Designer and Romantic Socialist*. New Haven and London, 1985.

Davey, P., *Arts and Crafts Architecture*. London, 1981.

Dawber, G., *Old Cottages, Farmhouses and other Stone Buildings of the Cotswold Region*. London, 1905.

Dormer, P., Harrod, T., Hill, R. & Roscoe, B., *Arts & Crafts to Avant-Garde*. London, South Bank Centre, 1992.

Farleigh, J. (ed.), *Fifteen Craftsmen on their Crafts*. London, 1945.

Fees, C., *A Child in Arcadia: The Chipping Campden Boyhood of H.T. Osborn 1902–1907*. Chipping Campden, 1985.

Fine Art Society, *The Arts and Crafts Movement 1890–1930*. London, 1973.

Gordon, C.A., *Gazetteer of Arts and Crafts Architecture in the Cotswolds Region*. CAGM, 1992.

Jewson, N., *By Chance I Did Rove*. Roundwood Press, 1973.

Joel, D., *Furniture Design Set Free*. London, J.M. Dent, 1969.

Lambourne, L., *Utopian Craftsmen*. London, Astragel, 1980.

Leicester Museums, *Ernest Gimson*. 1969.

Lethaby, W., *Architecture, Mysticism and Myth*. London, Architectural Press, 1979.

Lethaby, W., *Philip Webb and His Work*. London, 1987.

Lethaby, W., Powell, A. & Griggs, F.L., *Ernest Gimson, His Life and Work*. Stratford on Avon, Shakespeare Head Press, 1924.

MacCarthy, F., *The Simple Life: C.R. Ashbee in the Cotswolds*. London, Lund Humphries, 1981.

Marsh, J., *Back to the Land: The Pastoral Movement in Victorian England*. London, Quartet, 1982.

Marsh, J., *Jane and May Morris*. London, Pandora, 1986.

Masse, H.J.L.J., *The Art-Workers' Guild*. Oxford, 1935.

Morris, M. (ed.) *The Collected Works of William Morris*. London, Longmans, Green & Co., 1910–1915.

Myerson, J., *Gordon Russell*. Design Council, London, 1992.

Naylor, G., *The Arts and Crafts Movement*. London, Studio Vista, 1971.

Pevsner, N., *Pioneers of Modern Design*. London, Penguin, 1960.

Robinson, S., *A Fertile Field*. Guild of Gloucestershire Craftsmen and CAGM, 1983.

Rogers, J.C., *Modern English Furniture*. London, Country Life, 1930.

Rothenstein, W., *Men and Memories*. vol. 2. London, Faber and Faber, 1932.

Rothenstein, W., *Since Fifty*. London, Faber and Faber, 1939.

Ruskin, J., *The Stones of Venice*. London, 1851–3.

Russell, G., *Designer's Trade*. London, Allen & Unwin, 1968.

Saint, A., *Richard Norman Shaw*. New Haven, Yale University Press, 1976.

Sedding, J., *Art and Handicraft*. London, Kegen Paul, 1893.

Service, A., *Edwardian Architecture and its Origins*. London, Architectural Press, 1975.

Shaw, N., *The Whiteway Colony*. C.B. Daniels, 1933.

Stansky, P., *Redesigning the World*. Princeton University Press, 1985.

Tanner, R., *Double Harness*. Impact Books, 1987.

Thompson, P., *The Work of William Morris*. London, Quartet, 1967.

Verey, D., *Gloucestershire*. vol. 2. Buildings of England Series (ed. N. Pevsner), London, Penguin, 1970.

Watkinson, R., *William Morris as Designer*. London, Studio Vista,1967.

Weaver, L., *Small Country Houses of Today*. London, Country Life, 1930.

Wilgress, J., *Alec Miller: Guildsman and Sculptor in Chipping Campden*. Chipping Campden, Campden and District Historical and Archaeological Society, 1987.

Articles

Aslet, C., 'Rodmarton Manor, Glos. I and II', *Country Life*. October 1978.

Baker, S., 'Gimson's Cotswold Furniture and its London Origins', *Apollo*. January 1979.

Batkin, M., 'Twentieth Century Cotswold Furniture Painted by Alfred and Louise Powell', *Antique Collecting*. March 1989.

Burrough, B.G., 'Three Disciples of William Morris', *The Connoisseur*. 1969.

Carruthers, A., 'Like Incubi and Succubi', *Craft History Two*. April 1989.

Darwent, C., 'Collectivism in the Cotswolds', *Country Life*. 27 October 1988.

Derrick, F., 'Sapperton Craftsmen 1–4', *Illustrated Carpenter and Builder*. October–November 1945.

Derrick, F., 'After Gimson 1–4', *The Illustrated Carpenter and Builder*. October–November 1952.

Hill, R., 'Nostalgia or New Wave', *Crafts*. July–August 1992.

MacCarthy, F., 'The Inheritance of Diffidence: Crafts in Britain between the Wars', *Craft History One*. 1988.

Pevsner, N., 'Roots and Branches', *Design*. December 1959.

Powers, A., 'Oliver Hill as Exhibition Designer', *The Thirties Society Journal*. no. 7, 1991.

Index

Illustrations are shown in italic.

Abbey, Edwin, Austen, 45, 11
Adams, Katherine, 96, 156, 157
Adeney, Bernard, 97, 125, 129
agriculture, 7, 89, 173
   depressed, 44, 78
alcohol, 86–7
Amberley, 73, 75, 76
Anderson, Mary, 82, 84, 155
antiques trade, 155, 156, 157, 164
apprenticeship system, 31, 34, 36, 142, 148, 150, 168
Architectural Association, 162
architecture
   Arts and Crafts commissions, 61–70, 74, 75
   characteristic Cotswold, 7–8, 44, 45, 59, 74, 76–7
   conservation and repair, 70–4, 108, 167: see also Society for the Protection of Ancient Buildings (SPAB)
   thatching, 60, 63, 68
   traditional local 60, 61, 72, 76
   weather boarding, 60
artisans see craftsmen
art nouveau, 1, 16, 51
Arts and Crafts Exhibition, 102, 158, 172: (1896) 25, 51; (1906) 101 (1910) 168; (1916) 113, 140

Art Worker's Guild, 13, 117, 142, 184
Ashbee, Charles Robert, 13, 14, 15–16, 19, 57, 60, 74, 78, 85, 86, 125, 141, 142, 158, 173, 179, 180, 181
   architecture, 60, 61, 65–7, 71–2
   character, 55
   domestic life, 58
   emigrates to Jerusalem, 58, 140
   establishes Guild at Campden, 45–6, 48, 79, 82, 89, 155
   furniture design, 48, 49
   jewellery design, 51–2, 55, VI
   lectures, 58, 184
   publishing, 53–4
Ashbee, Janet (née Forbes), 46, 48, 55, 58, 82, 83, 86, 87
Ashendene Press, 41

Back-to-the-land movement, 78, 84
Bailey, Jack, 48, 56
Baillie Scott, M.H., 16, 48
Barnsley, Alice, 23, 24, 81
Barnsley, Edward, xiii, 10, 26, 28, 29, 36, 41, 43, 55, 85, 146–7, 151, 166, 179, 180, 181
Barnsley, Ernest, 12, 13, 22, 23, 25, 36, 54, 55, 79, 81, 92, 128, 148, 179

architecture, 32, 60, 61, 70, 71, 73
   Rodmarton, 64, 64–5, 84
   break with Gimson, 32
   character, 23–4, 65
   death, 43
   domestic life, 32, 41
   furniture design, 29, 31–2, 40, 159
Barnsley, Grace (later Davies), 29, 102, 105
Barnsley, Herbert, 25, 81, 82
Barnsley, Lucy (née Morley), 23, 24, 29, 81, 87
Barnsley, Mary, see Jewson, Mary
Barnsley, Sidney, 12, 17, 19, 22, 23, 24, 55, 78, 81, 85, 91, 92, 100, 128, 146, 148, 150, 181
   architecture, 60–1, 64, 67, 70–4, II
   Byzantine studies, influence of, 17, 39
   character, 26–7
   death, 43
   domestic life, 30, 41, 87
   furniture design, 28, 32, 37–40, 102, 113, 140, 159, III
   working methods, 31, 32, 41, 79
Barnsley, William, 81, 82
Barron, Phyllis, 64, 89, 122, 124, 130, 132, 133, 134, 135, 177, 183, 184, X

appearance, 123
character, 124
death, 138, 139
early experiments in printing, 126, 128–9
exhibiting, 128–9
work after Larcher collaboration, 137–9
Bateman, C.E., 61, 71, 73, 156
Bathurst, Lord, 24, 29, 70, 77, 78
Bedales School (Hants), 92, 102, 146
Beechanger (S. Barnsley's home at Sapperton), 67, 68
Biddulph, the Hon. Claud, and Margaret, 32, 64–5, 77, 85, 108, 150
Birmingham, 7, 12, 13, 23, 45, 61, 177
Birt, Peggy, *133*, 134
Bisley, 75, 148
block-printing *see* handblock printing
Blomfield, Reginald, 17, 19, 21, 179
Bloomsbury circle, 97
Blow, Detmar, 60, 61, 63, 64, 68, 70, 76, 128, 129
Bodley, G.F., 8, 15
bookbinding, 92, 156
Book of Cottages and Little Houses, A (Ashbee), 66
book production, 53–4: *see also* bookbinding; typography
Bosence, Susan, 137, 183
Braithwaite House (Campden), 46, 54
Brewery Arts (Cirencester), 177
British Crafts Council *see* Contempoary Applied Arts
Broad Campden, 56, 58, 142
  Norman chapel at,

71–2, 84, 125, 128
Broadway, 45, 61, 63, 70, 71, 142
  restoration, 73
  Russell in, 155–62, 165
  workshop, *163*, 169
  visitors to, 82, 111, 155
Broadway Tower, 5, *5*, 84
Brookes, Jack, 58
Brook Street Gallery (London), 128
Bucknell, Alfred, 34, 36, 74, 148
Bucknell, Norman, xiii, 74, 148, 153
Builder, The, 61, 65, 181
Burchett, Percy, 31, 148, 150, 151
Burne Jones, Edward, 3, 96
butterfly joint, 28, 76
Byzantine style, 17, 39

Cabinet-making, 15, 17, 26, 27, 31–2, 36, 38, 48, 150, 158, 159, 164
Cadbury family, 41, 113
Cadbury, W.A., 75, 77, 152
calligraphy, 96, 156, 158
Cambridge, University of, 13, 15, 93, 136
Campden School of Arts and Crafts, 54, 89, *90*, 142, 181
Campden Trust, 75, 167
Cardew, Michael, 168–70, *170*, 185
Cardew, Mariel, 170–1, 175
Carpenter, Edward, 15, 54, 82
carpentry, 3, 27, 28, 40: *see also* woodwork
Carruthers, Annette, xiii, 179, 184
carving *see* Simmonds, William; woodwork
Central School of Arts and Crafts, 21, 93, 96, 97, 101, 106, 147, 172

ceramics *see* pottery
chair-making, 9, 33–4, 36, 95, 144: *see also* ladderback chairs
Chalford, 144, 146
  Waals' workshop at, 147, *147*, 148, 150, 151, 152, 161
chamfering, 19, 28, 30, 37, 159
Cheltenham, 119, 121, 158, 172, 174, 184
Cheltenham Art Gallery and Museum, 139, 158, 172, 177, *178*, 185
Cheltenham School of Art, 151
Chipping Campden, 1, 75, 81, 84, 119, 125, 180
  Ashbee at, 44–6, 78
  Ashbee's architecture and, 61, 66, 71, 72
  Campden Trust and, 167
  Guild workshops, 46–58, 87, 141, 142, 144
  Russell at, 155, 156
Cirencester, 1, 29, 108, 112, 173, 174
Cirencester workshops *see* Brewery Arts
class, social, 3, 7, 78, 168
  divisions broken through crafts, 79, 106
  patronage and, 77
Clisset, Philip, 13, 159
Cobb, Casty, 116, 117, 118, 183
Cobbett, William, 7
Cockerell, Douglas, 54, 92
Cockerell, Sydney, 96, 111, 156
Comfort, Elijah, 169–70, *171*
Contemporary Applied Arts (London), 177
Coomaraswamy, Amanda, 56, 58, 71, 72, 84, 125, 168
Commaraswamy, Ethel *see* Mairet, Ethel
Cotswold Co-operative Handicrafts, 158, 172

'Cotswold Tradition, The' (1951 exhibition), 173–4, 185

cottage design and repair, 65–7, 68, 71–2, 76

Council for Industrial Design, 166

Council for the Preservation of Rural England, 167

Country Life, 62, 181

Coventry Cathedral, 57, 144

Crafts Council, 177

craftsmanship, 42, 172
  at Chalford, 150–1, 159
  industrialization and, 2
  local traditions and, 32, 65, 76
  Morris' influence, 93, 94
  preserving, 59, 60, 79, 91, 100, 153

Craftsmanship in Competitive Industry (Ashbee), 19, 179

craftsmen, 3, 10–11, 15
  at Chalford, 147–8, 150, 152
  employment of, 31, 34, 36, 150
  and mechanization, 40–1
  in pottery-making, 99

Craftsmen of Gloucestershire, 172

Crafts Study Centre (Bath), 112, 177, 183

crafts traditions, 109, 155
  local, 32, 44, 65
  surviving industrialization, 8, 78

Crane, Walter, 54, 110

Crawford, Alan, 67, 179, 180, 181

Daglingworth, 75

Daintree House (Campden), 66–7

Daneway House and Workshops, 7, 25, 29, *30*, 31, 33–4, 36, 40, 140, 147–8, 150, 152
  architecture, 68, 173

impact of WWI on, 41
  visitors to, 41, 44, 82

Dartington Hall, 137, 138, 183

Davies, Tony, 121

Davies, Grace *see* Barnsley, Grace

Davies, Oscar, 105

Davoll, Harry, 31, 102, *147*, 148, 150, 152–3, 175

Dawber, Guy, 59, 61, 62, 63, 69, 73, 181

Debenham, Ernest, 41

Debenham & Freebody, 41

decoration, 2, 13, 15, 40, 48
  furniture design and, 29, 32, 34, 39, 166
  metalwork and, 40, 49, 159, *164*
  pottery design and, 92, 102, 107
  woodwork techniques and, 37–8

demography, 2, 7, 60, 65

De Morgan, William, 49

Denning, Toni *see* Russell, Toni

Derrick, Freda, 24, 180

Description of the Work of the Guild of Handicraft, A (Ashbee), 45, 47

Design and Industries Association (DIA), 41, 140–1, 151, 158, 169

design, British
  industrialization and, 2, 141
  position in Europe, 1, 154
  Russell knighted for services to, 166
  see also furniture design: pottery; textile design

design motifs, 19, 52, 135
  Gimson's, 40, 147
  Louise Powell's, 97, 100, 105, 113: *see also* pattern design

nature as inspiration for, 40, 49, 51, 113

Dickinson, Goldsworthy Lowes, 15

Ditchling (Sussex), workshops at, 1, 168

Dixon, A.S., 71

Dolmetch, Arnold, 116

Downer, Charlie, 56, *85*, 142, 144

dress styles and rural life, 81–2, 89

Dumbleton, 68, 69

'Duopour' pot, 105

dyes
  textiles and, 126, 133–4, 135
  vegetable, 6, 128

Dyrad Handicrafts (Leicester), 41, *XII*

Eadburgha Bindery, 156: *see also* Katherine Adams

East Midlands Training College, 151

Eaton Hall (Cheshire), 117

Edgeworth, 45, 148

Edsall, Emily, 134

education, promotion of, 54–5, 65, 85, 89, 102, 106, 142, 158, 177
  Barron's contribution to, 138
  public sector, 167
  Waals' posts, 151
  see also Central School of Arts and Crafts

Edward Barnsley Educational Trust, xiii, 179, 180

Eiloart, Arnold, 90

Elm Tree House, 54, 89

embroidery, 40, 52, 64, 81, 89, 93, 113, 123

employment 3, 36, 55, 150
  and WWI, 102, 148
  see also apprentice system; craftsmen

enamel colouring, 49, 51, 52, 53, 56, 98, *VI*

English Tradition in Design, The

(Gloag), 172

Essex House, 15–16, 45 (London); 46, 53 (Campden)

Essex House Press, 53–4, 55, 56, 86, 89, 180

Essex House Song-book, The, 86

Evans, Alan, xiii, 177, 178

Evenlode, 62, 63

Everett, Ethel, 140

exhibitions, 19, 41, 100–1, 102, 108, 119, 121, 128–9, 132, 136, 139–40, 144, 148–9, 172, 173; *see also* Arts and Crafts Exhibitions; 'Cotswold Tradition, The' (exhibition); Paris International Exhibition

Fabianism, 89

Fairford, 70, 111

Far Oakridge, 112, 115, 118, 121, 126

Falconer, Thomas, 75–6

Fels, Joseph, 56

Festival of Britain (1951), 173, 174

Few Chapters in Workshop Reconstruction and Citizenship, A (Ashbee), 48

Fifield, John, 68

Finch, Ray, xiii, 172, 174, 175, 176, 185

First World War, 70, 102, 111, 144, 159
  effect on craft activity, 1, 142, 148, 154, 167
  impact on Daneway, 43, 144

Fisher, Alexander, 49

Fletcher, Benjamin, 55

folk art and tradition, 81, 84, 118

food, 87, 175

Forbes, Janet *see* Ashbee, Janet

Foster, Fred, 91, 173

Forsyth, Gordon, 106, 171

France, 126, 136, 139, *X*

influence of, in design, 62, 97, 132

Froxfield workshop, 43, 146, 147: *see also* Barnsley, Edward

furniture, 25–6, 28, 48, 65, 92, 102, 156: *see also* cabinet-making; chair-making

furniture decoration, 29, 32, 34, 39, 48, 159

furniture design, 3, 13, 17, 19, 27–9, 41, 48, 148, 159, 163–6: *see also* Barnsley, Ernest; Barnsley, Sidney; Gimson, Ernest

Garden Craft, Old and New (Sedding), 65

garden design, 65, 73, 113, 121, 166

Gardiner, Edward, 13, 33–4, 144, 159

Gardiner, Derek, 150

Gardiner, Fred, 115, 136, 144, 148, *X*

Gardiner, Harry, 36, 159, 161

Geddes, Patrick, 54

Gere, Charles, 82, 118, 183

Gilford, Noël, 125, 128

Gill, Eric, 86, 88, 115

Gimson, Emily (née Tompson), 29, 36, 81, 85

Gimson, Ernest, 12, 13, 20, 22, 23, 24, 29, 30, 35, 55, 82, 92, 128, 136, 146, 148, 173, 179
  architecture, 60, 61, 63, 70–2, 74–5
  break with E. Barnsley, 32
  character, 23, 33, 40, 43, 86–7
  death, 43, 144
  decorative designs, 40, 147
  furniture design, 17, 19, 31–2, 34, 36–7, 39–40,

41, *42*, 43–4, 102, *103*, 140, 144, 157, 162, 163, 177, *I, V, XI*
  domestic life, 29, 32, 41
  and Powell, 93, 95
  work methods, 36, 79

Gloag, John, 146, 158, 172

Gloucestershire County Council, 54, 57

Grainger, Percy, 85

Great Exhibition (1851), 2

Great Pottery, 169

Grevel, William, 44, 45

Griggs, Fred, 41, 54, 57, 70, 75, 85, 105, 142, 167, 179, 180

Griggs, Nina, 105, 113, 118, 182, 183

Guild of Gloucestershire Craftsmen, 172

Guild of Handicraft, 1, 15–16, 17, 18, 71, 136, 155, 159, 180
  collapse and reformation at Campden, 55–6, 56–8, 141
  established at Campden, 45, 46–58, 65, 79, 82, 84, 87
  workshops 46, *47*, 140–2
  entertainment and cultural life, 54–5, 84–5

Gwynne, John, 113, 121, 183

Gyde Almshouses (Painswick), 67

Hallidays' Mill (Chalford), 147

Hambutts House (Painswick), 122, *122*, 123–5, 132
  workshops at, *133*, 137

handblock printing, 64, 122, 126, 129, 134–5, 137–8

Harrison, Richard, 27

Hart, George, 56, 141, 142, 156, 158, 174, 176, *VI*

Hart, Will, 48, 56, 57, *85*, 87, 142, 144, 156

Heal, Ambrose, 41, 158
Heal and Sons (London), 41, 101, 158
Herdman, D.W., 158, 172, 174, 185
Hesse, Grand Duke of, 16, 55
Hewitt, Graily, 96
Hill, Oliver, 7, 173
Hilles House (Harescombe), 63–4
Hindshaw, Margery, 101
Holland, Rob Martin, 46, 54, 71, 77
Holst, Gustav, 85
Hornby, C.H. St John, 41, 96
Horwood, Ted, 56
Houseman, Laurence, 53
Hunt, Bert, 148, 152
Hussey, Christopher, 173
Huyshe, Reynell, 56, 142

India, Larcher in, 126, 132
Indian arts and crafts, 84
industrialization
    and design, 2, 12
    and rural decline, 71
    see also mechanization
Iles Farm (Far Oakridge), 75 76, 82
Industrial Revolution, 2, 154
Influence of Building Materials upon Architecture, The (Morris), 61
Izod's House (Campden), 66

James, Henry, 82, 84, 111
jewellery, 3, 16, *52*, 142, 177
    Ashbee's designs, 51–2
Jewson, Mary (née Barnsley), *23*, 24, 120
Jewson, Norman, 24, 27, 33, 36, 43, 64, 65, 71, 72, 74, *74*, 76, 82, 86, 87, *120*, 148, 167, 174, 176, 180, 181
Johnston, Edward, 96

Kelmscott Manor (Lechlade), 4, 6, 8, 61
Kelmscott Manor Cottages, 68
Kelmscott Press, 53
Kenton and Company, 17, 19–20, *20*, 21–2, 26, 31, 32, 39, 93

ladderback chairs, 25, *26*, 33, *44*, 159
Larcher, Dorothy, 64, 89, 122–4, *124*, 125, 127–9, 131, *132*, 134, 136, 139, 174, 177, 183
Leach, Bernard, 168–9, 177
leadwork, 74, *75*
Leicester College of Art, 54, 58
Leigh, Ray, 165
Lessore, Louise *see* Powell, Louise
Lessore, Elaine Thérèse, 95, *95*, 96, 97–8, 111, 125
Lethaby, William, 12–13, 19, 20–2, 26, 28, 41, 60, 93, 96, 97, 101, 141
Liberty's (London), 55
limestone, 6, 8, 59, 68
Little Gallery, The, 129, 136
London, and Arts and Crafts, 12, 15–17, 22, 46, 56, 61, 111, 122, 128, 177
    Barron and Larcher in, 129, 132
    exhibitions, 41, 101, 170
    Guild of Handicraft in, 48, 53, 55, 84, 142
    Powell and Wedgwood collaboration in, 101
    Russell in, 158, 164, 166
Lupton, Geoffrey, 146, 147, 182
Lutyens, Edwin, 63, 148
Lygon Arms (Broadway), 73, 155–7, 164

McCarthy, Fiona, 81, 88, 180, 181, 182, 184
Macartney, Mervyn, 17, 21
MacDonald, Ramsey, 85
Mackintosh C.R., 61, 82, 181
Mackmurdo, Arthur Heygate, 13
Madresfield Court, 48
Magpie and Stump (Chelsea), 16, 49
Mairet, Ethel (née Partridge, then Coomaraswamy), 84, 128, 136, 168, *VII*
Mairet, Philippe, 57, 125, 168, 183
Manchester Cotton Board, 133
manual skills, 2, 3, 13: *see also* craftsmanship
Mansfield, Leslie, 166
Mare, Walter de la, 84
Mark, William, 51, 56, *VI*
Marshall, R.E. and C. Ltd, 158
Martyn, H.H. and Co., 158
Masefield, John, 54, 84
Mayor, Fred, 126, *X*
mechanization
    and craftsmanship, 2, 40–1, 91, 100, 161, 169
memorials, 57, *70*, 167
metalwork, 3, 13, 15–16, 41, 73, 93, 108, 148, 158, 177
    decoration and, 40, 49, 159, *164*
    Guild of Handicraft and, 48–9, 50, 52–3, 56–7, 144, *VI*
    see also jewellery
Middle Ages, 3, 7, 44, 93, 97
Miller, Alec, 48, 56, *57*, 58, *85*, 142, 144, 156, 158
Miller, Fred, 56
Millet, Frank D., 111
Milne, W.O., 93
Minchinhampton, 61, 70, 76
Miserden, 67, 89

Mitchell, Arthur, 152
Modern English Silverwork (Ashbee), 55
Montagu Scott, Walker, 61
Morley, Lucy *see* Barnsley, Lucy
Morris, Jane, 4
Morris & Co., 3, 7, 13, 34, 40
Morris, May, 5, 70, 96, 140, 179
Morris, William, 1, 3–4, 5, 6, 8, 23–4, 40, 53, 59, 61, 64, 86, 93
  designs, 89, 106
  influence on Movement, 12, 13, 15, 28, 39, 44, 60, 94, 96, 110, 178
  publications, 5–6, 61, 96, 179, 182
  tours and lectures, 12, 13
  work with SPAB, 12, 60, 71
Muggeridge, Malcolm, 89, 182
mummer's plays, 86
music and folk tradition, 84–5, 118, 174

nature
  architecture, building traditions and, 60, 75, 113, 115
  inspiration source for design, 2, 6, 22, 40, 81, 93, 102
Nailsworth, 147
National Trust, 167
Neal, Neville, 144
Nether Lypiatt Manor (Glos), 119
Nether Swell Manor (Stow), 61–2
New, E.H., 45, 47, 53
Newbolt, Henry, 82
News from Nowhere (Morris), 5–6
Newton, Ernest, 61, 69–70, 71
Northleach, 122

Oakridge, 150, 152: *see also* Far Oakridge Old Cottages, *Farmhouses and Other Stone Buildings of the Cotswold Region* (Dawber), 61
open construction, 19, 28
Orton, Fred, 144, 148
Ould, Ted, 164, 165
Overbury, 45, 61, 69, 71
Owlpen Manor, 75

Painswick, 61, 67, 119, 122–5, 128–9, 133, 135, 137–9
Palaces, The (Dumbleton), 68–9
Paris cabinet, 159, *160*
Paris International Exhibition (1925), 106, 159, 160, 182
Partridge, Ethel *see* Mairet, Ethel
Partridge, Fred, 48, 82, 84, 87, 168
pattern design, 40, 97, 100, 102, 106, 107
Patterson's Gallery, London, 100
Payne, Edward, xiii, 91, 110, 111, 113, 176, 182, *IX*
Payne, Henry, 72, 73, *IX*
Peach, Harry, 41, *XII*
Pearce, Maresco, 170
Pearson, John, 49
Peart, Eve *see* Simmonds, Eve
Pelper, Marian, 162, 164, 165
Pevsner, Sir Nikolaus, 165, 172, 184, 185
Pick, Frank, 151
Pinbury Park, 23, 24–5, 27–30, 32, 37, 44, 78, 81, 87, 95
Pioneers of Modern Design, The (Pevsner), 172–3
plasterwork, 13, *20*, 25, 31, 33, 36, 68, 74–5, 102, 148

Pleydell Bouverie, Katherine, 177
Plunkett, Charlie, 56
political beliefs, 89–91, 176: *see also* social reform, socialism
pottery, 92, 97, 121, 168–9, 177
  decoration 98, 170
  Grace Barnsley's, 105
  Wedgwood/Powell collaboration, 97–102, 106–7
  see also Winchcombe Pottery
Powell, Alfred, 6, 12, 22–3, 34, 39–40, 42, 85, 91, 95, 111, 112, 116, 125, 179, 180, 181, 182, *IX*
  architecture, 60–1, 63, 68, 71, 94, 108–9
  designs, 97, *103*, 106, 140, *III*
  early life, 92–3
  furniture design, 102, 108, *V*
  health, 94–5
  domestic life, 89
  pottery, 98–102, 105–8
Powell, Louise (née Lessore), 39, *95*, 100, 111–12, 125
  calligraphy, 95–6
  craftwork, 89, 95
  death, 109
  embroidery, 96, 98, 113, *VII*
  furniture design, 102, *104*, 140
  domestic life, 89
  pottery, 98–102, 105, 106–8, *V*
Powell, Margaret, 93, 97
Power, Statia (Annie), 54, 87
Prentice, Andrew, 61, 70, 73–4
Pre-Raphaelite Brotherhood, 3, 4, 110
Prior, E.S., 63, 76
Prospects of Architecture in Civilisation, The (Morris), 61

Protheroe, Sudbury, 91
Pugin, A.W.N., 3, 60, 181
puppets, 116–18, *IX*
Pyment, Jim, *47*, 142

railways, 78, 144
Ramage, Archie, 71, 89
Ramsden, Omar, 142
Randolph, S.L., 91
Redesdale family, 54, 89
Reeve, Sidney, 48, 55
Report on the Treatment of Old Cottages (Powell), 71
Richardson, Alice, 126
Rodmarton Manor, 32, 43, *64*, 64–5, 72, 84–5, 108, 116, 150, 151
Rodmarton Women's Guild, 89, 108
Roeginga Pottery (Rainham), 105
Rose, Muriel, 129
Rossetti, Dante Gabriel, 4–5
Rothenstein, William, 75–7, 82, 84, 86, 113, 117, 119, 140, 181, 182, *V*
Royal Academy, 97, 119, 140
Royal College of Art, 106, 110
Royal School of Needlework, 96
Royal West of England Academy (Bristol), 139
Rural Industries Bureau, 168
rural values, 22, 24, 44, 44, 45, 55, 78
Ruskin, John, 3, 15, 60, 71, 93, 178, 179
Russell, Dick, *145* 155, 157, 161, 162–4
Russell, Don, 155, 157
Russell, Sir Gordon, xiii, 77, 136, 168, 169, 172
   business exploits, 161, 163, 164–6

death, 166
designs, 156, 159, 161, 162–3
early life, 154–5
knighted, 166
marriage, 158
publications, 164, 184
war service, 157
Russell, Sydney Bolton, 155–6, 157–8, 168, 169
Russell, Toni (née Denning), 157–8, 164, 166
Rust, Frank, 148, 152
Ryland, Daisy, *133*, 134

Sapperton
   as centre for craft activity, 1, 10, 20, 24, 27, 29, 34, 43–4, 55, 67–8, 74–5, 86, 92–5, 144, 147, 155, 159, 173
   village hall, 70, 85
Sargent, John Singer, 45, 82, 111
Savage, Reginald, 53
School of Handicraft, 54, 56, 57, 142
Scrubey, Owen, 148, 153
Scrubey, William, 65, 148
Second World War, 129, 136, 166, 167, 173, 174
Sedding, John, 12, 13, 65, 93, 94
Seynckley House (Amberley), 72, *73*
Sharp, Cecil, 110
Shaw, Nellie, 90, 182
Shaw, Norman, 12, 69
Schultz, Robert Weir, 12, 13, 41
Sickert, Walter, 98, 111
Simmonds, Eve (née Peart), 110, 112, 115, 126, 128, 174, 183
   character, 113

death, 121
early life, 111
embroidery, 113, *114*, 117, *VII, XII*
domestic life, 111, 112–13, 119, 121
Simmonds, William, 10, 91, 124, 126, 174, 176, 182
carving, 112, 113, 115, 116
character, 115
death, 121
early life, 110
domestic life, 111, 121, 112–13, 119
theatricals, artefacts for, 111, 115–19, *IX*
wartime exploits, 111–12
Smith, Ernest, 31, 146–7, *147*, 148, 152–3
smocks, 81, 113
Socialism, 13, 90, 91
social reform, 13, 54, 20, 66, 89, 91
Society for the Protection of Ancient Buildings (SPAB), 8, 12, 60, 71, 72, 94, 167, 181
stained glass, 3, 17, 54
Stoke-on-Trent, Cardew at, 171–2
Stoke-on Trent Schools of Art, 106
Strang, William, *14*, 53, *83*, 140
Stroud, 89, 135, 138
Stroud School of Art, 121, 138
Studio, reviews in, 51, 98, 182

Tanner, Heather, 139, 177, 182
Tanner, Percy, 148, 150
Tanner, Robin, 123, 138, 177, 182, 184, 185
Taplin, Millie, 105–6, *107*, 107–8
Tarlton, 94, 108, 112
textiles, 3, 177

Barron's and Larcher's
  work in, 126–36
design, 13, 108, 165
dyes for, 6
printing, 123
Thimble Cottage (Glos), 69,
  69
Things we see – Furniture, The
  (Gordon Russell), 156,
  172
Thornton, Bill, 56, 142,
  143, 144
Times, The, reviews in, 129,
  170
Tolstoy, Leo, 89
tourism to Cotswolds, 45,
  78, 82, 111, 142, 155,
  164
Toynbee Hall (London),
  15
Trevelyan, Sir George, xiii,
  33, 150–1, 152, 180,
  184
Troup, Francis, 41
Tunley, 68, 92, 95, 97,
  125, 148
Tustin, Charlie, *171*, 172
Tustin, Sidney, 170, *171*,
  172
typography, 53, 161, 164

USA, 1, 111, 129, 144,
  156, 164
  Ashbee and, 55, 58
Upper   Dorvel   House
  (Sapperton), 29, 68, 72

Varley, Fleetwood, 51, *VI*
Vegetable Dyeing (E. Mairet),
  128
Vaughan Williams, Ralph,
  84, 85
Victorian   and   Albert
  Museum, 49, 126,
  128, 158
Voysey, C.F.A., 67, 148,
  158, 162

Waals, Peter van der, 31,
  33, 36, 39–40, 91,
  104, 115, *146*
  at Chalford, 144,146–52,
  176, 184
Wall, William, 56
Warmington, Harry, 56,
  58, 142
Waterlane, 148, 150
Waterlane House, 72, 75
Weaver, Lawrence, 62
Weaving, 168, 173
Webb, Philip, 3, 8, 12, 13,
  23, 24–5, 27, 30,
  78–9, 93, 179, 180,
  182
  architecture, 60, 92
Wedgwood & Sons Ltd, 92,
  97, 100–2, 103, 106,
  109, 165
Wedgwood, Cecily Stella
  'Star', 106, 107
Wedgwood family, 2,
  92, 99, 100, 154,
  171
Well's Folly (Evenlode), *62*,

62–3
Wesker, Arnold, 88
Westminster, Duke of, 128,
  129, 130
Whitefriars'   Glassworks,
  100, 165
Whiteway Colony, 89–91,
  158, 172, 177
Whitworth Art Gallery, xiii,
  136
Wilde, Oscar, 178
Wilson, Henry, 12, 94
Winchcombe   Pottery,
  169–70, 174–5, 177
Winchester   Cathedral,
  Barron/Larcher
  commission at, 136
women, role of in Move-
  ment, 87–9,168
Woodroffe, Paul, 53, 54, 57,
  71, 81, 156, 158
woodwork, 27, 46, 56–7,
  108, 148, 155
  carving, 112–13, 115,
  116, 119, 121
  furniture design and, 37,
  48
  mechanization and, 147,
  150
Woolstaplers' Hall (Camp-
  den), 46, 89
wooltrade, Cotswold, 7, 44,
  59, 173
Wright, Alfred, 65

Yeats, W.B., 82
Young, Rowland, 148